Wiley Global Finance is a market-leading provider of over 400 annual books, mobile applications, elearning products, workflow training tools, newsletters and websites for both professionals and consumers in institutional finance, trading, corporate accounting, exam preparation, investing, and performance management.

Additional Praise for
The Facts of Business Life

"Who better to talk about business ownership then someone who has done it, lived it, loved it, and left it? *The Facts of Business Life* is not just a book about how to be successful, it's a book that challenges some commonly believed entrepreneurial myths, and in my case, made me rethink my role as a business owner. Bill's book will surprise some with facts such as 'Protecting Your Assets is Your First Priority;' what asset protection means and why it's important; and his explanation of the 'War Zone' and how all these facts work together to create unbelievable success. If this isn't enough for one book, Bill gives us more; the business life cycle makes so much sense, and when you understand it, it makes my role as an owner so much clearer."

—Gil L'Hommedieu, founder, President, and CEO,
Net Claims Now

"Bill McBean is the consummate business executive. Just ask the manufacturers he represented so successfully, the competitors from whom he regularly grabbed market share, or the employees who were fiercely loyal to him. But Bill also has an amazing capacity to reflect on his business experiences and convey the lessons he's taken from those experiences. The five levels of a business life cycle is a perfect example of this. It's Bill's concept, simple to understand, and makes perfect sense. Two of these levels, 'Creating Your Company's DNA' and 'Moving on When It's Time to Go' are worth the price of a dozen books."

—Fritz Kern, former SVP and General Manager,
U.S. Passenger and Commercial Vehicle Operations,
American Isuzu Motors

"Bill McBean is one of the best business owners I've ever come across. I think so much of his ability that I seek out his opinion on my own business issues, and have referred some of my best clients to him for his expertise. Every page of *The Facts of Business Life* has something owners can use in their business, but I found the 'War Zone' and 'Marketing' facts to be especially powerful, as are the levels on DNA creation, opportunity and its Analysis, and the maintaining of success. This is a great book, and the way Bill describes the business life cycle concept, like a light switch being turned on—it made so much else make sense. It will be a wonderful gift to my customers and a great introductory tool for my sales force to pass out to prospective customers."

—Tony Fincannon, CEO and President, Dealer Associates

"What impressed us most about Bill was the clarity he brought to complicated business issues. Bill's book, *The Facts of Business Life*, does just this; it discusses the priorities business owners need to concentrate on to be successful. The life cycle Bill describes is brilliant and brings clarity where there was none. His book makes business ownership easy to understand for the rest of us."

—Victor Papazov, Chairman, Bulgarian Stock Exchange,
and Irena Komitova, Managing Partner and Publisher,
Creative Solutions; Sophia, Bulgaria

"Bill McBean is a self-made businessman. He started with little and turned it into a lot. I've been able to closely watch how he takes troubled businesses and turns them into successes, then uses their collective successes to create a competitive advantage in the marketplace. Bill is a competitor who attacks a market with preparation, skill, and determination. His book is a must-read for every business owner because the seven Facts of Business Life and the five levels in an ownership life cycle are the summation of his four decades of experience and success, and a tribute to the great business owners who mentored Bill. Level Five, 'Moving on When it's Time to Go,' is a must-read, because Bill's exit was as good of one as I've ever seen."

—Tony Nolan, former President and CEO,
NCM & Associates

"Bill is a great businessman who delivers a strong message, simply and to the point. The seven Facts of Business Life give owners the priorities they need to concentrate on to be successful and profitable. The five levels of a business (and/or owner) life cycle is something I've never thought about, but makes perfect sense and gives me a structure or boundaries to work within, as well as a clearer focus on where I am and where my business is headed. When you read this book, you quickly recognize why Bill was so successful, and there is no doubt that you're talking to a business owner who has been where we are, and won the battle. This is simply the best business book I have ever read."

—Dave Resendez, Director, Texas Towing Association

"Many people have common sense, but few people can turn common sense into uncommon success. Bill McBean is one of the few who can. As a successful businessman, Bill has demonstrated an uncanny ability to maintain integrity and honor in both his business and personal life. Because of that, his employees love to work for him, his customers trust to buy from him over and over again, and he endears himself to his friends. His book is a must-read and should not be limited just to entrepreneurs, but to individuals who are running any type of organization."

—Jess Cole, Senior Pastor, Grace Community Church, Corpus Christi, Texas

"Understanding the entire realm of business—marketing, sales, costs, employees, and products—is a trait few business owners have. But Bill McBean can not only see the whole picture, he understands the small things as well. This is reflected in his book, *The Facts of Business Life,* and particularly in how he describes the seven facts and why they are important singularly, and then shows you the real strength of the facts—how they work in tandem with each other to create great success. Add this to the description of the five levels of the business life cycle and the result is a source of great knowledge for business owners large and small. A must-read business book."

—Ted Oakley, Director, American Bank

"As a successful, hands-on entrepreneur, Bill has done a masterful job of presenting the essential elements for successfully running and growing a business. His presentation is straightforward and compelling, and anyone who owns, manages, or is considering starting a business should grab a highlighter and start reading his book."

—Mike Lewis, CEO, Office Arrow

"Bill has a wonderful business mind and an uncanny ability to cut through the 'noise,' clearly see a problem or opportunity, and then attack it. His businesses are successes because he is a visionary, a leader, a motivator, and a focused manager, and because his employees believe in him. When you read his book you'll know why. Bill sees the complete macro picture of owning a business and puts it all in an orderly, easily-understood, sensible format."

—Tim Keen, Vice President, Sonic Automotive

"Bill McBean is humble, honest, has a great sense of humor, and is a sincere friend to all of us here at his alma mater. He was and is a hard working professional and a leader amongst his peers. It is little wonder that this former captain of his hockey team is now a captain of his team in the business world. *The Facts of Business Life* explains how Bill has taken some of the hard lessons sports teaches and used this knowledge in his business career. Particularly telling is the 'The War Zone' business fact, which tells about the competitive spirit needed to succeed or the business fact concerning the importance of protecting your business assets, which reminded me of how critical defensive play is to winning and becoming champions. Bill's book is not just reserved for business owners; it should be read by managers in every occupation."

—Bill Seymour, former Athletic Director and Men's Hockey Coach, University of Saskatchewan

The Facts of Business Life

The Facts of Business Life

WHAT EVERY SUCCESSFUL BUSINESS OWNER KNOWS THAT YOU DON'T

Bill McBean

WILEY

John Wiley & Sons, Inc.

Published by John Wiley & Sons, Inc., Hoboken, New Jersey.
Published simultaneously in Canada.

For general information on our other products and services or for technical support, please contact our Customer Care Department within the United States at (800) 762-2974, outside the United States at (317) 572-3993, or fax (317) 572-4002.

Wiley also publishes its books in a variety of electronic formats. Some content that appears in print may not be available in electronic books. For more information about Wiley products, visit our web site at www.wiley.com.

Library of Congress Cataloging-in-Publication Data:

McBean, Bill, 1951-
    The facts of business life: what every successful business owner knows that you
    don't/Bill McBean.
      p. cm.
    Includes index.
    ISBN 978-1-118-09496-9 (cloth); ISBN 978-1-118-22360-4 (ebk);
    ISBN 978-1-118-26189-7 (ebk); ISBN 978-1-118-23699-4 (ebk)
      1. Entrepreneurship. 2. Success in business. 3. New business enterprises.
      4. Management.   I. Title.
  HB615.M3728 2012
  658.4'09—dc23   2012017202

Printed in the United States of America
10 9 8 7 6 5 4 3 2 1

This book is dedicated to
my mother and father, Bill and Nona McBean;
my aunt and uncle, Mark and Margie Hulings;
and my wife and friend, Lynnda McBean.
Thank you.

Contents

Foreword   xi

Acknowledgments   xv

Introduction   xix

Chapter 1:   The Facts of Business Life   1
              The Facts   3
              The Business Life Cycle   9

Chapter 2:   The Five Levels of Business Success   13
              Level 1: Ownership and Opportunity   17
              Level 2: Creating Your Company's DNA   22
              Level 3: From Survival to Success   27
              Level 4: Maintaining Success   32
              Level 5: Moving on When It's Time to Go   37

Chapter 3:   Fact 1: If You Don't Lead, No One Will Follow   45
              Level 1: Ownership and Opportunity   50
              Level 2: Creating Your Company's DNA   56
              Level 3: From Survival to Success   62
              Level 4: Maintaining Success   72
              Level 5: Moving on When It's Time to Go   77

Chapter 4:   Fact 2: If You Don't Control It, You Don't Own It   87
              Level 1: Ownership and Opportunity   89
              Level 2: Creating Your Company's DNA   93

Level 3: From Survival to Success	98
Level 4: Maintaining Success	103
Level 5: Moving on When It's Time to Go	111

Chapter 5:   Fact 3: Protecting Your Company's Assets Should Be Your First Priority   121

Protecting Tangible and Intangible Assets	125
Protecting Products or Services	126
Protecting People	127
Level 1: Ownership and Opportunity	129
Level 2: Creating Your Company's DNA	134
Level 3: From Survival to Success	142
Level 4: Maintaining Success	150
Level 5: Moving on When It's Time to Go	159

Chapter 6:   Fact 4: Planning Is About Preparing for the Future, Not Predicting It   167

The Elements of a Proper Business Plan	170
Level 1: Ownership and Opportunity	172
Level 2: Creating Your Company's DNA	175
Level 3: From Survival to Success	179
Level 4: Maintaining Success	182
Level 5: Moving on When It's Time to Go	187

Chapter 7:   Fact 5: If You Don't Market Your Business, You Won't Have One   193

The Elements of Marketing	196
Level 1: Ownership and Opportunity	198
Level 2: Creating Your Company's DNA	204
Level 3: From Survival to Success	212
Level 4: Maintaining Success	218
Level 5: Moving on When It's Time to Go	224

Chapter 8:   Fact 6: The Marketplace Is a War Zone   235

The Products or Services You Sell	238
How Your Business Operates	240
How Your Business Competes—The "X" Factor	241

Level 1: Ownership and Opportunity   242

Level 2: Creating Your Company's DNA   250

Level 3: From Survival to Success   256

Level 4: Maintaining Success   264

Level 5: Moving on When It's Time to Go   272

**Chapter 9:   Fact 7: You Don't Just Have to Know the Business
You're In, You Have to Know Business   279**

Product   281

People   282

Accounting and Finance   283

You   284

Level 1: Ownership and Opportunity   285

Level 2: Creating Your Company's DNA   293

Level 3: From Survival to Success   300

Level 4: Maintaining Success   307

Level 5: Moving on When It's Time to Go   314

Conclusion   323

About the Author   325

Index   327

Foreword

Congratulations, entrepreneur-minded reader. In your hand is a terrific book with real-life, ready-to-use-now lessons that should help you see more success and tackle life more comfortably.

In my 40-plus years in the investment business—most of which has been as head of my own firm—I've read over 100 books on starting and running a business—some useful, others less so. Most business books fall into one of two camps: how to start a business, or personal ruminations on business leadership from some widely recognized figure. There's nothing wrong with either, and many of those are great, but if you're a would-be entrepreneur or a business owner embroiled in the day-to-day business of business, there's not much that speaks to the full life cycle of what it means—truly means—to be an owner, manager, CEO, and board chairman.

That's where Bill McBean comes in. I know Bill personally—have for years—and he's a sharp, shrewd, no-nonsense businessman. Most folks are lucky to find business success once, but Bill has met repeated success in a variety of venues, geographies, business lines, you name it. One time is luck and more than once is skill, but if you're as repeatedly successful as Bill has been, that takes serious acumen and drive. Oh, and by the way, he's a heck of a nice guy. His experience alone would probably make a good business book.

But this book isn't memoir or rule book. It's a usable, open kimono look at the nitty-gritty of what's truly required not just to start a business, but to take it from a new business to a surviving one to a thriving one. And once you've got a thriving business, he covers what few people have ever done in books I've seen—he describes how to decide whether to exit the business, when, and how. Sometimes foldin' 'em is better than holdin' 'em.

I don't want to give away too much of the book, but another important lesson Bill delivers—another I've not seen well covered elsewhere—is the need to create your company's DNA. This is a key lesson—critical—for building a business that lasts.

In fact, this is how I think about my own firm. Over the years, we've built processes to ensure that my firm's DNA is embedded in each employee so no matter how far we expand geographically and no matter how far into the future, I can be assured our clients continually get the kind of service (or better) they get now and that I've wanted them to have since the beginning—and with it, the culture gets carried forward and is self-perpetuating. If you don't build an enduring culture now that you'll be proud of in the long-term future, you'll have a long-term future with a culture that mildewed on you en route. That alone is a lesson worth the price of this book. Get that and his other Facts of Life in your bones, and this will have been time well spent.

Entrepreneurs are a special breed. They get, inherently and without effort, the myriad benefits of being the boss. They have vision—without it, you can't hope to even think about starting a firm. But where I see folks fail is in their lack of grit. Grit is what it takes—and that's what Bill takes you through in this book. It's no-holds-barred. It's not sugar-coated. And if you walk away thinking, "Nope, that's not for me," then this, too, will have been time well spent, saving you (and your spouse, kids, next-door neighbor, and dog) the future multiple heartaches inherent in starting a new venture. But if you've truly got it in you, and my guess is you do, or want to, or you wouldn't be reading this book, then Bill gives you some clear to-do, think-this-through steps to help you on your way to success.

One more thing: In my 2008 book *The Ten Roads to Riches*, I make the point that entrepreneurship and failure go hand in hand. The most successful founder-CEOs have often failed a few times at no-go ventures. Nothing wrong with that. Failure is a great way to learn—again, nothing wrong with it, so long as you learn from it and fail differently next time and learn still another perma-lesson. But the lessons Bill gives here will help you learn still more from your failure and make a better go next time (and the time after that). And I hope you do try—and succeed—because the entrepreneur road is insanely rewarding, not just in money but in every other part of life, when done right. Bill will help.

Enjoy the read.

—Ken Fisher
Founder and CEO of Fisher Investments
28-year *Forbes* "Portfolio Strategy" columnist
New York Times bestselling author

If you are attracted to the seductive magnet of business ownership, there are only two possible outcomes. Either you resist it, and for the rest of your life say, "It might have been," or you give in to it. But once you choose the ownership path, you had better be prepared to say, "I gave it everything I had" or you won't succeed.

—Bill McBean

Acknowledgments

I owe a great deal of thanks to many people who not only helped me shape this book but showed me how to become a successful business owner.

To begin my acknowledgments without mentioning Rob Kaplan just wouldn't be right. Rob started out as my editor and, over the course of our working together on the book, became my friend. I had first come to him with a rough manuscript, but despite its flaws he saw something in it that I had not seen, and he made a number of suggestions that led, finally, to the book it is today. Rob took my business knowledge and guided me through the process of writing, editing, and rewriting until, at last, I had a book worthy of a publisher like John Wiley & Sons. Every page of this book has Rob's imprint on it in one form or another, and for this I am most grateful, as I am for his friendship.

Second, I want to thank Ken Fisher for writing a flattering foreword. His encouragement and mentorship in this book's development, particularly in the beginning when his wisdom was needed the most, was invaluable. In his own way, Ken was a significant factor, because without his enthusiastic support this book may have never been published. Thank you, Ken, for all you have done.

I also have to thank John Wiley & Sons for their patience as I struggled to meet deadlines, and for their belief in this book, especially Laura Walsh, Judy Howarth, Tula Batanchiev, Sharon Polese, Jeff Gould, Melissa Torra, and Steven Kyritz.

I also want to thank the many partners I've been fortunate to be associated with, who have remained long-term friends: Bill Sterett, a great guy and a good man, who supported and helped me in taking broken businesses and turning them into powerhouses; Al McKay and Walter Wilkenson, my first partners, who believed in me and gave me the money needed to open a new business, and unselfishly allowed me to lean on them for their experience; Gil L'Hommedieu, my current partner, who has been patient with me as I dedicated so much of my time to writing this book; and Mark Hulings Sr., Mark and Janet Hulings, and Mary Sterett—each a wonderful partner in his or her own way.

One of the important factors in every businessperson's success is their competitive instincts and knowing what it takes to win on a consistent basis. I was fortunate to play for some great coaches, who led us to multiple championships and taught us how to win, overcome adversity, and be leaders on a winning team. To coaches John Mooney, Blaine Knoll, Bill Seymour, Terry Bicknell, and Lyn Bannister, thank you for teaching us how not just to win, but to win championships. Of course, coaches can't do it on their own. There were some great athletes and "character" players who have remained lifelong friends. So thanks for the great times we had to: Dr. Greg "Nick" Homenick, Bruce "Buc" Buchan, Ross "Rocky" Johnson, John "Scotor" Allen, Ron "Logie" Logan, Billy "Roomy" Thompson, and all the hundreds of players I competed with over the years, as well as enjoyed beverages with throughout the seasons. And I can't forget two good friends, Jim Peplinski and Terry Labonte, NHL and NASCAR champions, who through our friendship have shown me time and time again how great champions transcend their sports by demonstrating their class and the character that made them winners both in their sports and away from them.

Thanks, also, to my many business mentors: Jerry Gleason, Doug Spedding, Mike Maroone, Tony Noland, Bob Du'Chalard, Bruce Axleson, Gordon Mann, Richard Gallagher, Blayne Lensen, Charlie Thomas, Fritz Kern, Gordie Bell, John Spellen, and Uncles Stu and Don McBean; and gentlemen like Carlos Ledezma, Steve Hincliff, Ed Tonkin, Dave Solmun, Ron Brown, Joe Serra, John Bowman, Mike Boyer, Bob Myers, and all the fellows I was in Business Owners Twenty groups with in both Canada and the United States

Special thanks to: Pat "PJ" Johnson, Cheryl Jaeger, Brian Campbell, Debbie Elicksen, Debbie Meadows, Lynnda McBean, Shauna Butts, Scott McBean, Tony Fincannon, Dave Resendez, Sean

Butts, Blair Upton, Kristy and Walter Wright, and of course, my sister, Susan Nazarenko, for helping and encouraging me in one form or another to eventually get me to the point of writing this book.

Thanks to the scores of people who taught me so much and had fun with me so often: Dorothy Cram, Harold Whitbread; Doug Grey; Bill Yard; Harry Apps; Harvey Coates; Ken Chatwin; Stone Avery; Kenny Brown; Brian Sweeney; Bob Todd; Blair Upton; Barry Kuntz; Brent Dewar; Dave Ashton; Jerry Daniels; Bill Davies; Steve Blake; Rob Hutchison; Brian McVeigh; Ken Boa; Bobby Cavanaugh; Grant Rodgers; Judge Pat Koskie; Scott Brower; the Rusnak brothers, Dave and Wayne; Wayne Jensen; Stu McFadden; Ken Chyz; Rollie Wilcox; Bruce Keith; George Marlette; Ron "Rookie" Robinson; Ed Chynoweth; Doug Lindsay; Dave "Pick" Picket; Rick "Fergy" Jackson; Don "Crapper" Harapchuk; Wayne Knowles; Brian Vasey; Dave "Kingster" King; Bill and Carol Pettus; Glynda Fincannon; Jess and Jackie Cole; Craig Dunn; John and Julie Buckley; Nick Hardcastel; Roy Nazarenko; Don Wheaton Sr., Dave Windsor; Bridget Werner; Tim Keen; Stu Esplen; John Esplen; Greg Campbell; Doug Clark; Kent Harleson; Gary Bentham; Walter Hilderbrant; Bob "Art" Faulkner; Pete "Pistol" Badyk; Orest "O" Kinderchuck; Murray Fairweather; Donny Kozak; Mel Gross; Howie Hicks; Charlie Carins; Bobby Will; Mickey Shaw; Eldon Cooke; Bob Korpan; the Houston brothers, Greg and Kirk; Dennis Breker; Paul Monarch; Steve Hyatt; Will Sodski; Cathy Peplinski; Doug "Spitz" Spitzig; Don "Crapper" Harapchuk; John Laskoski; Scott Atkinson; Mason Cox; Stanley "Frenchie" Patoine; Mike Lemire; Doug Colville; Mary Cole; Ted Oakly; Arnie and Sharon Boeyen; Ken Jaeger; Brian Vasey; Skip and Irene Kretschmar; Mike and Jane Lewis; Jeff Dyke; Ron Gall; Mitch Lanier; Ken Laxdal; Mike and Tina Jones; Ray Schmaamn; Victor and Irena Papazov; Russ Vanden II; David Dunn; Ed and Bev Bacak; Doug Balfor; Dr. Keith Crocker; Cliff Wright; Jim Gibson; Dr. George Fisher; Michael and Toni Conte; Shannon Wilde; Scott Sherman; Chris and Cindy Duval; Tom Gauley; Judy Newman; Jack and Patty Bradfield; Shirley Pagen; Jeff Amidon; Jack Powers; Carlos Keeling; Pat Kasperitis; Rick Dames; Randy Sonnier; Laurie-Anne Rusnak; Mike Collins; Mike Ferlet; Frank Gleason; Pat "Dunner" Dunn; Jim Gentry; Randy

Hicks; Preston Douglas; Patti L'Hommedieu; Terry and Phyllis Cox; Dave Brown; John and Diane Doyle; Walter Meadows; Bill Goodman; Lawrence "Frenchy" LaBonte; John Hobbs; Tom Flores; Donny Orcutt; and all my employees, past, present, and future.

And, finally, a special thanks to Lynnda and Scott McBean, and Shauna Butts, and the soon-to-be newest arrival, "Keiki" Butts, for giving me the time and space to write this book.

Introduction

Business ownership is a seductive magnet. It promises success, wealth, and a life full of rewards for you and your family. The fact is, though, that the reality is very different from the dream, even when you are successful. That's because most would-be owners don't have a very clear picture of what it actually takes to be successful. *The Facts of Business Life* is designed to remedy that. It is accordingly a unique business book that focuses on what needs to be done to create success, how to do it, and when to do it. And I know these business concepts will work for you because they've done so not only for me but for hundreds—if not thousands—of other successful business owners.

One of the reasons it's unique is that it provides a series of seven facts without which no entrepreneur's business can succeed. These facts are:

1. If you don't lead, no one will follow.
2. If you don't control it, you don't own it.
3. Protecting your company's assets should be your first priority.
4. Planning is about preparing for the future, not predicting it.
5. If you don't market your business, you won't have one.
6. The marketplace is a war zone.
7. You don't just have to know the business you're in, you have to know business.

As you can see, some of these facts cover traditional areas like leadership and control or management, while others are less conventional, like those concerning the war zone and the importance of protecting business assets. As the book explains, each of these facts is important, but as important as each one is, their real strength lies in how they are interrelated and how they work together. That is, in addition to their individual value as guidelines for entrepreneurs, they demonstrate that being a successful owner isn't about being good in one or two business disciplines but in all seven of them, as well as about understanding how they depend on each other.

You may understandably ask why I've chosen these seven facts out of the many disciplines of business. When you own a business, and I have owned several successful ones, you learn that you must be able to prioritize, and these seven facts, or concepts, represent the priorities I believe every owner, new or experienced, should never lose sight of. In addition, these particular concepts benefit both would-be and experienced owners in several different ways: (1) they are easy to implement; (2) they are easy for employees to understand and work with; (3) the more you understand them, the better chance you have for success; (4) they work in unison and form a solid foundation on which to build a business; and (5) they will produce the desired results.

The other important point to bear in mind regarding the seven facts is that they are organized strategically. That is, the first fact concerns leadership because without leadership and vision you cannot define success. In other words, it's leadership that determines the company's eventual destination and what it will look like when it gets there. Leadership is always followed by control, or management, which essentially outlines the day-to-day blocking and tackling that must be accomplished in order to achieve success as you have defined it. The third fact concerns protecting assets, because if your assets aren't protected, you are essentially leaving your investment at the mercy of your employees and forces in the marketplace over which you have little or no control. After protecting assets comes planning, because planning creates the road map, based on objectives and goals, that determines how your business will attain success, as well as maintain it. The fifth fact covers marketing, because very little can happen without customers and the sales revenue they provide, and marketing and advertising focus on attracting customers and creating a market presence. The fact that the market is a war zone comes next because, while it's one thing to attract customers, it's another to sell them and keep them as customers, and it's important that you understand this distinction. And, finally, the seventh and last fact—the importance of having a good general understanding of business—makes it clear that implementing all the previous facts can be done most effectively only when they are used together and backed up by a broad understanding of all the various facets of business.

The other reason *The Facts of Business Life* is unique is that it introduces the concept of a business life cycle, and the five levels every successful business goes through as it starts, grows, and matures. These five levels are divided into two groups. The first, which represents planning levels, includes "Ownership and Opportunity" and "Creating Your Company's DNA." The second, which represents the action levels, includes "From Survival to Success," "Maintaining Success," and, finally, "Moving On When It's Time to Go." Understanding this life cycle enables owners to pinpoint where they are at any given time, what has been done, and what has yet to be accomplished. The levels are progressive in nature, and owners carry their experiences with them from one level to the next.

It is important to note, however, that these levels are not quite as linear as they appear to be. As planning levels, Levels 1 and 2 are about deciding if you want to own your own business and, if so, what kind of business you want; and, having decided to become an owner, creating the processes and procedures under which your company will operate. Level 3, the first of the action levels, is where you implement the plans you made at the earlier levels and actually begin operating the business. Level 4 occurs when, having achieved success, you look for ways to maintain that success, and Level 5 is when you begin thinking about selling the business, passing it along to a successor, or closing it down. However, nothing is ever that straightforward in business. For example, it is possible for a successful business at Level 3 to slip back along the survival–success spectrum, in which case the owner has to return to Levels 1 and 2 to remedy the situation. In fact, it's necessary at all the action levels for owners to occasionally revisit the first two levels in order to review opportunities and evaluate threats, keep up with changes in the market, and make changes in their own processes.

Finally, the book explains how the application of the Facts of Business Life changes over the five levels. For example, "leadership" is always a business constant, but how an owner leads a business is significantly different when he or she is just starting to become successful than when the business has had years of back-to-back success. Similarly, the way an owner attacks the war zone is totally different when the business is working to maintain success than it is when the company is relatively new. This is, of course, common sense, but no business book has ever identified or addressed these issues as this one does.

There are few guarantees in life, especially if you're a business owner. Markets change, government regulations make it harder to do business, customers want more for less, competitors force you to adapt and innovate, and on and on. With all the changes that engulf owners in today's business climate, it's more important than ever to build a stable platform of business concepts on which they can operate their businesses. *The Facts of Business Life* provides that platform.

—Bill McBean
Corpus Christi, Texas
April 17, 2012

CHAPTER 1

The Facts of Business Life

Just as there are facts of life that affect us on a personal level, there are facts of life that affect us as businesspeople, and business owners who ignore them are essentially setting their businesses up for failure rather than success. These Facts of Business Life apply to every aspect of owning and managing a successful business—from maintaining control to strategic planning, from protecting assets to marketing, and from leadership to establishing and managing appropriate policies and procedures. And when these facts are recognized, understood, and acted on appropriately, they can literally make the difference between success and failure.

The sad truth is that less than 30 percent of businesses last more than 10 years, and most failures occur in the first few years of operation. Some of those businesses are doomed from the start because they are ill-conceived, poorly planned, or lack the working capital to attain success. Still others fail because their owners sabotage their chances to succeed through arrogance, lack of ethics, or misunderstanding what the role of an owner actually is. There are, though, other businesses—which I believe to be the majority—that could be successful but aren't, simply because their owners don't understood these Facts of Business Life.

1

And what are these facts? They represent the seven business concepts that every entrepreneur or business owner who hopes to succeed must have in his or her toolbox, including exhibiting leadership, maintaining control, protecting the company's assets, planning, marketing effectively, having a warrior mentality, and understanding business. There are, of course, other important business concepts, but after many years of running a number of successful businesses and studying successful businesses managed by others, I have come to the conclusion that these are the seven essential concepts without which no entrepreneur can succeed or reach his or her potential.

But it's not enough for you, as a business owner, to just understand these seven facts. It is equally important that you recognize how these facts are interrelated. Very few things in life work in isolation, and that's true of managing a business as well. If, for example, you are very adept at planning or marketing, that's a good start. But being able to develop strategic plans or market your product or service well will mean little if you don't have a good understanding of business in general. Similarly, while possessing leadership skills or knowing how to maintain control in an organization will be of enormous help in enabling you to manage your company, unless you're equally good at protecting the company's assets and have a warrior mentality, it's unlikely that you will ultimately be successful. In other words, you have to be good at all these things if you want to make sure your company will still be here 10, 20, or even 30 years from now.

Finally, although understanding the facts and recognizing their interrelationship are essential, there is one other concept you must understand if you hope to attain success. And that's the concept of the business life cycle—that is, there are various levels through which every successful business must progress over the course of its lifetime. Businesses, like people, go through various stages of life, and it's important to understand both what these stages are and how they affect the implementation of the Facts of Business Life. In this chapter, I provide an overview of the seven facts, and in the next I discuss what the business life cycle is and how it impacts making use of the facts.

The Facts

As I've already mentioned, there are many things an owner needs to know if he or she wants to start, build, maintain, and eventually sell a successful business. And because there are so many, no book—or, for that matter, series of books—could possibly teach you all of them at once. As with the facts of everyday life, some of them have to be learned at the beginning, and some can be learned as you go along. The following seven facts are the ones you need to understand right from the start if you want to build a strong foundation for your business.

Fact 1: If You Don't Lead, No One Will Follow

Good business leadership begins with defining both the direction and the destination of your company. But it doesn't stop there. It also requires you to quickly develop a set of skills and to continuously improve on them as your company moves forward. These skills include being calm under pressure, disciplined, motivational, realistic, and able to effectively communicate your vision of success, among others. In other words, as with all the other Facts of Business Life, leadership is something that must be recognized, understood, and acted on every day.

One aspect of leadership is developing a culture in a company that's based on expectations, and rewarding those who meet or exceed these expectations. A good leader makes sure that such employees are not only recognized but also financially rewarded, as this kind of positive reinforcement helps focus the entire company on the things that really matter. Another is developing a culture that enables employees to deal constructively with the kind of problems that inevitably come up in any business. For example, imagine a patron in a restaurant who complains to the waiter that he is not satisfied with his meal. If the owner has developed an appropriate culture, the waiter will apologize without hesitation and do whatever is necessary to satisfy the disgruntled customer. As a result, the customer is not only satisfied, but because he was treated so well he is considerably more likely to come back. The owner who has developed this kind of culture has made it possible to turn a negative situation into a positive one, in the process strengthening the entire company.

Some people argue that leaders are born, not made, and there is probably at least a bit of truth in this. However, there are a great many aspects of leadership that can be learned, and if you are intent on making your business a success, it is imperative that you develop them.

Fact 2: If You Don't Control It, You Don't Own It

If you don't control your business by defining the key tasks that must be handled every day, and dictating how those tasks will be handled, you don't control anything, you don't own anything, and you probably won't be in business for long. The concept of ownership control is this simple. This kind of control, however, can be achieved only through teamwork, which occurs in successful companies when people (employees), products (or services), and processes (internal procedures) work in unison. Essentially, people deliver the products by following the company's internal procedures, and it's these processes that operate the business.

A good example of why this is so important is what happens when an owner fails to establish procedures at the point of delivery. If there are no specific procedures, every employee handles customer delivery based on his or her own standards, which means every customer is handled differently. This presents a problem not only because it's never good for customers to be handled inconsistently, but also because the customer delivery point triggers a series of important internal events, including customer follow-up, inventory control and reorder, financial accounting, and others. And if these aren't triggered in a consistent and correct way, not only will the company not have the inventory its customers want, the company itself won't have the critical data it needs to make sound decisions.

But even if you do tell employees how you want the business to operate, it will never happen unless proper controls are designed and implemented to make sure employees do what's required.

Without controls like these, there is a good chance that serious problems will develop, and you may not recognize them until they've become crises. Unfortunately, when owners are faced with crises, they have to act on them immediately, but at this point they have relatively few options available to them. Similarly, if you don't establish and maintain a professional dress code, your employees are more than likely to use their clothing to express their individualism. Of course, doing so is perfectly acceptable outside of business hours, but business isn't about individualism, it's about conformity and a common goal, and it has to be controlled. The fact is that even though you may have your name on the business, if you don't control how the business operates, all you're really doing is observing a business you've invested in. And that's no way to run a company.

Fact 3: Protecting Your Company's Assets Should Be Your First Priority

Many people are likely to be surprised by this Fact of Business Life, because they think that a company's first priority should be sales, profits, and growth. But while sales, profits, and growth are important, it is equally if not more important to focus on protecting your assets because they power your sales, profits, and growth. Assets include equipment, accounts receivables, cash, and all the other items on your business's balance sheet. But there are other assets on which you can't put a dollar value, like your skills and experience; your employees and their skills and experience; the company's processes, customer base, and reputation; and others. And even though these assets do not appear on any balance sheet, they all have value and should accordingly be treated as if they had a cash value. And this means you must do whatever has to be done to manage and protect them.

For example, in order to build and maintain a company's customer base, you have to focus on developing processes for keeping existing customers as well as training employees to find new ones. If, however, you concentrate on finding new customers at the expense of providing after-sales service to existing ones, it's likely that those existing customers will go elsewhere. Protecting and managing a company's assets is one of the most underappreciated business issues today and, if mismanaged, can be one of the most damaging ones. But if you understand what *all* of a company's assets are, and that they *all* have to be protected, you are much more likely to see your company not only survive but succeed.

Fact 4: Planning Is About Preparing for the Future, Not Predicting It

Nobody knows what the future will bring, but you can make educated guesses based on the most current, accurate information available as well as your own past experiences. That means gathering and making use of such information as past sales, expenses, and profit results; the size of the market; and competition and customer demographics, just to name a few. Doing so enables you to look into the future and start anticipating what opportunities or threats may present themselves, as well as to make sure that you have whatever is needed to prepare for them. Although people frequently think planning is limited largely to the early stages of a business, it's actually an ongoing activity, or at least it should be.

It's important to remember, too, that planning is both a science and an art. The science is in gathering pertinent information, and the art is in taking that information and turning it into a plan that will move the business from "here to there" over a specific time period. In fact, being able to plan better than one's competitors is such an important skill that it can provide a company with a competitive advantage in the marketplace. If, for example, an owner knows there is a new product coming on the market and proactively plans for it ahead of time, he or she can "own the market" before the company's less aggressive competitors are even thinking about it. This is similar to something the Ford Motor Company did in 2008 and 2009 when careful planning enabled it to see the coming restriction on bank lending. Being proactive, they were able to raise capital before the tightening of lending regulations, which their competitors, General Motors and Chrysler, did not. And because Ford's management "read the tea leaves," unlike GM and Chrysler, their company didn't run out of cash and need a government bailout. They knew, as you should, that planning is important because it focuses owners on what's important and prepares them for what lies ahead.

Fact 5: If You Don't Market Your Business, You Won't Have One

Marketing and advertising are business realities. Without marketing and advertising there are few sales, and without sales there is no company. If you can't or don't want to work to market whatever product or service the company is going to provide, you should seriously reconsider the decision to become an owner. It doesn't matter if your company has the best product available or is the best at whatever it does. If not enough people know about it, it won't make any difference. The need to make potential customers aware of your company—to get the company's message out into the marketplace—never goes away, and only companies that are relentless in doing so remain successful.

For example, an owner of a new company has the huge challenge of letting the marketplace know that a new business is open. At times like this, money is usually very tight and large expenditures, such as marketing, tend to make owners extremely nervous. But the fact is that if marketing isn't done, very little good will happen. And if you understand this, and will make the necessary effort, you will have a big advantage over those who are afraid to spend their money or who view marketing as an expense rather than the investment it is.

Another example of the importance of marketing is the situation in which a company has been offered an opportunity to buy some merchandise at a significantly discounted price, but only if they will order twice as many of the items as they normally would. All things being equal, under normal operating conditions the company would likely be unable to take advantage of an opportunity like this. But if they were to develop a marketing and advertising campaign to sell the item and pass on the discount to the customers, they would be able to attract new customers, increase their market share, and in the process create additional profits. In other words, marketing and advertising are weapons that businesses can't afford to not take advantage of because of the potential they have to drive sales and profits.

Fact 6: The Marketplace Is a War Zone

Every company has competitors, and if it doesn't and it's successful, it soon will. Successful owners know they have to fight not only to win market share but to retain it as well. In fact, the reason they've become successful is that they've developed a warrior mentality, and it's this mentality that enabled them to survive and succeed in the first place. Successful owners also know that past success is no guarantee of future success, and that the only way to remain successful is to maintain their fighting mentality.

If, for example, a new competitor arrives in the market either by buying one of your competitors or starting a new business, the marketplace is likely to change. In a situation like this, you may well have to be more aggressive if you want to protect what you have, that is, retain your market share, much less increase it. But the market will also change if a competitor closes down his or her business. In that kind of situation, a void is created in the market, and it will be only the more aggressive owners who step in to fill that void, take advantage of the opportunity, gain market share and new customers, and at the same time increase sales and profits.

In other words, as an owner, in order to be successful or remain that way, you have to continually focus on the market, react to it, and fight for what you believe should be yours. The marketplace *is* a war zone, and if you don't think of it that way, your competitors will, and they will be the ones who win the war.

Fact 7: You Don't Just Have to Know the Business You're in, You Have to Know Business

Understanding one's industry is obviously a must, but in order to become successful in any business an owner must also understand how business itself works. That means he or she has to not only understand the Facts of Business Life but must also be familiar with the various aspects of business, such as accounting, finance, business law, and personnel issues, to name just a few. In addition, an owner must understand how the facts, and the various aspects of business, impact on each other so that he or she can make intelligent decisions.

A good example of the importance of this might be when an owner, seeing a market opportunity, buys a competitor by using a significant amount of working capital from his or her existing business. As a result, both companies are strapped for cash and limited in their potential for growth or expansion, if not in even more dire circumstances. If this owner, however, had a better understanding of accounting and finance and had completed a working capital analysis, as well as doing cash flow calculations, he or she could have foreseen the cash squeeze problem and avoided it by finding other means of funding the purchase.

If any proof is needed of the importance of having a good understanding of business, all you have to do is look at what often happens when the owner of a business decides to retire and turn it over to one of his or her children. More often than not, when this happens, the son or daughter who takes over has spent a few years working in the business and a few more helping the owner run it. But a lot of family businesses don't do as well when they are passed on, and one of the primary reasons for this is that, even though the new owner has some experience in the business, he or she often doesn't understand the various facets of business and how they are all interrelated. And the result, unfortunately, is that a perfectly viable company, one that its original owner spent years building up, now has a questionable future.

Colleges and universities understand the importance of having an overall understanding of the many concepts of business—it's why they insist business students choose a major but also take other core business courses. The fact is that if you don't have a good general idea of how business works, it puts you and your company at a distinct disadvantage when compared to competitors who have developed this understanding.

The Business Life Cycle

In business, as in life in general, nothing remains the same. There are so many variables beyond our control that, when it comes to ourselves as well as to our businesses, the only way we can be sure to not only survive but flourish is to adapt to the changes that are taking place around us. There is, however, one aspect of both business and life in general that we can expect and, to some extent, prepare for—and that's maturing. Of course, people don't mature in exactly the same way that companies do, but both people and organizations go through a life cycle. In life, we start as newborns, then grow into infants, toddlers, children, teenagers, young adults, adults, middle-agers, and, eventually, seniors. Companies, by comparison, go through five stages—or levels—of life:

1. Ownership and Opportunity
2. Creating Your Company's DNA
3. From Survival to Success
4. Maintaining Success
5. Moving on When It's Time to Go

I will provide more explanation about these five levels in the next chapter. For the moment, though, it's important to recognize that, just like people, businesses need guidance as they go through their life cycle, and it's the owners who are ultimately responsible for providing that guidance. It's equally important to recognize that, just as the guidance a parent provides a child must change as the child grows older, the guidance an owner provides over the lifetime of a company must change as the company moves up from one level to the next.

The seven Facts of Business Life are essentially a means of providing guidance for a company. What that means, though, is that while the facts are always true, their application will change depending on where the business is in its life cycle. We have all seen businesses that come out of the gate hard and fast, have a big impact in the market, and then fizzle out, never reaching their potential. What that means is the owner provided appropriate guidance to enable the company to get off to a good start, but wasn't able to adapt that guidance to the successive levels of business. Making that transition successfully, ensuring that your company will continue to be successful, requires an understanding of how these seven concepts change as the business matures, and your ability to adjust to those changes.

The Levels of Business Success

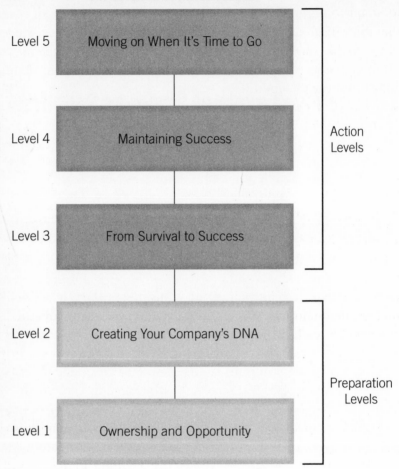

CHAPTER 2

The Five Levels of Business Success

Walt Disney's hit movie and Broadway show *The Lion King* features a wonderful song called "The Circle of Life," which reminds us that we are all born, grow up, get older, and eventually pass away. But it isn't only living things that go through a life cycle—businesses do the same. Just like human beings, new businesses start, grow, achieve success, maintain that success, and eventually come to an end. This business life cycle is not always apparent, but it does exist, and it's going on around us every day and everywhere. And it's very important for business owners to understand this life cycle, because it gives them parameters or structure, which in turn forces them to focus not only on *what* is important but also on *when* it's important.

Trying to manage a successful business without taking this concept into account is like playing a baseball game without knowing what inning you are in, if you are winning or losing, where you rank in relationship to other teams, or how far into the season you are. But if you understand the business life cycle, you are able to look at your company and determine where you are, how far you have to go, and what you have to do to get there. Having this understanding also helps you define what success means to you, determine appropriate objectives and goals, plan and strategize to achieve those goals, measure your efforts, and make adjustments and improvements as necessary. Finally, it makes it possible for you to see threats as well as opportunities, recognize options for overcoming the threats, and take advantage of the opportunities you might have otherwise missed. Unfortunately, though, the vast majority of business owners operate without this understanding. And there is no doubt, at least in my mind, that this lack of understanding contributes significantly to the extremely high failure rate of American businesses.

The fact is that, whether you are aware of it or not, every successful business inevitably passes through five levels over the course of its lifetime:

1. Ownership and Opportunity
2. Creating Your Company's DNA
3. From Survival to Success
4. Maintaining Success
5. Moving on When It's Time to Go

The first level, Ownership and Opportunity, is the one in which individuals seek out or create an opportunity in a market because they believe their ownership skills can produce a reasonable profit based on their investment. At Level 2, Creating Your Company's DNA, owners create processes and procedures that determine how the company will be run on a day-to-day, month-to-month basis, which in turn dictate how employees will perform their jobs and how they will interact with each other and the company's customers in order to create the expected outcome. These first two are essentially planning levels, although owners also have to refer back to them as their companies go through the business life cycle.

The third level, From Survival to Success, is the period during which those day-to-day processes are put into effect, results are measured to make sure that what's accomplished is what was expected, and steps are taken to modify them if necessary. During Level 4, Maintaining Success, owners protect their businesses from threats and create or seek out additional opportunities in order to solidify the company's foundation and build on its success. Finally, at Level 5, owners finalize and implement their plans for winding down their careers, and if they've done it right, exit the business on their own terms and with maximum payout. Levels 3, 4, and 5, then, are action levels in that at these levels the company is actually in operation.

These five steps in the business life cycle, the five levels of business success, are successive in nature. That is, a business must successfully complete Level 1 before it can go on to Level 2, Level 2 before going on to Level 3, and so on. In this respect it's very much like going through school. You can't go to middle school without first having gone to elementary school, attend high school without having finished middle school, or enroll in college without having completed high school. In addition, in the same way that the information you gather and the skills you develop in the lower grades continue to be used in the higher ones, everything you learn at the various levels of the business life cycle continues to be used as you move through it. That is, rather than leaving the levels behind, you actually bring them with you, and expand and improve as you go from one level to the next.

It's important to remember, too, that even though you use the same skills in school from one grade to the next, you don't necessarily use them in the same way. For example, you learn how to read in elementary school, but as you go through middle school, high school, and college, you use that skill to read different kinds of things. Similarly, you start to learn arithmetic in first grade, but by the time you're finished with your schooling, you've learned how to solve much more advanced mathematical problems. The seven Facts of Business Life work exactly the same way. That is, although the facts—the skills you develop—remain the same from one level to the next, the way you apply and implement them changes as your business moves through the life cycle. Take, for example, Fact 4, "Planning Is About Preparing for the Future, Not Predicting It." At Level 1, Ownership and Opportunity, most of the plans you make will be concerned with the overall profitability of the opportunity, how long it will take to become profitable, and how much cash you'll need to get the business up and running. However, at Level 4, Maintaining Success, the plans you make are much more likely to be strategic and tactical in nature, and focused on market share and profit. In other words, the skill remains the same, but its use changes. And that's why the level a business is on at any given moment—that is, where it is in its life cycle—has a significant impact on how it operates and what its owner's role is.

There is also, however, an important distinction that needs to be made among the various levels. In his book, *The Seven Habits of Highly Successful People* (Free Press, 1990), Steven Covey discusses how everything is essentially created twice—first as a mental concept and then as a physical concept. This is true of the business life cycle as well. Levels 1 and 2 represent the mental creation of the business—that is, thinking and preparing—while Levels 3, 4, and 5 represent the physical creation of the business—that is, taking action to implement those thoughts and preparations. The truth of this will become clearer as you learn more about the Facts of Business Life and how they are implemented at the five different levels.

While in a perfect world every owner would begin at Level 1 and move easily on to Level 2, Level 3, and so on, life in the business world is seldom perfect. While most businesses do basically move from one level to the next, there are always instances in which, for one reason or another, they have to temporarily return to earlier levels. For example, if a company at Level 3, From Survival to Success, finds that one of its competitors has developed a better way to deliver its product to customers, it would be in the company's best interests to go back to Level 2, Creating Your Company's DNA, and reconfigure its own process for delivering its product, thereby keeping up with a competitor's challenge. Similarly, if a company at Level 4, Maintaining Success, decides to expand its business, it has to go back to Level 1 to analyze whether the proposed expansion will be profitable, and, if so, return to Level 2, Creating Your Company's DNA, to rework its processes to handle the expansion. In fact, it's only by going back and forth from one level to another that companies can continue moving successfully through the business life cycle.

In order to provide a clear and concise overview of each of the five levels, I have divided the discussion of each one into five general areas: (1) Leadership, (2) Management, (3) Planning, (4) People, and (5) Marketing and the Customer. Although there are other, more specific aspects of running a business, I've chosen these five because I feel that together they represent the basic elements of business ownership and that by reviewing them you will get a good idea of what happens at each level.

Level 1: Ownership and Opportunity

The owner's objective at Level 1 is essentially to determine if an opportunity exists—or can be created—that would be attractive based on how much profit it can generate and how much cash will be needed to do it, the owner's criteria for success, and the owner's tolerance for risk. Notice that I use the word *risk* here. Ownership and opportunity is a "risk versus reward" proposition and has nothing to do with the generally accepted belief that going into business for yourself is a gamble. Gambling is what happens when a potential owner goes into an opportunity without proper research. However, if you do your homework and understand what needs to be done to make money, and how much money the opportunity will require, it becomes a risk versus reward decision.

As I mentioned earlier, although Level 1 is where every business starts, since you bring each level with you as your company moves through the life cycle, you must continue to execute the tasks at Level 1 even as you move on to succeeding levels. That is, these tasks don't have to be done only when a prospective owner first researches the market for his or her product or service. They are also required when a current owner wants to determine whether market factors have remained the same. All successful owners know they have to keep on top of the market and are constantly visiting Level 1 so they can stay ahead of competitors by keying on market shifts, trends, and opportunities.

Leadership at Level 1

One of the most important skills of leadership is self-analysis, but it is particularly critical at Level 1. This is especially true for the first-time owner because not everyone is cut out to own his or her own business. But it also applies to current owners who are thinking about expanding their companies or starting new businesses. That's because even though a great opportunity may present itself, it may not be the right opportunity for you and your situation. And unless you take the time to analyze yourself and your abilities realistically, you won't be able to make an informed decision about pursuing it. So, particularly at this level, you need to stop and think about who you are and who you want to be, and you need to do it before you sign a bank note or negotiate a purchase.

Management at Level 1

The first thing any businessperson needs to know about management is that it always comes after leadership. Leadership points the way, but it's management that gets you where you're going. Once you've analyzed yourself and determined that you are ready to pursue an opportunity, management takes over. At Level 1, the primary task of management is to gather information and develop financial forecasts in order to determine if an opportunity exists, what the potential profits are, if the market is expanding or growing, the possibility for additional opportunities in the market, and the possible threats to achieving the desired results.

The information you will need to gather includes market size, the strengths and weaknesses of your competitors, potential sales, ease of competitor entry, market demographics, typical gross profit margins in the industry, typical expenses, and expected profits as a percentage of sales. By the time you have gathered all this information, you will have essentially become not only an expert on the market but will also have developed an understanding of both national industry trends and future prospects for the industry. Once you have this information, you will be able to produce realistic financial forecasts detailing "most likely" sales, gross profits, expenses, and net profits. You will also be able to determine cash flow, cash burn, working capital, and the total amount of investment required. All of this will, in turn, lead to a return on investment (ROI) number and indicate how long it will take the company to become debt free on the operating side.

Finally, ownership and opportunity decisions should always be based entirely on up-to-date facts or, at the very least, educated assumptions. Emotions, guesses, dated information, uneducated assumptions, or what you imagine life as an owner might be like should never be part of any business decision. And the simple truth is that the better the information you gather, and the better you analyze it, the more likely the decision you make will be the right one. This process is the same regardless of whether it's the first business being bought or the fifteenth. The only difference is that the more you do it over the years, the better you get at it.

Planning at Level 1

At this level, as at every level, planning addresses the question of how you are going to accomplish what you're expecting to accomplish. But at Level 1, planning's primary purpose is to determine if the financial forecast you've completed is realistic, and if it isn't, what that means for the future of your potential business. Of course, every business plan is different, both because markets are different and because every owner's definition of success is different. There are, however, some elements that are common to every successful plan.

The first of these are goals and objectives. Goals are where you ultimately want your company to be, and objectives are the intermediate steps you have to attain before you can get there. At Level 1, for example, you might set a goal of increasing sales by 10 percent. In order to achieve that goal, you could set up a series of objectives such as increasing sales by 5 percent a year for two years; increasing inventory, marketing, and advertising by 5 percent a year; hiring additional employees to handle the increased volume; increasing employee training; buying new equipment; or updating processes to handle the expected sales increases.

The next common element in a successful business plan is the analysis. The goal of this analysis is to determine if what needs to be done in order to be profitable is realistic. In other words, it's one thing to put numbers down on a piece of paper, but it's quite another to make it happen. Such an analysis should consist of several key questions, including:

- What is the size of the overall market?
- What percentage of the market will I have to capture and keep in order to make a profit?
- Is the market growing or contracting, and how will this affect profits in the future?

- What will happen if the business doesn't perform up to my expectations?
- Do I have enough cash to last through some unforeseen difficulties?
- Do I have the talent and experience to lead my business to success?
- Is the expense structure likely to support the expected results?

Answering these questions is particularly important because they "slow" you down; that is, they remove emotion from your calculations and force you to focus on the facts and the realities of the situation.

The last of the common elements of a successful business plan is the development of strategies. Strategies are, simply put, the means by which you will accomplish the goal and objectives you've set for the company. That means, for example, if one of your goals is to capture the business of one of the market's top-volume customers, you might develop such strategies as assigning a specific employee to handle their business, fast-tracking their orders, or perhaps setting special pricing or discounting for certain products or for purchasing in specific volumes. Similarly, if one of your goals is to increase gross profit margins, your strategies would have to include increasing your selling price, lowering your product cost, or some combination of the two. You might supplement this with a short-term objective of increasing training for your salespeople, and a long-term goal of eliminating some of your competition by buying or squeezing them out in order to dominate the market.

Planning at Level 1, as at all levels, is essentially a step-by-step process that enables you to determine if and how you will be able to attain whatever goal you have set for your company. At Level 1, though, it is also about preparing yourself for what may occur if you decide to move toward ownership or expansion, and to provide you with more information on which to base that decision.

People at Level 1

Employees are not only a major part of any business but also, in most companies, one of the largest expense categories—if not the largest. Owners accordingly want to get their money's worth by hiring the best people they can find. Unfortunately, there is a limited number of such people, and even if you can find them, they may not want to work for you. And even if they did, you probably wouldn't be able to afford all of them. However, since you aren't actually hiring anyone at this level, you have time to identify these people, recruit them, and work their cost into your expense structure.

When you are thinking about employees at Level 1, there are essentially three issues you must take into account. The first is their overall cost, including payroll taxes and benefits. Because employees constitute such a large expense, their cost will have a major effect on profits, which means that estimating the cost correctly is important as it can affect the opportunity decision, either positively or negatively. The second issue is that every business has key positions, and it's essential to identify these key jobs and make sure they get filled first. The fact is that not every job is equally important, so it's best to know which ones are vital, identify some candidates for those jobs, and be realistic in terms of the salary and benefits they will demand. The third issue concerns training. In any new opportunity, training is important, and sometimes employees have to be hired even before the first customer walks in the door. For that reason, the cost of training has to be taken into consideration, especially if processes have to be designed and coordinated with each other. The bottom line, so to speak, is that setting a limit on personnel expense is a tool you must use at this level if you want to be able to make an informed opportunity decision.

Marketing and the Customer at Level 1

After you've done all the research and analyses you need to determine if a particular opportunity is right for you, there is one last area on which you need to focus—who your customers are and how you can reach them. As an owner you have to get this right, because if you don't, even if you do everything else right, your chances for success will be slim at best. Of course, at this level the opportunity is still a mental concept rather than a physical one, and you have yet to fight any real marketplace battles. But marketing and the customer have to be one of your focal points, both before and after you start your business, because without customers there is no business. And if you don't know your customers, you will never be able to reach them to tell them that you exist and are ready to fill their needs.

Once you know who your customers are, assigning and developing a marketing budget should become your focus. Like employee salaries, marketing and advertising can be a major expense, so your estimate of its cost has to be realistic. It also has to include the cost of getting the word out about your business as well as keeping it in front of your potential customers. Marketing is one of those expenses owners tend to minimize, especially at this level, and my suggestion would be to first determine what you consider a realistic budget, and then add a certain percentage to cover unforeseen marketing opportunities.

Marketing experts often describe marketing and advertising as an investment in your business, and for a good reason—it is. But before you begin that marketing effort, it is essential that you know where your customers go for information and/or how to reach them, what their important buying motivations are, how to drive them to your business, and what it will cost. This is one of those aspects of business you have to get right from the beginning because if you don't, nothing else is going to matter. You can be wrong in some other areas and survive until it gets fixed, but if you're wrong in the marketing and customer area, failure can happen so quickly that you won't even have time to make corrections.

Level 2: Creating Your Company's DNA

Creating a company's DNA is essentially about determining and mapping out how the business will operate on a day-to-day, week-to-week, and month-to-month basis. This is done by establishing procedures and processes that will enable you to realize the results you forecasted at Level 1. These range from determining how cash sales are recorded to how customers are handled and treated, from developing an internal code of conduct to how job descriptions are written, and from how training is conducted to how salaries are paid out. In other words, DNA includes any task that requires some kind of procedure in order to make sure that your business operates in a manner consistent with your definition of quality.

Establishing processes like these is extraordinarily important for several reasons. First, it enables owners to show their employees how they want the business to be operated. This is essential because, as I noted earlier, it is ultimately these processes that operate the business. In addition, processes by definition demand accountability, which in turn results in job expectation and performance standards, and makes it easy to evaluate an employee's performance. Finally, when there are processes in place, it is much easier to spot problems and to fix them before they become serious. Unfortunately, establishing these processes—creating a company's DNA—is perhaps the least understood and most underappreciated macro concept for business owners. It is also, though, one of the most essential.

Leadership at Level 2

A good leader has to have a toolbox full of skills, but at Level 2 the predominant skill required is vision, that is, the ability to look into the future. An owner has to be able to visualize how the company will operate in order to exploit the opportunity to its fullest and achieve the success forecasted. What that means is that you have to visualize what tasks must be accomplished, determine those areas in which processes must be established, assign accountability for them, and develop means of determining whether the processes are working the way they should be. This is the first step in creating a company's DNA.

If as an owner you cannot do this, your company will essentially be operating on the philosophy "If you don't know where you're going, any road will take you there." And those roads lead to failure. However, by defining what needs to be done, designing processes to match that definition, and dictating how the processes will work, you will be exhibiting the kind of leadership that's necessary at this level. It's important to note, though, that determining what processes are needed can be a very complex task. If, for example, your company operates primarily on cash sales, everyone should understand how these sales are recorded and what happens from the time the customer hands the money to an employee to the time the money is deposited into the business's bank account. One of the obvious benefits of establishing such a process is that it protects the business from theft and normal human absent-mindedness. What's less obvious is that it's also important to develop processes that determine how employees treat customers, when inventory should be replenished and when it shouldn't, and when and how the customer should be contacted after the sale, as well as many other items.

Management at Level 2

Once an owner has determined what tasks must be accomplished and which of these require processes to be established, creating the step-by-step procedures and determining how to measure the results of those procedures is essentially a management function. For instance, in the preceding example, if you want to develop a procedure to follow up with a customer, it could be something as simple as sending an e-mail to thank them for their business. You could also contact them after some particular number of days to make sure they are satisfied and give them a special discount on their next purchase. Similarly, you could set up a procedure in which you inform them of a product or products that complement what they bought, or tell them about what other customers who bought what they did also bought. The point is, regardless of what you choose to do, it is important to set up a process for doing it— or nothing will get done.

But setting up processes also helps you develop the company's DNA in another important way—by helping you develop a clear picture of the kind of talents employees will need to ensure competent operation of the processes. This will in turn better enable you to determine the number of employees needed, the training required, the discipline you must have to make the processes work, appropriate performance expectations, and the means by which employees will be held accountable for results. And all of these things become part of the company's DNA.

Planning and People at Level 2

As I mentioned earlier, in any successful business, it's the processes that operate the business. But it's the owner's job to define these processes, and the employees' job to operate them. At Level 2, DNA creation accordingly brings together leadership, management, and planning in that it connects the definition of success (leadership) and the step-by-step processes needed (management) to an organized format (planning) in order to make the success goal a reality.

Planning for a business is actually similar in many ways to planning for a trip. When you're planning a trip, you first decide where you want to go, then decide on the route, and then determine how long it should take to get there. Once you've accomplished this, you will know how many nights you will have to stay in a hotel, the number of meals you will have, and what your other expenses will be. When you're planning a business, you also start with where you want to go—in this case, the success you are hoping to attain. Then you decide how you're going to get there, how long it will take, and what you and your employees will have to do to accomplish the expected results, that is, how much sales revenue and gross profit you will need to meet your expenses and make a profit. And just as you need a map when you're planning a trip, you need a plan when you're starting a business so that you know which road to take, where to turn, and what you have to go through in order to get where you want to be.

Employees are, of course, also an important aspect of DNA creation, but they also have to be controlled. That means they must have the appropriate skills and a great attitude, be adaptable to change, and be willing and able to work within the guidelines you establish. If, for example, you want your customers to feel that your organization is a professional one that they can trust, your staff must present themselves accordingly. If your company sold medical equipment and a customer came into your business and was greeted by an unshaven, 60-year-old man dressed in leather and covered with tattoos, the customer would not in all likelihood be favorably impressed. The important thing to remember is, where DNA creation and employees are concerned, the tail can't wag the dog. That is, how your company operates must be your decision, not your employees'. Creating a company's DNA is hard; enforcing it is even harder. But if long-term success is your goal, you really don't have any choice.

Marketing and the Customer at Level 2

Nothing happens without the customer. And customers won't know that your company—or the products or services you provide—exists without marketing. This is one of those business laws that you just can't ignore, and one that, fortunately, most people know. What you may not realize, though, is that your company's DNA has a very considerable influence on how your company markets and delivers its products or services. What that means in practice is that the kind of message delivered through your marketing should reflect the ethics and professionalism of your company.

Virtually everyone expects politicians to make promises and then not deliver on them—it's part of the game. But it doesn't work with customers. If you make a promise to a customer and don't deliver on it, he or she is very unlikely to come back. And because of this, it's essential for your company's DNA be a reflection of your marketing. That is, if the message your marketing sends to your customers makes a promise, you must develop your DNA to make sure both your products and services deliver on that promise. This is an important point that can easily be forgotten in the busy day-to-day operation of a business. You might be able to realize some short-term gains by making promises you can't back up, but it's one thing to attract a customer and quite another to bring a dissatisfied customer back to your business. And having a clearly stated DNA makes it easier to keep your marketing from making exaggerated or misleading claims that can get you in trouble with your customers.

Marketing and customers go hand in hand, but the overall purpose of attracting customers is to get them to buy from you, then come back and buy again, and then tell their friends and relatives what a great business you have. Most customers are decent, law-abiding, moral people, and if you want to attract and keep the majority of them, your business has to operate in accordance with their values. What this means is that everything about the way your business is run has to reflect those values, including how honest your advertising is, how a customer is greeted, how well employees are trained to respond to customers' requests or questions, and literally hundreds of other aspects of your operation.

Creating your company's DNA begins at Level 2 but is actually an ongoing activity. Because the market and your customers are always changing, as your company moves through its life cycle you will have to periodically come back to Level 2 to create or recreate processes that reflect those changes. That's one of the reasons it's so important for you to think through and develop the kind of processes that your company will need to operate successfully at Levels 3, 4, and 5.

Level 3: From Survival to Success

The third level, From Survival to Success, is the point at which all the planning and preparations that were done at Levels 1 and 2 are implemented. It's here that you must be relentless in your pursuit of putting those day-by-day processes into effect by measuring the results to make sure they're accomplishing what's expected, modifying them if necessary, and continuously working with your employees until those processes become second nature to them. The goal at this level is to move the business from the survival to the success end of the spectrum. That may sound simple enough, but the reality is that the majority of businesses that start Level 3 don't make it past the survival end of the spectrum, and only 3 out of 10 survive more than 10 years. This means that Level 3 is not only where businesses begin, it's also where most entrepreneurial dreams die.

Although most of the failures at Level 3 can be traced to a lack of preparation in identifying appropriate opportunities and/or in designing how the business will operate, the fact is that some of those businesses could have been saved if their owners knew what to do, that is, revisit Levels 1 and 2 and make corrections. When problems arise at Level 3, failure is by no means inevitable, and owners have to understand that they have to fight to be successful. In fact, most owners become successful because of how they handle adversity. Things seldom go as planned, and Level 3 is more about working hard, being smart, and focusing on building a successful business one step at a time—sometimes by trial and error—than it is about being an overnight success.

If, for example, you should find that your Level 3 business has stalled, or is not delivering the desired profits, you can go back to

Level 1, look again at the information you gathered at that point, and determine if the opportunity you thought was there still exists. If it doesn't, you can research the market again, find out where the opportunities are, and then change your company's direction. However, if you find the opportunity does still exist but the company is not operating the way it should in order to take advantage of the market, you can return to Level 2, find the operational problems, and then create or recreate processes and procedures to enable the company to operate the way it should.

Leadership at Level 3

Level 3 puts an owner through more turmoil and change than any of the other levels of the business life cycle, and accordingly requires him or her to exhibit a variety of leadership skills. There are, however, three of those skills that are particularly important at this level: (1) defining reality, that is, making sure you have a good understanding of where the business stands right now; (2) determining what has to be accomplished and in what time frame; and (3) motivating employees to buy in to the owner's vision and continue working to help move the company forward. Doing this is no easy task, and it doesn't get any easier. In addition, the leadership that's required at the survival end of the spectrum is different than what's needed at the success end, which means the owner's leadership qualities and skills have to grow and improve as the business moves along the spectrum.

As you move your company along the survival–success spectrum, you will probably find that one of the most difficult battles is the one you have with yourself. Effective leadership means staying calm in the face of adversity, remaining consistent in your ethics and discipline, having the patience to see the plan through, maintaining the courage it takes to make decisions, and being continuously enthusiastic about the future. And that's not easy, especially when your knees are knocking, you have to reinvest profits time and time again to feed the growing beast, you're constantly faced with self-doubt, and you have to deal with all the other issues that ownership brings with it. Moreover, these battles erupt frequently and rarely let up, and it takes time before you become comfortable in the knowledge that the business can meet its goals and objectives.

There is, however, one more important aspect of leadership that begins at Level 3 and continues through the end of the business life cycle. Although when you first start a business you cannot delegate leadership, as you become more skilled at it, it is essential that you begin—and continue to—develop as many leaders as possible among your employees. Doing so makes the company stronger because the more people you can develop as leaders, the more horsepower your business will have to pull it forward. And more horsepower means you will get to your destination faster and have a healthier business when you arrive there.

Management at Level 3

Because at Level 3 the business is "live," that is, it's become active, and its destination has been defined, it becomes management's job to implement the processes created at Level 2 so the company can achieve its objectives and goals for sales and gross profit. In other words, at this level, management is about the day-to-day blocking and tackling of managing sales and profits, keeping on top of expenses, watching for changes in the market, managing the customer base, creating more customers, and improving processes, among many other tasks. However, important as all these functions are, the most important thing to remember is that results matter, and if the company is not achieving the results you intended it to, it's essential you find out why and fix the problem. That's because in the end results are what it's all about, so results have to be your main focus from the time you open the doors in the morning until you close them at night.

Planning and People at Level 3

Although Level 3 is where the plan you developed for the business is put into action, the plan itself is not the main focus. As I've mentioned before, a lot of people can design a plan, but what's more important is how you implement it and how you react to both successes and failures. This is because while the plan you formulated at

Level 1 is essentially the road map showing you how your business will get to its destination, it has to be changed and upgraded as new information is accumulated. That is, even though the destination remains the same, time frames may have to change. For example, if your business has been slow in attracting and training people to work for you and you're bringing in less revenue as a result, it will affect your financial forecast, and your plan will need to be revised to reflect the change. In fact, the key to planning at this stage of the business is recognizing the exceptions to the plan, both what is working better than expected and what isn't, taking advantage of those things that are, and improving those that are not. In other words, developing a workable plan is important, but plans are about results, good and bad, and the skill of the owner and the employees in adapting to the results is where the "rubber meets the road" and success is created.

Of course, in order for any plan to work, you need employees, and that's not only a challenge, it's frequently a problem as well. While some employees are likely to surprise you and others to disappoint you, both groups need constant attention. This is because at Level 3 the business goes through constant change as it moves along the survival–success spectrum, and employees tend to fight change because they don't understand that it's to their benefit, both in terms of pay and job security. If, however, you have designed processes within which your employees can work, those processes will keep them focused on their jobs rather than running around doing things they think are important or like doing, neither of which may have a great deal to do with the results you expect of them. In addition, processes give you a means of measuring what your employees are doing. For example, if your plan and supporting processes call for 100 items to be shipped per day, and your measurement shows you are shipping an average of only 80 per day, you have a problem that needs fixing. The great thing about processes is that they measure output, and they can be an early warning of things going wrong or of things going better than expected, both of which need management input.

Ultimately, particularly at this level, constant motivation, communication, and education are critical components for employees.

This is because at Level 3 so much is happening it's hard for employee's not only to keep track of all the changes but to keep up with them. Making sure they are in the loop as far as information is concerned, and doing whatever you can to help motivate them, will go a long way toward keeping your company on an even keel.

Marketing and the Customer at Level 3

At Level 3, marketing is aimed primarily at the market in which your research at Level 1 indicated there was an opportunity. The challenge at Level 3 as far as marketing is concerned is that marketing costs money, and cash is usually tight when you are still on the survival end of the survival–success spectrum. It takes ownership courage to spend money without being sure of a return on the money spent. And because of that, it's always a temptation to cut back on marketing at this level. However, the reality is that marketing is more critical at Level 3 than at any other point in your business's life cycle because it's marketing that leads to sales, and sales that supply the money you need to continue moving along the spectrum.

Targeting your customer base is critical, as is the message that explains to your customers why they should buy from you. That is, potential customers need to know why your business deserves their attention and consideration, and this has to be the focus of your marketing at Level 3. In other words, you have to be constantly aware of who the message is targeted to, how this market learns about your business, and what kind of advertising hook attracts them. And once you've attracted them, you have to focus on how your employees make the sale and how they follow up on it to make sure those customers will come back.

Of course, at the end of the day, everything a business does has to be done with the customer in mind. And although this is especially important at Level 3, it's also particularly difficult to do because the business goes through so many changes at this level that it's hard to keep the focus on the customer. This may sound crazy, but it's true. This is because as the business moves along the spectrum, the way it operates changes, and when things change, problems occur. The focus then is usually on fixing the problems so the business will operate more efficiently and the employees' jobs will be easier. But this is the wrong way to go about it. You obviously have to correct any problems that come up, but if there are any changes to be made, the first question you have to ask yourself is how those changes will affect the customers, not the company.

Your business will have attained success at Level 3 when it has a clear and unequivocal track record of consistent profits and success in reaching the goals and objectives you set for it. By the time it gets to the success end of the survival–success spectrum, the company will have developed a habit of continuously finding or creating new opportunities, defending itself against threats, and constantly making improvements in its processes and procedures. Success, however, is fleeting. Competitors will react to your improved market position, your customers' wants will change, new products will emerge, and old tried-and-true products will fade away. Keeping a business on top is not as easy as many people think, and it's at Level 4 that you will have to contend with these new challenges.

Level 4: Maintaining Success

The fourth level, Maintaining Success, is the period during which owners build on what they learned at Levels 1, 2, and 3 in order to ensure their company's continued success. Achieving this requires the owner's constant vigilance in order to make sure that processes and procedures are adhered to and improved on, leaders are developed internally, and challenging goals and objectives are established and met. It also requires that employees be continuously held accountable for their results, performance expectations be achieved, and all of the company's departments move in the direction in which the owner wants the company to go. In other words, the owner and the company's employees have to do everything that was done at Level 3 to become successful in the first place, but do it at a higher level and a faster pace.

When your company attains Level 4, you will find that it presents you with many challenges. But there is one thing you can do to help overcome at least some of those challenges: develop a mentality, a drive, or a thirst to compete at every level of your business, and pass that mentality on to others. Competing at Level 4 doesn't mean being satisfied with being successful or average. It means putting unrelenting pressure on your competitors using the strength that only a strong, profitable, and well-run business possesses in order to compete in every market your business participates in, every day and all day. Competitiveness is like measles— they are both contagious—and if you want your company to be competitive then you have to lead the charge. In business there is no trophy for just showing up—the trophy goes to the business that understands and values the qualities competing brings with it. Competing aggressively becomes a way of life and a valuable tool in avoiding some of the traps you'll find at Level 4.

Continuing to be competitive at Level 4 is important because there is a surprise awaiting unsuspecting owners who think that once their businesses becomes successful they can take it easy and relax. The surprise is that they can't. The simple truth is that success today does not guarantee success tomorrow, because your competitors will always want what you have and will fight to get it, and if you stand pat or relax, you will make it easier for them to do it. Unfortunately, it's not only owners who tend to think they can relax once their companies have attained success: the people who work for those companies often start to think so, too. And the apathy that sets in, in both owners and employees, can have serious consequences for a business. Just look at sports. Championship athletes will tell you the first championship was extremely hard to achieve, but staying on top and winning another is even more difficult. It's the same with business, and as an owner you have to overcome your own apathy before you can deal with it in your employees.

In reality, if you own a successful business and don't continue operating it with the same vigor you did to make it successful, it's entirely possible—even likely—that your company will slide back down the slippery slope from Level 4 to Level 3, and you will again find yourself fighting for survival. Think, for example, about General Motors, the most successful company of the twentieth century, collapsing and filing for bankruptcy in 2009. Or think about Fannie Mae, a company described as "great" in Jim

Collins's bestseller, *Good to Great* (HarperBusiness, 2001), which not only failed in 2008 but took a leading role in creating the housing bubble. The point, of course, is that it's one thing to create a successful business but quite another to keep it successful. Obviously, if two business giants like these can fail, so can any privately owned company.

Leadership at Level 4

In their book, *The Leadership Challenge* (Jossey-Bass, 2002), James M. Kouzes and Barry Z. Posner say that leaders "imagine what is possible," and quote one owner as saying, "I'm my organization's futures department." This pretty much nails the definition of leadership at Level 4. More than at any other time in the life cycle of a business, at this level an owner has to look toward the future and focus the company on operating on an above-average level. This is accomplished essentially by overcoming apathy, continuing to gain market share and increasing profits through expansion, buying up competitors, finding a competitive advantage, or a combination of these.

Management at Level 4

I said earlier, in the discussion of Level 3, that management is the daily blocking and tackling that must take place in order for a business to achieve the owner's success goal, and that is equally true at Level 4. It is also true that in every decision management makes, financial performance and customers must continue to be your main focal points. The best way to make sure that happens is to keep the following six questions in mind:

1. How can we keep the customers we have and attract new ones?
2. How can we be more profitable, and how will we reinvest these profits to make us even better?
3. Is our product at least as good as our top competitors', and how can we make it better?
4. What processes do we need to improve, and how can we improve them?

5. How can we improve the caliber of our employees?
6. What are our competitors doing, and how can we develop both defensive and offensive strategies to deal with their tactics?

Being able to answer these questions and act on those answers requires you to have two overriding traits: you must be proactive and competitive. If you are not proactive at this level, you will be constantly fixing problems rather than anticipating them and limiting their effects. And if you don't maintain your competitive spirit, your company's forward momentum will stall. Of course, even if you consistently exhibit both of these traits, it's essential that your key employees do as well. You can't do it all yourself. Though you may succeed for a while, over time it's the leaders within your company who will have to carry the flag. You can help bring this about by demonstrating these traits yourself, as well as by motivating the leaders to embrace the competitive will and demand it of themselves and their staff.

Planning and People at Level 4

To be fair, a business can't be running at full throttle all the time, so putting your company into a holding pattern from time to time is not only advisable, it's necessary. You and all your employees have to take some time to collect yourselves and have some fun before getting ready to take on the next challenge. And in most cases the fourth level is the first one at which you can do that. Being in this kind of holding pattern not only enables you and your key employees to refresh yourselves, it also provides you with time to deal with any internal concerns you may have.

At the same time, it's important that you maintain what you've fought for and gained up to this point. That's why your planning at this level should reflect some aggressive objectives and goals, particularly in the areas of training, leadership building, and employee evaluation, as well as a complete evaluation of your processes and what you want them to accomplish—all of which add to making your business a tough competitor as well as a market and profit leader. In fact, if you want your business to continue to be successful, at some point you have to set what your managers and employees may consider to be unreasonable goals and objectives. This is true because if you allow them to stay in their comfort zone rather than challenge them, you will never find out how good your people and/or your company can be. In any case, the fundamentals of planning remain the same. Your plan has to be defined by reality, and clear objectives and goals have to be established throughout the business, just as they have at every other level.

Also, as at other levels, people are important at Level 4, but what is most important at this level is their ability to work together. Teamwork in itself can be a competitive advantage for your company because it can be so powerful, and even more so because it's so rare. But turning your staff into a team has to begin with you. That means you have to understand how powerful teamwork can be, and then have the courage to build and develop your staff into a team. It's not easy, but it can be done, particularly if you enlist the help of other leaders in your company. If you do, you will find that teamwork can be an invaluable tool in your efforts to attain the "impossible" and maintain your company's success.

Marketing and the Customer at Level 4

Peter Drucker has said that "There is only one valid definition of business purpose: to create a customer," and creating customers is a marketing responsibility. However, as your business grows and attracts new customers, you eventually run into the law of diminishing returns. That is, at some point it becomes harder and harder to attract—and keep—those new customers. In order to overcome this, you have to be creative, which means, among other things, considering all the possible means of marketing and advertising, particularly those you haven't considered before. For example, if some of your competitors are weak in social networking, there may be opportunities in it for you to attract new customers. It's also important to bear in mind that when you do hit on something that works, you should pour resources into it and try to get as much out of it as you can before your competitors jump in.

One of the keys to keeping both old and new customers satisfied, as I mentioned earlier, is always thinking about how the customer will be affected whenever you make a management decision. What you need to do, once you've made a sale, is focus on the customer and find ways to develop a relationship with him or her. The fact is that no matter how technologically advanced you may become, how big your company gets, or how it evolves and changes, at the end of the day what it's really all about is the relationship you have with your customers, the trust they have in you, and their sense that they are important to you and everyone in your company. To the extent that you can develop this feeling in your customers, you will have provided yourself with a very substantial and very important market advantage. And that's because a company's most effective marketing and advertising is always through word of mouth—the good things your customers tell others about your company.

Level 5: Moving on When It's Time to Go

The fifth and final level, Moving on When It's Time to Go, comes when an owner begins to think about his or her exiting the business and whether to sell the company, pass it along to a successor, or simply close it down. Although thinking about leaving raises emotional issues for most owners, the reality is that they should treat the decision just like every other important decision they've made during their careers. That is, it should be well thought out and based on facts. The one difference is that the owner has to take into account not just what's best for the business but also what's best for him or her, because, for the first time since the company began, what's best for the business and what's best for the owner are not necessarily the same thing.

To my mind, selling a successful business, or turning it over to a family member, should be the highlight of your career because it epitomizes the entrepreneurial dream—go into business, become a success at it, and leave under your own terms. Unfortunately, though, that's not always the case. Some successful owners find it hard to walk away because they like the lifestyle and/or the attention and respect they get because of their positions. Also, the uncertainty of the future, particularly the question of what you will do with the rest of your life, can be unnerving to someone who has controlled his or her environment for many years.

Curiously, compared to other business topics, very little is written about the reality of an owner's exiting his or her business, and few owners are willing to openly discuss the subject. Business owners aren't usually shy about discussing their business operations with their peers—as long as they aren't direct competitors—but in all my years of ownership I cannot remember a single instance in which an owner talked openly about what he or she was thinking in terms of exiting the business. This is very unfortunate for two reasons: (1) if you don't pick the time to exit, someone or something else will; and (2) the best time to sell, or enact a succession plan, is when you don't have to. And there is no escaping these two realities. That means any owner who doesn't take his or her exit seriously is leaving to chance one of the most critical business decisions he or she will ever make, and that doesn't make sense.

Leadership at Level 5

At this level, leadership requires you to fulfill two tasks. The first, which benefits everyone, is to continue being the leader you have been all along. This is important because making sure your business continues to perform at a high level will be critical to your payout if you choose to sell, and critical to your successor if you decide to pass the company along to one or more of your children. The second task, which is essentially only for your benefit, is to decide exactly what you want to do as far as exiting is concerned, and how you want to do it. To achieve this task you will have to determine:

- A reasonable market value for your business.
- The various tax and legal implications.
- How much money you will need to live a full life, and how much money you want to pass on—if any.
- The best time for your exit, based on the company's market value, the optimum selling or succession point, and your personal time frame.

- Whether it's best to sell, pass the company along to a successor, or close down and sell the company's assets.
- The best buyers, if you are selling the business, that is, those who have the ability to pay and would benefit most from owning your business.
- The best successor or successors, if you are passing the company along, based on their aptitude and desire to be an owner, ability to motivate and work with others, understanding of your business, and understanding of business in general, among others.
- What former owners have successfully exited their businesses, and ask them for guidance.

In other words, as with the decisions you have to make at all the earlier levels, you should make this decision based not on emotions but on reality. That is, you have to review your situation, determine the facts, evaluate those facts, and then choose the option that makes the most sense for you and your future.

Management at Level 5

Aside from continuing to run your business on a day-to-day basis, albeit with help from your key managers, your primary management task at Level 5 is to learn and manage the exit process. The first step in this process, as suggested earlier, is to determine what you want to do with the company. The next step, depending on which route you choose to take, is to either prepare yourself for the buy/sell negotiation or design a process under which you will educate your chosen successor. Regardless of what you decide, however, among the steps you will need to take are the following:

- Determine exactly what is for sale, which in most cases includes real estate, assets, and goodwill or blue sky.
- Determine the value of the company, taking into account its past profit history, how much free cash it generates, the industry standard for goodwill, the appraised value of the property, and the value of your assets—either book value, market value, or a combination of the two.

- Make sure your financial statements are accurate and provide justification for your valuations.
- Consult with a business lawyer regarding a standard buy/sell agreement, as well as about any specific items you would want included and any you would not accept from a buyer.

The point is that management at Level 5 is primarily about defining the exit process and preparing yourself so you can be in a position to control the buy/sell process from the time it begins until the moment you walk out the door, no matter what you choose to do with your company.

Planning and People at Level 5

At Level 5, as with every level in your business's life cycle, in order to get what you want when you want it, you have to make plans. That means you have to gather the appropriate information, analyze it, develop the plan, and then implement it, just as you've always done. Interestingly, in some ways the exit plan you develop at Level 5 is similar to the plan you developed at Level 1. This is because both plans are about creating an opportunity for yourself—at Level 1 it's about buying, and at Level 5 it's about selling. The big difference is that by the time you've reached Level 5 you will have become very skilled at the art of planning, and that gives you a real advantage. Your understanding of the process not only gives you an edge with a buyer who may be less skilled, it also provides you with the kind of knowledge you need to pick the right successor.

It's important to remember, though, that even while you are making your exit plans, you must continue to make sure your visibility is high by watching over the monthly business plan and objectives, applying pressure where necessary, and seeing to it that your managers are appropriately focused on the day-to-day blocking and tackling to obtain the overall results you want. This is essential because no matter how carefully you make your exit plans, they often take longer to work through than you expect them to, and in the meantime the business has to keep operating at a high level. If you neglect the ongoing operation of the business, you are likely to find the company going off course in the absence of the leadership and input your staff has come to depend on. And the longer the exit process continues, and the more your employees—especially your key employees—feel your detachment and lack of focus, the more the business will drift off course and the sooner it will begin to slip backward.

As at all the other levels, people are important at Level 5. However, at this point the most important people are not the company's employees. Rather, they are the people the owner surrounds him- or herself with as the exit process moves ahead. Foremost among these are attorneys who have experience handling business buy/sell contracts or legal succession issues, and accountants who can provide tax advice and tax planning. The importance of these professionals and the advice they can offer should never be minimized, as they can protect you from both heartburn and heartache well beyond the sale or succession. For example, as a seller, you have to protect yourself from any problems the buyers may have after the sale, and you will want strong legal language in the agreement guaranteeing that you will be held harmless in whatever the new owner may get involved in. Similarly, having an accountant work with you before and during the sales process, and then filing your tax returns, will usually lessen the chances of a battle if the government tax collectors want more than you paid.

Some owners also hire brokers to help them find buyers from outside the local area, price the business, negotiate the transaction, and keep it quiet and relatively rumor free. Some owners also hire experienced negotiators or mentors to help them set up the negotiations and get them started, while others rely on their own skills to price the business, pick the best buyers, negotiate the sales contract, and so on. This is usually a personal decision based on the owner's comfort level. But what can't be understated is that once the business is sold, it's gone, and a serious mistake during the negotiations or in the contract will be very difficult if not impossible to undo. That means the people you surround yourself with to guide and protect you through the process should be of the highest caliber you can find or afford. This is true for both sales and succession scenarios, but in some ways it's even more important in the latter. That's because in a succession family dynamics are at stake, and, as with selling, sometimes things can't be undone, and sometimes family members will neither forgive nor forget.

Marketing and the Customer

When you're in the process of selling your business, it can be tempting to back off on marketing and advertising. After all, once you're out of the business you don't have to worry about the future, so why not let the new owner worry about it. However, until the money is deposited in your banking account, your business hasn't been sold, and since any number of things can keep that from happening, why take the chance? Moreover, it's important for the buyer to see, as reflected in your financials and sales figures, that the business isn't slipping backward. Not surprisingly, a buyer is likely to see a business that's falling off in a less positive light, and may start looking for ways out of the deal. And if you are planning a succession, since the objective is to make a transition as seamless as possible, backing off on your marketing would not, under normal conditions, be considered a wise thing. In fact, in some cases ramping up marketing may be the best way to go, using it to promote the fact a new generation is taking over.

Selling a business, turning it over to a successor, or closing it down is never easy and always has emotions attached to it. The fact remains, however, that eventually it will be your time to move on. The choices you will have are simple—do it under your terms or have it forced on you one way or another. But choosing the way to make your exit and when it should happen are important decisions, and ones for which you should seek professional advice. If it's done right, it's a great feeling, but if it's done wrong, it will haunt you. In the end, it's a decision that only you can make, but if you prepare yourself so you know the road ahead, and where the bumps and curves are, it's much more likely the choice you make will be the right one for you.

■ ■ ■

As you can see, the five levels of business that every successful company goes through are not only progressive in nature, they also serve as building blocks to create a strong foundation for the company. It's this foundation, carefully built up one layer at a time, that gives a business the kind of strength it needs to not only become successful but to stay successful. As an owner, understanding this concept provides you with a scorecard that enables you to recognize where your company is in the business life cycle, what you can expect to happen, and what you have to do to develop and maintain success. It also enables you to understand that although the Facts of Business Life in themselves don't change, how they are applied changes as the business moves from one level to another. And that is essentially what the remainder of this book is about.

3

Fact 1: If You Don't Lead, No One Will Follow

The words *leader* and *leadership* have become part of our everyday language. But as common as these words are, the reality is that among businesspeople, real leaders and leadership are very uncommon. Leadership is one of those things everyone believes a successful business has to have, but few people understand why, or what leadership actually is. The bottom line is, if you're an owner or about to become one, with money and pride on the line, you have to know what leadership is, and be ready to put it into practice. If you don't, the likelihood of your business's surviving is slim. And even if it does survive, at best only a small percentage of your business's potential will be realized.

Of course, leadership is not only a business issue. One extraordinary example of leadership is the story of Apollo 13, the NASA moon mission launched on April 11, 1970, and later chronicled in an Academy Award–winning film. When an oxygen tank exploded two days into the mission and the crew was put in grave danger, it was flight director Eugene Kranz and mission commander James A. Lovell who stepped up and provided the leadership needed to save them. When Kranz insisted that "failure is not an option," it set up a leadership chain of events, from properly analyzing the overall situation, to focusing on the right issues, to picking the best of the worst choices, to solving each problem in an orderly fashion.

He pushed people to their limits, stood firm in the face of adversity, and motivated and challenged the NASA crew to do what some thought was impossible. Commander Jim Lovell, on board the command module, picked up the flight director's lead, and despite the crew's dire circumstances, remained optimistic, refusing to give up. Leading by example and maintaining a firm resolve to overcome every challenge and setback, Lovell continuously worked to find ways to save the mission. In the end, it was these two men's leadership that enabled NASA to get the crew safely back to earth.

Unfortunately, many businesses wind up being "lost in space," often because, unlike Kranz and Lovell, their owners don't step up and provide them with the leadership they need. What's worse, these businesses frequently end up being replaced by other businesses that also lack leadership, and they fail as well. And the cycle goes on. However, when a leader takes on an ownership role, things change because leaders are willing to make the hard choices, stand by their beliefs, and fight and win the battle for success.

The fact is that leadership is important not only in business but in any endeavor that depends on a group of people working together toward a common goal. Whether you're talking about a space mission, a business, a sports team, a nonprofit organization, or a church, no matter how skilled the employees or players are, or how devout the congregation may be, they all need direction, coordination, discipline, and someone to make the hard choices so they can move forward and flourish. Without a leader who can create order out of chaos, will be accountable, is able to prioritize and select a path, and can separate the "must have" from the "like to have," an organization will simply cease to move ahead. This is the essence of leadership, and the better the leader, and the more leaders an organization has, the better the outcome. And in a business, if the owner doesn't lead, no one else is in a position to do it. As in every other kind of organization, everyone in a company looks to the owner to define what the future is and to take them there. And this is one of the roles that an owner cannot shy away from.

The good news for owners is that leadership isn't genetic. It's a self-taught skill that people can develop, and the more one uses it, the more honed his or her leadership skills become. That is, the skills get better the more you exercise them, and combining those skills with increased business and ownership experience can provide an individual with an extremely powerful business tool. I have known a lot of successful individuals who are great leaders, and none of them started out intending to be leaders. Circumstances and their career choices forced the leadership ability within them to surface, and they had the courage and self-confidence to exercise it. In fact, in his book *On Becoming a Leader* (Addison-Wesley, 1989), Warren Bennis wrote, "More leaders have been made by accident, circumstances, sheer grit, or will, than have been made by all the leadership courses put together." That's not to say, of course, that leadership courses aren't important, but that leaders often emerge when circumstances demand it rather than as a result of formal training. This is a very significant point, and one that is usually forgotten when leadership is discussed.

But it's one thing for a business owner to know leadership is important, and quite another to know how to implement it in his or her business. The first step toward doing that, though, is developing a working definition of what leadership is. In *Managing for Dummies* (IDG Books, 1996), Bob Nelson and Peter Economy distinguish between managing and leading by saying, "Managers push their employees to achieve the goals of an organization," while leaders "challenge their employees by creating a compelling vision of the future and then unlocking their employees' potential." They also say, under a section titled "What Leaders Do," that leaders "inspire action, communicate," and "support and facilitate." In my own mind, leadership means defining the future, clearly stating the goals, and taking everyone there, and then, when they arrive, redefining the future and starting all over again. Leadership is, of course, much more than a definition, but it has to start with your defining what it means. You can borrow a definition from someone else or create your own, but regardless of where you get it, you must know what leadership is before you can go out and do it.

■ ■ ■

There are essentially five characteristics of great leaders. The first of these is being flexible. Not everything goes as planned.

Competitors change tactics, governments force new regulations on business, strikes stop the flow of products, and, occasionally, natural disasters occur. And at times like these, leaders have to be able to change course; that is, first make sure their businesses will survive, and then find a new way to reach their goals. The second characteristic is being able to communicate. Some leaders are great orators, but speaking well isn't all that's required of a leader. As we all know, there are lots of people who talk a great game but deliver nothing. Leaders who communicate well are those who not only share their thoughts with employees, but also let their strength and personal character show through in their communication, and empower those who work for them by defining the company's goal and showing how to get there. A third characteristic of great leaders—or, perhaps, group of characteristics—is having courage, tenacity, and patience. Having the courage to stand alone, the tenacity to not succumb to pressure, and the patience to keep fighting until you win the day—and sometimes being able to do all three at the same time—is something you will have to develop if you want to be a true and successful leader.

The fourth necessary characteristic is the combination of humility and presence. Acting aloof, or above your employees, does not make a leader. Leaders have to be able to talk and listen to their employees on all levels of the company. At the same time, they must have the respect of their employees, the kind of respect that's earned by being honest, having integrity, and being tough but fair. The fifth and final characteristic of a successful leader is being responsible. A business owner has to realize that, as the saying goes, "A skunk stinks from the head down," and a business does too. This means when there is blame to be accepted, the owner must be the first one to accept it. But it also means that when accolades are appropriate, they should be spread out among the employees. And when this happens, a leader is born.

The Benefits of Leadership

- Being a leader enables you to be effective and efficient in determining your company's destination and creating a team that focuses on getting it there.

- Being a leader means defining and exhibiting moral and ethical courage and setting an example for everyone in the company.
- Being a leader helps you teach leadership skills to your employees, who will then help do the "heavy lifting" of moving the company from where it is today to where it needs to be in the future.
- Being a leader enables you to recruit, hire, and promote employees who demonstrate leadership abilities.
- Being a leader forces you to analyze your own strengths and weaknesses, as well as those of the company, and enables you to develop a good sense of reality.
- Being a leader helps you dictate appropriate employee conduct while, at the same time, preventing employees from being too tough, ruthless, or mean to other members of the staff.
- Being a leader helps you emphasize the value of the company's customers, how they are treated, and the importance of their returning.

The Realities of Leadership

- Your company can meet the goals you establish only if you lead the way by motivating and encouraging your employees to become a coordinated team focused on the destination.
- When you are leading your company into a "New Frontier," because neither you nor your employees have been there before, mistakes, miscues, and inexperience add to the challenge, and your leadership is key to meeting that challenge.
- You have to understand and be good enough at leadership to teach it to your employees, both by example and by coaching. The more leaders you can develop, the stronger the business will be, and the less you will have to worry about how the business is operating.

In exhibiting leadership, there are essentially three things you must accomplish if you hope to make the company a success. These three things don't represent every facet of leadership, but they do form the foundation on which leadership is built and are an integral part of leadership at every level. The first of these is achieving the objective. This is not something you, or anyone, can do alone, which means you will have to work with others to accomplish it. The second is building and maintaining the team. Saying you need a team to accomplish something is one thing, but developing one, and consistently encouraging and motivating it, is something else, and something you must do. The third and final thing you have to do is develop individuals within the company. In order to accomplish this, you must lead by example, teach employees what leadership means so they can teach their direct reports, establish an environment for success by eliminating excuses, recognize when jobs are well done, have the courage to make the tough calls, and encourage empowerment within certain parameters, among others.

■ ■ ■

Leadership may mean different things to different people, but in a business, leadership must always start with the owner, who has to define exactly what leadership means to him or her, and then decide what success means to the business. However, being a leader also means articulating that vision to everyone else in the company, convincing them of its importance, and encouraging and motivating them to work together to achieve it. And while doing so may come more naturally to some than to others, it's never easy. In fact, as Vince Lombardi, the legendary Green Bay Packers coach, once said, "Contrary to the opinion of many people, leaders are not born. Leaders are made, and they are made by effort and hard work." If you want to give your business a good start toward success, it has to start with leadership, and leadership has to start with you.

Level 1: Ownership and Opportunity

Leadership is, of course, usually thought of as one individual providing guidance and/or direction to a group of other individuals. At Level 1, though, because there is no business yet, and there are no employees, there are no individuals other than you. That does not mean, however, that leadership doesn't play an important role at this level. In fact, it plays a critical role, because if you do not exercise leadership, there will never be a business. It's leadership, in the form of what I refer to as ownership and opportunity, that ultimately leads to the creation of a business.

As the name of this level suggests, it is somewhat different than the other four in the business life cycle because it essentially consists of two parts. The first of these, ownership, is the part during which you must decide whether being an owner is right for you. This also applies to current owners who are considering expanding their businesses or buying new companies. The second, opportunity, takes place only if and when you decide that ownership is right for you and is when you determine exactly where your best opportunity lies and how you can best exploit it. Both parts, however, rely on the leadership skill of analysis; that is, the ability to analyze yourself as well as a variety of opportunities, and then choose the one that's best for you. Unfortunately, although these analyses are an important first step, many owners don't take the time to do them because they underestimate the advantages of conducting them.

The Benefits of Leadership at Level 1

- Being a leader enables you to determine whether ownership is really for you.
- Being a leader helps you develop a vision of "what could be," that is, what success will look like.
- Being a leader provides you with fact-based information on the market and on your own needs.
- Being a leader requires you to collect and analyze information, which contributes to your being more confident in your ability to lead, manage, and grow a business.
- Being a leader keeps you from underestimating the challenges you must face in starting or expanding a business.
- Being a leader enables you to understand more clearly the kinds of opportunities that would be most beneficial for you.
- Being a leader provides you with an understanding of the key personal characteristics you need, such as competitiveness, discipline, and commitment.
- Leadership keeps you focused on what success means.

Nothing worthwhile happens without leadership. That's a bold statement, but one that's easy to defend, particularly in regard to Level 1. Without leadership there is no vision or success destination. Without leadership there is no assessment of your current reality, such as what obstacles or opportunities may lie ahead in the marketplace, how much working capital you will need to get started, and how you will hire and train employees, among many others. And without leadership there is no one pointing the company in the right direction. Leadership means action, and action means results. And for the business owner, leadership has to begin at Level 1 because if you get this level wrong, chances are that very little will work out the way you'd like it to.

There are three key leadership qualities that are particularly necessary at Level 1: (1) the ability to analyze yourself and to be realistic about your strengths and weaknesses, (2) the experience necessary to intelligently evaluate an opportunity, and (3) the strength to remove assumptions and emotions from the decision-making process and rely entirely on facts. Level 1 is not, however, the only place where these leadership qualities are needed. In fact, they are important qualities that an owner will use throughout his or her ownership career, and owners have to demonstrate these qualities beginning at the Ownership and Opportunity level of a company's life cycle.

Achieving the Objective or Goal at Level 1

Since this level of the business life cycle has two parts, it requires you to meet two different objectives or goals. The first, as I mentioned earlier, is determining whether ownership is right for you. In order to accomplish this, it is necessary for you to answer three key questions:

1. Do I have the talent and skills to be a great owner and leader?
2. Am I experienced enough to evaluate, or create, an opportunity?
3. Do I have the leadership courage to bet on myself?

These are important questions, and answering them honestly takes a prospective owner—or, for that matter, an experienced one—a lot of soul searching. It requires a kind of self-analysis that you may have never conducted before, but it is a critical part of the process. In fact, if you don't answer these questions honestly, and decide mistakenly that ownership is what you want, regardless of how promising an opportunity may appear, you will lack the passion needed to drive a business toward success, meaning, at best, the business and you will struggle. However, if after careful self-analysis you correctly decide ownership is for you, this self-analysis will help you visualize the kind of opportunity that would be best for you.

Once the ownership issue is decided, the goal is to decide what opportunities may be available to you and which you may have to create. You should bear in mind, though, that opportunity seldom falls in your lap. In most cases you have to create it. This is an important point, and one that new owners as well as owners looking to expand their businesses must take into account. For everyone who chooses ownership as a career, selecting the right opportunity is one of the most challenging aspects of the process, primarily because there are some opportunities that are questionable at best, and some that are certain to fail. The challenge is separating the good from the bad and the legitimate from the phony. This is why the focus on leadership and analysis at this level is so important—you want to get this right because there is little room for error.

Although it is important to review Level 1 for all the Facts of Business Life before you make an ownership or opportunity decision, as far as leadership is concerned there are essentially two questions you must ask yourself: (1) does the product or service I am considering have a long life span or life cycle, and (2) can a business selling this product or service make continuously sufficient profits? That is, is the reward worth the risk? There will be other questions that have to be answered before you make a final decision, but if you can't answer "yes" to both of these in regard to any particular opportunity; there is no point in pursuing it.

"Sufficient profits" is an important phrase, and one that is open to interpretation. Whether profits are considered to be sufficient is usually based on how much is needed to pay off the initial debt and to keep the business running for an extended period of time. But when you are answering this question, it's also important to take your personal concerns into account. If all you want is a business that will enable you to pay your bills and go out to dinner once a month, it would probably be relatively easy to find one. But you probably want more than that out of your own company, including the fun of owning and operating a continually successful business, and the ability to enjoy the freedoms that a significantly profitable business can provide. And if that's what you're looking for in becoming an owner, it is essential that you do the kind of thoughtful research and analysis at this level that will enable you to achieve it.

Finding the Right Opportunity

I knew even before I started a business that ownership was what I wanted—all I needed was the opportunity and some experience. My reality, though, was that I didn't have very much money. Recognizing, once I had gotten enough experience, that I would have to create an opportunity myself, I approached a number of business owners and offered to make a small investment in their companies, run the companies for them, and buy them out over time. To my surprise, several of the owners I approached offered me another option: to open a new business, or buy an existing one outside of their market area under a partnership arrangement.

This wasn't my ideal, but I recognized that since I had such limited funds, this option might be my best chance at ownership, and that eventually I might be able to get enough "meat on my bones," that is, enough capital, to either buy my partner out or enable my partner and me to purchase a larger business with even more potential. I investigated each offer and studied each market, and continued to gain industry experience. As I was preparing to make my decision, seemingly out of the blue another possibility opened up. One of the owners I was interested in partnering with called an equity lender on my behalf and suggested they approach me to partner, operate, and eventually take full ownership of a business they would buy or open. I knew from the self-analysis I'd done that this was exactly what I was looking for.

What I'd done was create an opportunity for myself by going out and talking to owners, telling them what I was looking for, and asking if they could help or guide me. As a result, I created several options for myself, and eventually got lucky with one I hadn't even considered. Sometimes this is how it works, but the point is that most ownership opportunities have to be created because if they were obvious, owners in the market would jump on them even before you knew they were there.

Building and Maintaining a Team at Level 1

Since at Level 1 your business is still in the preparation stage and doesn't actually exist yet, you obviously won't have a staff to work with. But that doesn't mean you don't have to put together a good team of mentors and advisers. You will need a group to help you determine whether you want to become an owner and, if so, which opportunity you should pursue. Since, again, there are two aspects of Level 1, the team you put together to help you achieve the first objective may not be the same as the one you build to attain the second.

Among the people who can help you make the ownership decision—or an expansion decision—are current business owners in your market or owners of similar businesses in different markets, as well as bankers and accountants who know the specifics of your industry. Once you've decided you do want to be an owner—or to expand your business—you begin analyzing the opportunities available to you. You can gather information from local business associations; owners outside your market area; people who are experienced in buying and selling businesses; owners who have already been involved in expanding businesses; suppliers within your industry, who know the cost of products and sales histories; and members of state, provincial, or national industry associations.

Regardless of which objective you are trying to attain, in selecting the people you ask to provide assistance, you should be looking for those who have certain characteristics, including experience in doing what you want to do, the ability to assess markets, knowledge of your specific industry, a history of success in their fields, an understanding of the important role owners play in a business's success, and a willingness to help you when your business becomes "live."

Developing the Individual at Level 1

At this level, the only employee you are likely to have is yourself. However, developing individuals starts with developing yourself. And if ownership is your goal, there are a number of abilities and/or skills that you should master in order to get your company up and running, and to keep it going in the future. Among these are:

- Understanding what being a leader entails.
- Becoming a great communicator, in both speaking and listening.
- Understanding your own core values and never compromising on them.
- Being able to clearly state, and stand by, your vision for the company as well as its operating goals and ethics.
- Understanding that setting a good example is the most valuable gift a leader/owner can give his or her company.
- Recognizing that at some point in the future you will have to switch from being a student of leadership to a teacher of leadership.

Level 2: Creating Your Company's DNA

For the new owner, Level 2 is the point at which the business stops being purely theoretical and starts becoming real. Having made the decision to become an owner or expand your business, and chosen an opportunity, the owner begins to create the company's DNA. That is, he or she begins developing how the business will operate on a day-to-day basis, guided by the sales and profits forecasts and other information gathered at Level 1. This is an extraordinarily important step in the life of a business, not only because the preparation the owner does will be a major factor in how the company responds to his or her leadership, but also because it will be reflected in how successful the business will be, both in the beginning and in the long term.

Like Level 1, Level 2 begins with a mental image rather than a physical action, that is, in the mind's eye. As with anything an individual wants to accomplish, the dream comes before he or she actually goes out and does it. For example, people who decide they want to lose weight start by visualizing how much healthier they will be and how much better they will look and feel. Then they define their reality—that is, they recognize that they are, say, 30 pounds overweight, and decide this will be their weight-loss goal. Next, they determine how long it will take to achieve this goal, set up intermediate objectives and goals, and develop exercise and eating programs to fit the timetable. It's only then that they begin to take physical action.

Creating a company's DNA is a lot like choosing to lose weight. Owners also start with a mental image—in this case, one of how they want their companies to operate on a day-to-day basis, how their employees and customers will be treated, how their employees will treat each other, their performance expectations, what the company's objectives and goals will be, and who will be responsible for them. That is, they visualize what they want their companies to be, create the steps to get there, assign accountability, and determine oversight and controls. This is a key point for ownership success, because the result of leading in the mind's eye—thinking through how they want their company and all its moving parts to work, separately and in unison—enables owners to create their own destiny.

Of course, unless you have a one-man or one-woman operation, you can't operate a business entirely on your own. And that means you and your employees must operate as a team. There, however, is the rub. Most people believe teamwork and success go hand in hand, but that's not necessarily correct. In fact, a lot of teamwork isn't productive at all. Teamwork is productive only when there is a strong leader who establishes clear goals, orchestrates behavior, demands performance with accountability, and can put a little fear into his or her employees so they will consistently do what they need to do. This, ultimately, is how to establish a successful company—a business that operates as a team and is led by an owner/leader who isn't afraid to make the tough decisions, and who knows the goal is not popularity but winning the market war and being a long-term success.

It is important to note, however, that while creating a company's DNA is an essential part of getting a company up and running, there are also times when the owner of an existing company might find it necessary to come back to this level. This happens when he or she feels it is necessary to change the company's operating systems for any one of several reasons. It may be because the existing systems are not operating as they should, or because the owner is planning to grow the company, and recognizes that its current systems have to change to accommodate that growth. It may also be because there have been changes in the market that must be addressed, or because the owner wants to lead a change in the market. In other words, while DNA creation is something that must be done early on in a company's life, it's also something that may occur many times over the course of the business's existence.

The Benefits of Leadership at Level 2

- Being a leader enables you to determine the company's DNA, that is, how things get done.
- Being a leader helps you define why things are done this way.
- Being a leader forces you to determine the company's goals and objectives and when and how they are to be met.
- Being a leader enables you to make sure the company's rules are applied equally to everyone regardless of title or position.
- Being a leader helps you make individuals accountable for their actions.
- Being a leader creates and promotes teamwork.
- Being a leader enables you to easily see when something is going wrong and eliminate unpleasant surprises.
- Being a leader helps you define what is considered acceptable and unacceptable behavior toward customers and other employees.
- Being a leader helps you determine the types of employees you should hire and, as a result, reduces employee turnover.
- Being a leader enables you to demand that scorekeeping and personal responsibility be part of the company's culture, and puts a little fear into employees who are not doing their jobs appropriately.

Achieving the Objective or Goal at Level 2

The main leadership priority at Level 2 is creating the business's DNA by defining how all the moving parts of the company will work, both independently and together. DNA also defines what success will look like, the ethics under which the company will operate, and what is expected from employees in terms of their performance, attitude, and professionalism in dealing with each other and with customers. Creating a business's DNA—as well as re-creating it—requires the owner to exhibit certain leadership skills, that is, brains, resolve, and tenacity, if everything is going to be done the way it should be.

DNA and its creation can essentially be broken down into two parts. First, you have to visualize how the business will operate on a day-to-day level and remain consistently profitable. This means you have to think through all the functions that must be managed in the company and devise processes by which they can be. Second, you have to implement these processes. And that's not easy to do. In fact, to accomplish it you have to be both tough and courageous, that is, not afraid to use an iron fist and a hard shoe. But it is these kinds of skills that separate the good owner/leader from the bad, or, to put it another way, the ones who make money from those who don't.

If you are going into your first business, or have just taken over a business, you should be prepared, on the first day, to prioritize and implement how the business will operate and how financial forecasts will be met, know how to react if operations are going badly or if they're going better than expected, and know what will earn employees a pat on the back or a promotion, as well as what will be cause for a kick of reality or dismissal. Starting with the first day, you have to create a presence, and you do that by setting the tempo and the rules, determining the work ethic and attitude, and dictating the plaudits and punishment. Doing so enables you to earn your employees' respect and make them want to follow your lead so they don't disappoint you.

If you are already in business and re-creating your company's DNA, the leadership goal is the same—visualize how the company will operate, make it happen, and earn your employees' respect by the way you act and react in both adversity and success. In a situation like this, though, you have an additional challenge—your employees already know you and you know them, warts and all. Opinions will also have long since been formed, and everyone will have gotten comfortable in their jobs and their surroundings. DNA re-creation, though, means change, and it's some of those tenured employees who are most likely to put up the most resistance. That resistance can, of course, be overcome, but it's an uphill battle, and you can be sure that when you find yourself in this situation your leadership skills are going to be tested. Again, though, as the leader it is your responsibility to make whatever changes in the company and its DNA are necessary in order to keep up or get ahead of the market, and serve your customers.

Building and Maintaining a Team at Level 2

Once a company has created its DNA and is maintaining it appropriately, the chances are that it will be performing relatively well and generating decent profits. And, in fact, a good number of business-people are satisfied at that point, and don't make any further efforts to build their companies. However, those who are willing to work on their businesses by building a team can take their companies to heights of profitability and performance that are experienced by only the most successful owners. Doing so, though, requires the owner to make sure that three important elements are present in the company: leadership, a sense of purpose, and chemistry.

Leadership plays a role in team building in several ways, perhaps the most important of which is making sure the business is running smoothly on all cylinders. Let's say, for example, that a Caterpillar franchise parts department is great at selling compressors and generators, but the repair side of the business is awful. Although good sales are clearly a plus, the poor performance of the repairs department is likely to have a negative effect on future sales. And since the parts department will get the heat for that, the two departments will have a rocky relationship, and it will do a lot of damage to the effort to establish team unity. In fact, if this problem is allowed to continue, it will be a drag on the rest of the company and make it even more difficult to create a cohesive team. However, if the owner demonstrates leadership and makes the tough choices needed to improve the repairs department, a team can be developed. This is very important to understand because it pinpoints why teamwork in business is so important and so rare. When the team does well, everyone does well, but the opposite is true as well.

Once a team is built, it is held together by two elements, the first of which is a sense of purpose. A team's sense of purpose is essentially a reason for the group to work together, and there are any number of things that can serve to provide such a sense. It could come from the team's being dominant in its market, from its having the highest customer satisfaction rating, or from taking pride in being the most knowledgeable and professional in the way it represents your product. This is extremely important because your marketplace reputation will not only help drive prospects to your business but will help convert them into loyal, long-term customers.

The second element that holds a team together is chemistry. Unfortunately, a lot of owners struggle with chemistry because they don't understand it. Building chemistry starts by defining what it is. The dictionary defines it, in this sense, as "a strong mutual attraction, attachment, or sympathy." What it means in terms of a business team, though, is a connection that's felt by a group of people working together, a connection that has developed because they've learned they can count on each other to do their jobs so the group can achieve its desired results. It's not about everybody being friends or holding hands and singing "Kumbaya" or Louis Armstrong's "What a Wonderful World." Creating chemistry is about performance, and about knowing you can rely on the person beside you to do what has to be done.

There are several ways this kind of chemistry can be developed. One way is through fighting marketplace battles together. Another is by facing adversity and succeeding. In the end, though, creating this type of chemistry takes leadership. It takes a strong leader to get all the company's employees on the same page and thinking along the same lines. It's not easy, but it is essential. And the best way to do it is to create leaders throughout the business who will help everyone focus on what's important to ownership and take pride in the job they are expected to perform. In the end, that's how teams are built, how they win, and how they continue to win.

Developing the Individual at Level 2

"If we are going to win this championship, the leaders on this team are going to have to step up and get it done." Every year, on every team where something important is on the line, the team's coach says this, or some version of it, to his or her players. Coaches said this to me when I was playing hockey in high school and college, and they still say it today. Owners who are successful leaders do the same thing, and they do it because they know the not-so-secret secret that the more leaders a team has, the better the overall performance will be. They know, too, that when any of a company's leaders step up and lead the business's performance to another level, it puts pressure on other leaders in the company to do the same. In sports these types of teams don't just win—they win championships. In business when employee/leaders step up and help the owner lead, the result is a truly great company, and everyone knows it, including the company's employees, its competitors' employees, and its customers.

Even at this early stage of your business, there are ways to determine who the company's future leaders are, and things you can do to help them develop their leadership abilities. There are essentially three ways to identify these people. First, they consistently perform at a high level and inspire others by their actions. Second, they are 100 percent committed to the team concept and exhibit it by doing things like stepping in to help a struggling employee or helping a new employee settle in. And third, they have certain character traits, essentially the same ones I discussed earlier for leaders in general, including flexibility, the ability to communicate well, courage, patience, tenacity, humility and presence, honesty, fairness, and a willingness to take responsibility. Again, these are not all the characteristics of a leader, but they include the most important ones. Once you have identified which individuals in your company have the necessary leadership skills, the next step for you is to find ways of helping them develop those skills. There are several ways you can do this, including empowering them, asking for their opinion on how to improve a particular situation, or getting their help in identifying and recruiting the best talent in the area.

Level 3: From Survival to Success

Level 3 is the period during which an owner moves his or her business from fighting to survive to becoming successful as he or she has defined it. And, as such, it's where all the work the owner did at the previous two levels is implemented. It is also, though, the hardest level to master—it's certainly the one where the largest percentage of business failures occur. A significant number of these failures occur because the owner has not provided the leadership necessary to succeed. Part of the reason for this is that as a company moves along the spectrum from survival to success, the changes it goes through are the most dramatic of any in the business life cycle, which means the owner has to adapt his or her leadership style in order to lead and control the change.

When a business is at the survival stage, owners have to focus almost exclusively on the short term because if they can't develop positive cash flow and at least a little profitability, they are not likely to remain in business for long. Companies at this stage tend to have very uncertain atmospheres, because employees know when they join a start-up business or an expanding one, or are working in a business that's going downhill, the future is tentative at best. In a start-up or expansion situation, this tentativeness actually works to the company's benefit, because owner and employee optimism translates into positive enthusiasm and energy. However, in a business that's sliding backward toward the survival end of the spectrum, this tentativeness reinforces negative energy and helps foster an equally negative attitude. At the same time, sales, gross profit, and expense forecasts are clouded with doubt and cautiousness. Processes are followed inconsistently, and accountability for results is rarely questioned. Crisis seems to be more the norm than the exception, and the owner's leadership ability is consistently challenged as he or she tries to navigate through his or her day-to-day, month-to-month existence.

At the success end of the spectrum, though, the situation is very different. Short-term planning is still important, but the focus has turned toward the future, and short-term plans are now a by-product, or factor, of the long-term success goals and objectives the owner has defined. The atmosphere is businesslike, and the anxiety employees felt over losing their jobs has long since disappeared. The owner is showing leadership by preparing and setting up the company for the future. Sales, gross profit, expenses, and net profit forecasts are done with confidence that's driven by the company's success in the past and a positive outlook for the future. Processes have become a habit, performance expectations are in place, and some future problems are visualized and corrected before they even materialize. Finally, the owner is leading the company forward with a quiet confidence, some employees are helping with leadership, and others have become leaders themselves.

There are, however, numerous obstacles and significant traps along the way from survival to success, and unless you provide the kind of leadership that's needed, and when it's needed, instead of moving along a straight and steady path, your business will move in a continuous circle of chaos and never get anywhere. Some of these obstacles come from outside the company, such as a new competitor who moves in down the street, consumers whose needs or wants change, a landlord who decides not to renew your lease, a long-term road project that blocks customers' access and severely impacts sales, or any number of other problems. There are also, however, interior traps that a company can unwittingly fall into at this level, and which must accordingly be guarded against. Among these are your becoming arrogant due to past successes, employees who develop a negative attitude toward management and ownership, ongoing resistance from employees to following processes and performing as expected, the business sliding backward along the survival–success spectrum after experiencing some initial success, and the company sliding backward even after years of success. All these obstacles and traps can, of course, be dealt with, but it takes leadership to do it.

The Benefits of Leadership at Level 3

- Being a leader enables you to provide your company with the drive and the means of controlling change that are particularly important at Level 3.
- Being a leader helps you create the kind of urgency needed to help the company break through the survival barrier and generate the consistent profits that will enable it to attain its success goal.
- Being a leader forces you to define success and describe what the company will look like when it gets there, in the process

bringing structure and order into what would otherwise be chaos.

- Being a leader helps you provide a map showing how the company can overcome the obstacles that can keep it from reaching the success end of the spectrum.
- Being a leader helps you prevent managers from managing to the status quo rather than pushing themselves or their employees to become better.
- Being a leader helps you get your employees to not only focus on the quality of their work today but recognize how it builds a foundation for the company's success tomorrow.
- Being a leader enables you to prepare others in the company for leadership roles.

Achieving the Objective or Goal at Level 3

Every successful company needs goals and objectives. They are the scorecard of business and are among the first things leaders implement in their companies. They do this because they understand that goals and objectives represent much more than just targets, and can make the difference between success and failure. In fact, the goals and objectives determined by a company's leader tells everyone else in the company where they are heading and the steps they must take to get there, which is essentially the blocking and tackling of business. Attaining these objectives isn't always easy to accomplish, but it's where real leaders shine and where prior experience shows its value.

Experienced owners know the bottom line is making money, and that profit has to be the focus. There are, of course, other things that are important as well, but they won't happen if the business can't sustain itself. A business that can't produce profit is of no benefit to its owner or to society. The overall goal is to make money; however, in order to attain that, other goals and objectives need to be created. Over the years, I've found it best to break up goals and objectives into two types, internal and external, for ease of managing and determining the kind of leadership and support the owner needs to provide in order to attain the goals and objectives.

Internal Requirements for Meeting Goals and Objectives

- Ample cash to operate the business as well as support the objective, that is, to pay for products, marketing, operating expenses, accounts receivables, capital equipment and facilities, and so on.
- Processes to support the objectives, and employees assigned responsibility for operating those processes.
- Expectations of employee output that match the company's objectives.
- Adequate high-demand product and sufficiently trained personnel.
- A scorekeeping system that tells the owner where the company is compared to the objectives and will alert leaders to possible problems and/or additional opportunities.
- Employee enthusiasm for exceeding objectives.
- An overall understanding that nothing happens without the customer and the money they spend.

External Requirements for Meeting Goals and Objectives

- Competitive products for which there is adequate consumer demand and sufficient availability to support sales objectives.
- Competitive pricing that can produce sufficient gross profit to support profit objectives.
- Developing ways to make your product or service easier to find and buy than your competitors.'
- An appropriately financed and targeted marketing plan to attract customers now and in the future.
- A program to continuously reinforce in your customers' minds why they bought from your business in order to protect them from your competitors.

These are by no means all the elements needed to support objectives, but they do provide a framework. More important, since it is ultimately the owner/leader who must make sure all these requirements are met, they emphasize the fact that leaders do not only have to create goals and objectives for their businesses, they also have to support them if the company is ever going to meet, much less exceed, those objectives. Even then, though, as a leader you have an additional responsibility, which is to follow up on the company's efforts, regardless of how successful it was in attaining its goals. There are obviously two possible outcomes to your efforts—either you have met or exceeded your goal, or you have failed to do so. And depending on which one has occurred, you have different questions to ask of yourself and your staff.

When you have met or exceeded your objectives, you are, of course, entitled to a certain amount of self-congratulation. However, even in circumstances like this one, there are questions you need to ask. Among these are:

- Was our objective aggressive enough?
- Could we have done better or worked smarter?
- What did we do well?
- Where can we improve?
- What did we learn about ourselves, the marketplace, and our competitors?
- What were our strengths and weaknesses?

Raising these questions can only help you ensure meeting or exceeding your objectives in the future.

You may, however, have failed to meet your objectives. If you have, the important thing to remember is that missing an objective is not the end of the world, unless you fail to learn something from it. In this situation, the questions you should ask yourself include:

- Was the objective the right one, or were we overly optimistic?
- What went wrong?
- What were the problems encountered?
- Do the decision makers all agree on what went wrong and the problems to be solved?
- Can we all agree on the remedies?
- Can the remedies be easily implemented? If not, what needs to happen?
- Does our overall goal need to change and be revised?
- What effect does this have on our financial picture?
- What did we do well, and how can we build on it?

Raising questions like this will help make sure these mistakes won't happen again.

Regardless of the outcome of your efforts, however, there are two questions it is imperative you ask about every completed objective: (1) what is our next objective, and (2) can we increase the objective and, in turn, increase our expectations and profit goals? In fact, asking these two questions should become habit forming. That is, it should become part of a regular pattern of creating the objective, analyzing the outcome, and then asking the two questions. And you have to keep doing it over and over again, because it's the only way you will be able to develop a rhythm of results that will enable your business to maintain and build on its success.

Again, these are not all the questions that require answers, but they do provide a framework for your decision making. The bottom line is that if you neglect to ask all of these questions, that is, if you don't analyze what's occurred, whether positive or otherwise, you are passing up an opportunity for continued success. At best, you might be dooming your company to an erratic and nerve-jolting ride along the survival–success spectrum. At worst, you could be setting yourself up for failure. However, if you focus your company on goals, objectives, and results management, you are much more likely to reach the success end of the spectrum and to remain there.

Building and Maintaining a Team at Level 3

The discipline you develop from leading, and managing results based on goals and objectives, sets the company up for continuous improvement, future success, and greater profits. That is, it will take you and your company to the success end of the survival–success spectrum, which is the goal of Level 3. However, if you want exemplary profits, there is another step you can take, and that's using the successes and discipline of results management to build a team in your company. Goals, objectives, and management of the results create the kind of solid foundation on which successful teams are built.

A team is essentially a group of people who know what the company's goal is and can successfully implement all the various processes designed to achieve that goal. In other words, a team is effective only when the company's expectations, processes, and performance are in sync with each other. For example, a football team's goal is to win. It does the team little good if its offense is above average but its defense is the worst in the league. Unless the processes—in this case the offense and the defense—support each other, the team can't win with any consistency, and neither can a business. Similarly, even if a restaurant offers the market's best selection at attractive prices, it's not going to mean anything if the kitchen is painfully slow in getting the food out to its patrons. However, if the kitchen's cooking processes can keep up with the demand, the restaurant is likely to be an extremely strong business.

Of course, no matter how strong and supportive the processes are, at some point people have to be involved, and it's ultimately people who create a team—or not. But having people who are "easy to work with" or can be described as "team players" isn't necessarily helpful when you're trying to build a team. You obviously want to work with people who have integrity and character, but teams are ultimately successful because they are made up of individuals who can produce results and in turn help everyone make more money. Think about that football team again. Let's say you're a player who has battled throughout the game and given it all you have. There are a few seconds left and you're down by two points, so a field goal can give you a win. Who do you want to kick the field goal, the team's most popular player or the one who has a history of making "pressure" kicks to win games?

If you are interested in building a team, and you should be, the first thing you need to do is create an atmosphere in which a team can thrive. And there are several ways this can be accomplished. For example, successful teams don't thrive operating in a dump, and while not every business can operate out of a glass tower, every business can be clean and continuously maintained. Every business can also make sure its equipment is in proper working order, both for safety reasons and to ensure employee efficiency. As the owner/leader, you can also foster team building by showing that you care about and respect your employees. One way you can do this is by training your employees, and rewarding good behavior and results—as well as punishing poor behavior and attitudes. Another way is to sponsor your employees' children in afterschool activities or help employees out when they're dealing with family emergencies. If the people who work for you know you have their backs, they will in turn have yours, which is a fundamental aspect of any team. Finally, you can encourage teamwork by making sure your managers and supervisors understand that their personal performances take a backseat to the performance of their direct reports. In other words, they will be judged on the "we" rather than the "me."

As all of this suggests, creating teams is not as difficult as some believe. And the good news is that if you want to do it, you don't have to reinvent the wheel. There are plenty of successful businesses you can learn from. The even better news is that if you are willing to make the effort, you will in all likelihood find yourself, and your business, in a position to attain a level of success that only a small percentage of companies ever reach.

Developing the Individual at Level 3

As I have said several times, good processes and systems are an integral part of every successful business. However, because neither processes nor systems can smile at customers or form relationships with them, they are of little value without the people who operate them. In fact, one of the main ingredients of any business's success is the relationship it has with its customers. Customers like businesses that welcome them, show them they are important, do little things like ask if they need assistance, and thank them for their business. But none of this happens by accident. And the only way to make sure that it does happen is for owners to establish standards for employee conduct and find creative ways in which to draw out the talent that lies within most employees.

One of the things that separates the experienced from the inexperienced owner is that the former knows the one thing you can't teach is attitude. No matter how talented an employee may be, if he or she has a bad attitude toward coworkers, customers, or life in general, you would be better off letting him or her go work for one of your competitors. Not only are people like that unlikely to change their attitude, but a bad attitude is like the measles, and the last thing you want is for that kind of contagion to spread. Of course, it's best if you hire people with positive attitudes in the first place, but even that's no guarantee that they will maintain those attitudes. That is, while some people seem to be positive no matter what's going on, most people have to have some reason to do so.

Just as you have to create an atmosphere that's conducive to building a team, you have to create one that will encourage people to be positive. One way to do that is through increases in pay, bonuses, and other forms of meaningful recognition. To accomplish this, though, you must start by clearly defining each employee's job and exactly what is expected from that employee. And when they succeed, you must reward them. At the same time, if they don't succeed, there must be consequences. This is important in employee development, because people have to see the benefits of a job well done, as well as what happens when they don't do their jobs well. In fact, a little fear of the consequences of poor performance is not a bad thing.

You can also help develop positive attitudes among your employees by empowering them with greater responsibilities and promoting from within the company. This type of transparency has a positive effect not only on the employees who receive these benefits but on the company as a whole, because other members of the staff see actions like these as additional encouragement to do their jobs well. Finally, and this may surprise you, another way you can develop individuals is by making sure your company is successful and has a good reputation in the marketplace. The fact is that, even in an age when people tend to move frequently from one company to another, many employees want stability and a place where they can build their careers. So in addition to the many other advantages of building a successful business, doing so helps you attract and keep good employees.

At the end of the day, employees want to have meaningful work, to enjoy and have satisfaction in what they do, to have fun, to respect those they work with and for, to be safe and secure in their jobs, and to be fairly compensated and recognized for the good work they do. Satisfying these basic needs of employees and developing those employees to their full potential is not easy, but it is doable. Just ask the successful owners you know.

Level 4: Maintaining Success

A strange thing happens when you realize you have reached the success you dreamed about when you first started out—you begin to reflect on where the business started, how far it's come, and where it is today. This reflection usually leads to the realization that your success is largely due to the leadership skills you developed. In fact, it's really only at this point that you can begin to fully appreciate the significance of leadership and the role it's played in your business's success. If you have brought your company to Level 4, it's because your leadership abilities have enabled you to achieve three things. First, you have successfully captured—and more than likely expanded on—the opportunity you chose to pursue at Level 1. Second, you have created the business's DNA, which now drives the company and guides the implementation of the processes you developed. And, third, you have defined the business's destination, developed goals and objectives to get you there, measured the results, and in the process created a disciplined management system that has produced consistent profits.

Now, having attained your initial goals, you are likely to feel that the hard work has been done and you can sit back and reap the rewards. And that's entirely understandable. There is, though, one thing wrong with that idea—it's not true. The truth is that once your business becomes consistently successful, that success itself creates some particularly cruel traps. And it's these traps that make Level 4 one of the most challenging levels for owners. Among the various traps lying in wait for successful owners are arrogance and the belief that success will continue no matter what they do, losing discipline and forgetting the importance of managing results, internal apathy, competitors' reactions to your business's success, losing the fear of failure and the motivation to be great, and losing enthusiasm for solving nagging problems and searching for opportunities. All of these traps represent serious challenges, and overcoming them requires the kind of leadership only an owner can provide.

The fact is that your business can't just stay where it is—neither these traps, not your competitors, will allow that to happen. What this means is from this point on there are only two ways you and your company can go. One, of course, is to go backward. And if these traps aren't dealt with, or you procrastinate about dealing with them, that's exactly what will happen—your business will begin to slide back along the same spectrum you worked so hard to move forward. In fact, I've even seen companies slide so far back that they end up at the survival end of the spectrum again. The other way you can go is forward. Deciding to do this, though, isn't easy. Moving ahead means your leadership skills will be tested as never before. You may, for example, find yourself in a position in which your personal loyalty to people in the company will conflict with your responsibilities as a leader. You may also have to risk a significant amount of the profits you have accumulated to enlarge your facilities, add more inventory, or buy some expensive equipment to make your business more efficient. Situations like these can be very difficult to deal with. Even so, unless you want to give up all you've fought to achieve, you have little choice other than to move ahead.

The Benefits of Leadership at Level 4

- Being a leader enables you to give the company focus and renewed purpose even after success has been achieved.
- Being a leader helps you identify the traps awaiting your company at this level.
- Being a leader enables you to drive a sense of urgency in the company.
- Being a leader drives change, and change keeps a business fresh.
- Being a leader enables you to overcome the traps of success.
- Being a leader helps you use the power of teamwork to move the company forward.

- Being a leader helps you develop individual leaders, which in turn strengthens the company and helps move the company ahead in a controlled fashion.
- Being a leader helps you prioritize which of the traps to tackle first.
- Being a leader helps you and your staff continue to focus on goals, objectives, and managing results.

Achieving the Objective or Goal at Level 4

The first leadership goal at Level 4 is to keep the company operating successfully and delivering profits as expected. To accomplish this, you must continue to determine the company's goals, create objectives and steps to meet the goals, record the results, and manage those results. As I mentioned previously, this represents the everyday blocking and tackling of a business, and is something that every business must do if it hopes to maintain its success. However, there is also a new goal at this level that every owner must establish, that is, finding or developing a competitive advantage and exploiting it. Competitive advantages include things like:

- Buying a competitor.
- Starting an entirely new business that has some relationship— and can provide benefits—to the current business.
- Purchasing or leasing new facilities in a better location.
- Buying new and more efficient equipment.
- Upgrading current facilities.
- Creating a complementary or parallel business, or buying your distributor so that you can take control of your supply chain.

Although it may seem that ideas like these are limitless, in reality they are not. There is only so much excess cash available, only so many opportunities that can provide support to a business, and only a few of these that will create a competitive advantage. But finding or developing a competitive advantage is a "killer" weapon for securing a business and creating additional incremental profits, and if you want to maintain your business, it is imperative that you try to develop this kind of weapon.

Building and Maintaining a Team at Level 4

Common sense tells us that a group of individuals working together to achieve a common goal is more efficient than a group of individuals working in their own interests. And it's this belief that has made the word *team* so widely accepted and used. But simply saying "We are a team" doesn't make it true. Creating a business team and maintaining it is actually extremely difficult to accomplish, which is why real business teams are few and far between. And in fact, the only way to build an effective team is through leadership, that is, through an individual who is willing to accept the responsibilities of leadership, who is prepared to make hard decisions for the common good of the business, and who is proactive. As an owner, taking on this role is your responsibility.

Despite the difficulties, there are several good reasons to develop a team at this level. First, one of the results of doing so is creating a dominant company that generates exceptional profits. Second, since it's hard to do, your competitors probably won't do it, which will be to your advantage. Third, having a team will help you overcome the traps of success. And, finally, teams help build individual leaders, and the more leaders you have who are focused on the right things, the more likely you are to succeed.

There are several things you can do as a leader to help build a team in your company. First, since teams are made up of individuals, the people you choose to work in your business are very important. You should accordingly look for people who have leadership qualities, such as being proactive, being willing to take responsibility for their actions, and having a positive attitude. Second, teams need to have a common, meaningful purpose, and you can provide them with that purpose by making sure they know how you define success and what you expect them to do to help achieve it. Finally, teams need to be coordinated, that is, every department's objectives have to support and promote the overall company's goals, and supplying that coordination is one of your responsibilities as a leader.

In other words, creating a business team isn't just dependent on one thing, it's dependent on a number of things. There are two common denominators, though. One is that a team can be built only by a leader, and as the owner you must be that leader. The second is that results must be the focal point; that is, individuals have to know what is expected of them and produce it. If these two things don't happen, trying to develop a team will be pointless.

Developing the Individual at Level 4

As at every level, at Level 4 building a team and developing individuals goes hand in hand. But it's especially true at this point in a company's life cycle. For example, at Level 4 most owners are getting tired, and a fairly large percentage of them are losing their passion and drive. So the more employees you have who can help with the heavy lifting of leadership, the better your results are likely to be. Similarly, a lot of successful companies outgrow their owners; that is, after a certain point, the owners' abilities are no longer sufficient to guarantee the company's long-term success. Developing people who have different skills and can pick up where the owner's abilities leave off can only be to the company's benefit. In addition, in the event that something should happen to the owner and he or she is no longer able to manage the company, developing other people who could take over if necessary can serve as a kind of insurance policy for the owner's family. At the end of the day, though, it just makes sense to develop individuals in your business because the more leaders you have pulling together for a common purpose, the stronger the company will be.

The key to developing leaders is empowerment, which is enabling leaders to work without the day-to-day interference of the owner and showcase their abilities. But empowering employees is a two-edged sword, because even though it lightens your load, it comes at the cost of giving up control. And after many years of running a business, that can be very hard. Some owners find it difficult because they have favorite things they like to do, and some because they have been burned in the past when they ceded control to others. But regardless of why you may be reluctant to give up control, if you want more leaders, you have to give them responsibility. It doesn't work any other way. Fortunately, there is one factor that should make relinquishing control somewhat easier. By the time you have reached Level 4, the chances are that you've already put sufficient controls into place to make sure that unpleasant surprises are unlikely to occur. And in the meantime, by developing multiple leaders and helping them learn and grow, you will have built your business into the strongest company it could possibly be.

Level 5: Moving On When It's Time to Go

For some owners, making an exit decision is very easy. They can't wait until they have enough money to retire, and as soon as they do they're very happy to wave it all goodbye.

But for many owners, the subject is one they don't even want to think about, much less discuss. And, to be fair, it's entirely understandable. Leaving a business, whether it's through sale, succession, or closing, marks the end of something owners are comfortable with, and moves them into a new area that may sound good but is still unknown territory. If that's not complicated enough, there is the question of which route they should take on exiting, as well as hundreds of others about the business that have to be answered. And to top it off, getting out of a business is something most owners know little, if anything, about. It's no wonder they don't like thinking about it.

To make matters even worse, deciding when it's time to exit is as far from an exact science as it could be. Most owners realize a business can lose momentum, become stagnant, and begin to stumble if they stay too long. Most also know that putting a business up for sale too early, if that's what they choose to do, can mean forgoing future profits and, possibly, a higher selling price. But it's not just a question of the best timing for the business—owners also have to think about the best timing for themselves. It's a difficult balance, a difficult decision, and owners have to face this reality the same way they have faced other difficult decisions in the past. Ironically, it's the same leadership skills that enable owners to power their way into ownership at Level 1 that are needed to power their way out at Level 5.

As I mentioned earlier, there are two unavoidable facts that every owner has to take into consideration as far as exiting the business is concerned. The first is that the best time to exit is when you don't have to. And the second is that if you don't pick the time to exit, someone or something else will. There is literally no escaping these two realities, which is why leadership is so important at Level 5. More to the point, after exhibiting leadership and exercising control for so many years, it doesn't make any sense to abandon your leadership role, give up control, and leave to chance one of the most critical business decisions you can make. Avoiding this, however, requires you to take two distinct and different leadership initiatives. The first of these is to continue leading and operating the business as you did at Level 4. No matter how you choose to exit, the timing of your exit will hinge at least partly on other people, and since you can't be sure of when it will occur, you have to stay focused and keep the business going strong until it does. The second leadership initiative you must undertake is to prepare yourself to set up the business for your exit.

Particularly at this level, being prepared and understanding what you're doing is the key, because selling a business, planning a succession, or closing down can be very unnerving, and you can easily end up way in over your head—and fast. Making these kinds of preparations and developing this understanding is something only a leader can do successfully. And the best way to do it is essentially by asking the right questions, making sure the answers are based on fact rather than emotion, and then using those facts as a basis for your decision making. Some of the basic questions you have to answer are the same whether you are interested in selling the business, passing it along to a family member, or closing it. Some, however, apply only to one or another of these situations.

Regardless of which kind of exit you are anticipating, among the questions you must ask yourself are:

- Who has done what I want to do, and what is the best way for me to seek guidance from them?
- How much is my business realistically worth?

- What is a reasonable time frame to get ready to begin the exit process?
- Am I exiting because it's a good time for me personally, because a sale is likely to bring in a particularly large amount of money now, or both?
- Who will I use for professional legal and tax advice, and how can they best help me structure the selling process to my advantage?
- How much money will I need to live out the rest of my life in the style I want to?
- Do I want a clean break, or do I want to exit gradually?
- What factors will determine the timing of implementing an exit plan?
- Do I want to sell the business outright, or do I want to implement a succession plan?

If you are planning to sell your business, you need to answer the following questions:

- What is the selling process and how can I maximize it and control it?
- Who will be my best buyer? That is, who will pay me top dollar, who will have the most to gain by buying my company, and who will have the most to lose if someone else buys it?
- What do I have to do to make the business worth the most in potential buyers' eyes?
- Would it be better for me to sell the shares of my business or to sell the business' assets?
- What are the tax consequences of a sale?
- What information do I need to show a potential buyer to get the top price for my business?
- How will I represent the condition of my assets so I will not be held responsible if a buyer later determines there is some kind of problem?
- What assets have to be fixed, painted, or replaced in order to impress a would-be buyer?

In the event that you are planning to implement a succession plan, the kinds of questions you have to answer include:

- Who will be my best successor? That is, which member of my family is most capable of stepping in and has the ability to operate the business over the long term?
- What kind of financial arrangements can I make for other family members to avoid a rift?
- What should I educate my successor about, and what will he or she have to figure out themselves?
- How will I integrate my successor into the business?
- Which key employees do I need to talk to in order to solicit their support and make the transition as smooth as possible?
- What oversight will I need to maintain during the transition process?
- What is a reasonable timetable for the total transition?

Even if you are planning to simply close down your business, there are a number of questions that you must answer, including:

- What current liabilities and long-term debt is the business responsible for?
- What are the tax and legal consequences of closing down?
- How long will it take, from a tax and legal standpoint, to close down the business once the doors are closed?
- Is it best to slowly ramp the business down or to pick a date and then close down all at once?
- Does the business's customer base have any value to a competitor?
- Do any of the business's assets have value?
- Do my skills have any value to a competitor or industry association?

These do not, of course, represent all the questions you must answer when you're planning to exit your business. They are, however, a good starting point and represent some of the large obstacles and issues owners will have to prepare themselves and their business for when planning an exit.

The Benefits of Leadership at Level 5

- Being a leader enables you to prepare mentally for the transition and at the same time prepare your business to be sold, passed on, or closed.
- Being a leader enables you to ask the proper questions and, in the process, slow yourself down so the decision you make is based on facts rather than emotions.
- Being a leader helps ensure that as little as possible is left to chance in the exit process.
- Being a leader makes it possible for you to keep your employees from losing their focus and dwelling on concerns about the future.

Achieving the Objective or Goal at Level 5

At this level, while it's extremely important that you keep the continuing success of the company in the back of your mind, planning and executing an exit strategy must be your main focus. The objective here, regardless of how you choose to exit the company, is to do it in as controlled and calculated a manner as possible. Like all important things, though, this is easier said than done. Perhaps surprisingly, the hardest part of the exit process is taking the first step. As discussed earlier, that first step is educating yourself and coming to grips with some of your soon-to-be realities. Not surprisingly, the more knowledge you have about your situation, the better your decision will be. For example, there is no point in contacting a potential buyer if you haven't made sure that after paying off your debt and paying taxes you will have enough money to live on. You would certainly not want to find yourself in such a situation. But the fact is that things like this happen more often than most people realize, and it's all because the owner didn't take the time to make sure what his or her situation was.

Having clearly assessed your current situation and determined that you want to move on, you have to develop a plan. At this point, even if you have not yet decided on a date for your exit, you should have a good idea of what you need to do to get the business ready to sell, pass along, or close. Developing a plan to do that starts with

answering the questions I raised earlier and subsequently dealing with the hundreds of other issues that must be addressed. The
important thing to bear in mind, though, is that whether you are
thinking about selling, passing your company along to a successor, or closing it, the process is going to take time—usually years,
in fact—if you want to do it right. And for that reason, the sooner
you start developing a plan, the better—there is really no downside.
Remember, too, that the goal here is to sell your business for as
much as you possibly can, turn it over to a successor in such good
condition that it will continue to be successful, or maximize your
earning power prior to closing it down. And as the leader, you are
the only one who can accomplish that.

Building and Maintaining a Team at Level 5

Humans are the most complex beings on the face of the earth. And
business owners, like all humans, have both positive and negative
traits. Some of those positive traits are likely to play a role in the
exit process, such as fairness, honesty, loyalty, a sense of humor, and
common sense. But some negative human traits can also come into
play when exiting a business, including being overly emotional,
unwilling to listen to other people's opinions, disinclined to deal
with difficult issues, and acting as if we know everything. In order
to counter these less-than-positive traits, owners at Level 5 need to
build a group of people around them who can remind them of the
goal, help keep them focused when things go wrong or unexpected
developments occur, and provide knowledge they might not otherwise have.

One of the people you need on your team at Level 5 is an
attorney. I know that, on the whole, attorneys don't have particularly good reputations, and perhaps with some reason, but the fact
remains that a good business lawyer will keep you out of trouble.
There is more to a sale, succession, or closing than negotiating a
price. The devil, as they say, is in the details, and where an owner's exit is concerned, the devil can be in the contract. And since
the contract has killed many a deal, making sure you have a good
lawyer on your team is essential. Another important member of

your team will be an accountant, particularly one who has experience in buy/sell agreements and understands the tax effects of the transaction, among other things. In addition, if negotiating is not your strong suit, it would be advantageous to have someone who can either do the negotiating for you or can at least help you set up negotiation parameters. Finally, as I mentioned earlier, you are much more likely to conclude your negotiations successfully if you have a counselor, or mentor, who has already done what you are trying to do and can provide you with advice on the entire exit process.

Obviously, whenever you choose advisers, you want people who are both skilled and experienced in their fields. But when selecting people to assist you in exiting your business, you want professionals who also have two other attributes. The first is leadership ability. This is important because the more leaders you surround yourself with, the keener the focus on the prize. Leaders are also not shy about voicing their opinions and at certain times in the selling process both the buyer and seller need to hear from someone other than themselves. The second is creativity. Having people around you who possess this trait is important because you may not be able to get exactly what you want in the negotiation process. However, since there is always more than one way to accomplish almost anything, if you have creative people on your team, they are more likely to be able to find an alternative that is acceptable to both sides or to think of ways to make additional money that hadn't occurred to you.

Developing the Individual at Level 5

At Level 5, developing the individual is a multifaceted process. As an owner, you must first develop the individual members of your team so they will work together and focus on what you need from them. And that's not always easy. Unlike the situations at earlier levels, the members of this team are not your employees. In fact, in all likelihood they have their own businesses and their own concerns, so while they will presumably do the best they can to assist you, your company is not their first priority. It is, however, your responsibility to make sure they are there when you need them, to learn from their experiences and turn it to your advantage, and to pressure them to outperform on your behalf. In other words, it's up to you to get the most out of them that you can. And the only way I've found to do this effectively is to prepare yourself by learning everything you can about the sales, succession, or closing process, knowing exactly what their roles are, defining those roles for them, making them accountable, and stepping on them when they are not.

If you are selling your business, though, there is still another individual you may have to develop—the buyer. If the buyer is someone who already knows what he or she is doing—that is, who understands the value of what you're selling and has a good general understanding of business—the process is likely to be easier than if he or she does not. If, though, you find yourself in a situation in which the buyer is not knowledgeable, it's your responsibility to remedy that. The reason it's your responsibility is that your buyer is likely to need help from bankers and/or outside investors to purchase your company, and as the leader of the sales process, your leadership has to extend through the buyer to his or her financing source. Only if your buyer has a solid understanding of your business will he or she be able to effectively present and sell it to others and guarantee that you get paid what your business is worth.

If you are implementing a succession plan, however, it might be equally necessary for you to develop a different individual—your successor. As the owner, you are responsible for making sure the successor knows the business and has a good general understanding of basic business concepts. This may seem obvious, but we've all seen or heard of sons or daughters who have taken over family businesses only to see them flounder, if not entirely collapse. And the truth is that in a lot of cases like this it's the outgoing owner who is at fault rather than the successor. But your successor doesn't only have to know your business—it's equally important that he or she knows how your business operates. And there's a difference. If your successor doesn't understand that processes operate the business, and people operate the processes, it will be your responsibility to make sure he or she learns it.

Finally, if you decide to close down your business, as I mentioned earlier, it is essential that you get the most you can from your attorney and your accountant. The best way to do this, as I also mentioned, is learning as much as you can about the process and then asking educated questions. Again, because these professionals are not your employees, and have their own priorities, it's up to you to not only get their undivided attention when you need it but, even more important, their best advice and counsel. Closing down your business may well be your last act as an owner, so you should do it right by hiring the most experienced professionals you can find and take a leadership role in getting the most you can from your investment.

■ ■ ■

It is no coincidence that the first Fact of Business Life is about leadership. Without leadership we wouldn't know what to manage or control, what assets we should protect, which processes have to be developed, what our goals and objectives should be, who will be accountable, or about virtually any other aspect of running a business. In fact, leadership is such a powerful tool that virtually every element of success depends on it. Unfortunately, while leadership is one of those words that gets tossed around very frequently, I believe that only a small percentage of owners and businesspeople have a real working understanding of what it actually is and when and how to use it. Oddly enough, that can work to your advantage. By exercising your leadership skills you will be able to attack your market, create an opportunity, expand your ownership role, add quality to your life, and, eventually, exit your business on your own terms. If you have any doubts about this, ask yourself if you've ever heard anyone blame a business failure on having too much leadership. Chances are that you haven't, and that's because when you exhibit leadership, when you have the courage to step out from the ordinary and use it, it can mean the difference between failure and success—not only in your career but in your life as well.

4

Fact 2: If You Don't Control It, You Don't Own It

What does control, or management, mean for an owner? If you asked a dozen business owners that question, you could get as many as a dozen different answers. That's because control, and what it means, differ not only from one industry to another but from one owner to another. As a working definition, we can use the one offered in Burton Kaliski's *Encyclopedia of Business and Finance* (Macmillan, 2002), which defines internal control as "any action taken by an organization to help and enhance the likelihood that the objectives of the organization will be achieved." Regardless of how you define it, though, it's important to bear in mind that more companies go out of business because there is too little control than because there is too much. This is a point you cannot afford to ignore.

To my mind, control means developing and implementing procedures and establishing parameters around which employees are expected to do their jobs and be motivated to excel at them. This doesn't mean that the owner should be a dictator who determines every move each of his or her employees makes. What it does mean is that he or she decides what needs to be controlled, that is, in which areas processes are needed; determines exactly what those processes or procedures should be; and makes sure they are followed. The fact is—and this is something that every business owner knows or should know—that without control a company's sales, expenses, gross profits, and net profits will never be consistent. Without control there will constantly be chaos within the company, an ongoing need for crisis management, and continuous employee and customer dissatisfaction, all of which are a recipe for disaster. And as a business owner, it's your responsibility to establish that control. As I've mentioned before, and will again, ownership is not for the faint of heart. If defining what to control and consistently enforcing it—that is, managing an organization—is not in your personal DNA, then ownership won't be a good career choice for you.

There are a good many people who view control as something distinct from management and, because of that, place less importance on it. But as far as I am concerned, establishing and maintaining control over how your business operates essentially is management, and as such is fundamentally critical not only to an owner's success but to his or her enjoyment of that success. To my mind, then, control must stand on its own alongside leadership, marketing, and other important business disciplines. In fact, once a leader has determined where a company is going, decided how the company is to be an operated, and established processes to make sure it is operated that way, it is control's function to make sure the business is run along the guidelines established by the owner. In the end, it's the only way owners can guarantee that the way their companies perform will satisfy not only their customers but themselves as well.

The Benefits of Control

- Being in control forces you to determine and define what you want.
- Being in control means that employees know what you want and expect of them, and how they will be rated.
- Being in control makes it easier for you to pinpoint problems when employees are not performing as expected.
- Being in control provides you with a platform on which to base job performance and evaluation.
- Being in control eliminates most of the unpleasant surprises that businesses are prone to because it enables you to look into the future and see problems before they become crises.

- Being in control enables you to provide consistency in delivering your products to the customer, which is a key to customer satisfaction.

The Realities of Control

- Establishing and maintaining control is difficult to do.
- Establishing and maintaining control is not something you can do on your own; it requires others in the company to help.
- Establishing and maintaining control requires patience, constant coaching, and sometimes a firm and unrelenting hand.
- Establishing and maintaining control requires you to reward those who do it right and discipline those who do not.

There are four areas in which it is essential that ownership control or management be implemented—information, processes, people, and products. But since every level has different requirements, control must be exercised differently at each one. The one constant, though, is this: You must inspect what you expect. Regardless of where your company is in its life cycle, unless you, as the owner, constantly watch what's going on and make sure that the company is running as you want it to, it will run away without you.

Level 1: Ownership and Opportunity

At Level 1, as Steven Covey has noted, a business is only a mental concept rather than a going concern. Given the four areas in which control should be exercised, it might then be difficult to see exactly how it can be an important factor at this level. And to be honest, control does play a less significant role than leadership or planning at this point in the company's life cycle. That does not, however, mean that control is unimportant in the ownership and opportunity phase. In fact, it's an essential tool that aids owners in the decision making that takes place at this level. This is because control helps pinpoint the relevant data and makes sure it is accurate and factual. It also plays a major role in holding the owner's emotions in check, and giving him or her the patience needed to review and analyze all the relevant data. In other words, control enables owners to make sure that the decisions they make at this level are based on rational thought rather than emotion.

The Benefits of Control at Level 1

- Being in control enables you to keep your emotions in check.
- Being in control helps guarantee that decisions are made based on facts rather than incorrect information or assumptions.
- Being in control enables you to identify what can be controlled as well as what can't be controlled, both of which need to be factored into any decision.
- Being in control focuses you on what needs to be controlled and which of those areas are most critical for the business's success.
- Being in control makes it easier for you to identify conflicts in the information gathered and gives you the patience to sort them out.
- Being in control gives you advance intelligence regarding potential opportunities or potential threats by keying in on current market trends regionally and nationally and enabling you to act on that intelligence.

Control of Information at Level 1

Controlling information at this level is essentially a matter of determining which information is important in making ownership and opportunity decisions and which is not. Doing so is basically a three-step process. The first step is prioritizing and defining the kind of information you need to make an informed ownership decision and evaluate the opportunity. The second is gathering and compiling the data, and making sure it is factually accurate, current, and from a wide range of sources rather than just one or two. The third step, which is often the hardest to do, is focusing on the facts rather than on your emotions. In fact (no pun intended), if you are at all uncomfortable with the decision you make, it would probably be a good idea to have someone else review the information as a kind of reality check. While controlling information is essential at every level, it is particularly important at this one because here you are making fundamental decisions on whether you even go into business and, if you do, what kind of business it will be—decisions that can have a long-term impact on your life.

Control of Processes at Level 1

The ownership decision process at Level 1 essentially consists of two steps. The first is simply laying out the reasons ownership is attractive to you, listing your alternative career choices (both current and future), and matching them up. Doing so enables you to focus on the first two questions that have to be answered: "Is ownership for me?" and "Is this my time?" No one can answer these questions except you, and that's why the ownership decision process (or the expansion decision process) starts here.

The second step is looking at the reality of the situation and asking yourself a series of important questions, such as:

- Do I have the experience for ownership or expansion?
- Do I have someone to go to for advice?
- Will I be able to raise the needed capital?
- What burdens will getting the money put on my current business, my family, or both?
- Can I make money right from the start?
- Do I like this business?
- Can my kids take over for me someday? Do I want them to?

These and other reality-based questions have to be answered before you can make a decision about whether you want to be an owner.

The opportunity decision process at Level 1 is much like the ownership decision process, but it "feels" like it has more of a foundation. This is because the business and the industry have some history, and you can see and touch your competitors. Even so, as in the ownership decision, the opportunity decision basically requires gathering information, that is, answering questions about the various opportunities you are considering, such as:

- Will it make money? How much money?
- What needs to happen to make the business profitable?

- Is the industry healthy?
- How long will it take me to pay back my debt?
- What are the threats to this opportunity? Can I overcome them, or do I have to live with them?
- What can turn this opportunity from a good one to a great one?

As with ownership, you have to keep yourself firmly grounded in reality when evaluating an opportunity. And it's the process of asking questions like these that slows you down and forces you to look at the facts realistically.

Control of People at Level 1

At Level 1, since you are still only in the planning stages of your business, "people" means you. So controlling people means controlling your emotions, exercising patience, employing common sense, and keeping a balanced and unbiased point of view. Doing so, in fact, is a key component in getting what you want, because it enables you to intelligently analyze the relevant data you have collected for both the ownership and opportunity decisions. But there is more to it than that, because there are always doubts, or should be, where opportunity is concerned, even for the most experienced owners. The more times you face the situation, the wiser you become, but that doesn't mean it gets any easier. It just makes you more aware of the importance of being in control of yourself and relying on facts rather than emotions.

Control of Product at Level 1

Although at Level 1 your business doesn't actually exist yet, you still have a product, and that product is you and the talents and capital you bring to the table. And in order to sell that product, you have to control it, which means you have to control how you present yourself to others. If you are trying to borrow money from a bank, the bank is looking at "you" as a risk, and is primarily concerned with your ability to do what you say you can do and pay them back. If you are purchasing a business, the owner is looking at "you" in terms of your ability to pay, your chances of success, and how much you want what he or she has. In situations like these, if you present yourself as a calm, intelligent, mature, experienced, and talented individual—or as close to that as possible—you are much more likely to be able to convince these first "customers" that they should "buy" what you're selling—yourself.

Level 2: Creating Your Company's DNA

Although control plays what might be considered a supporting role at Level 1, it's considerably more important at the remaining four levels. In fact, control plays such a major role in creating a company's DNA that, without the help of control, very little of what the owner wants to accomplish will happen. That's because when DNA creation and control intersect, or join together, they form the "backbone" of the company. And it's the quality and strength of that backbone that will separate success from failure and moderate from great success.

A company's DNA represents the established procedures through which the owner wants the company to operate, as well as how employees interact with each other and with customers. Control at Level 2 is simply the reporting mechanisms that show the owner, and his or her key employees, which processes are being run correctly and which aren't. These mechanisms, in turn, generally force owners and/or those key employees into some sort of action or reaction. And that action, reaction, or, for that matter, inaction sends a clear message to every employee about the strength, passion, and resolve the owner has when things don't work the way they should—hence the development of the business's backbone, which lets employees know how far they can push before you push back.

Most owners actually understand the importance of procedures and controls as well as the effects of combining them. Unfortunately, though, because some owners do whatever they can to avoid confrontation with employees, they continue to tell their people how they would like to have things work but fail to put in any controls. Not having controls does decrease, if not eliminate, confrontations, but it also decreases or eliminates the likelihood of the owner's having things done the way he or she wants. At the other extreme are those owners who micromanage their businesses and try to put controls on almost everything, which chokes the life and character out of a business. Obviously, neither extreme works over the long term.

As an owner, then, you have to find your "control balance," that is, a point between the two extremes where both you and your staff are comfortable. And when you find that balance, you've not only given your business a great gift, you've given yourself one as well. Because once a business's backbone is formed, proactive employees will use it as their guide to doing their job, and the company's character—the one you want—will start being created. And when that happens, sales and profits soar, and the workplace is functional, efficient, teamlike in operation, and consistent, all of which are vital to customer loyalty.

The Benefits of Control at Level 2

- Being in control enables you to put your "stamp" on the business.
- Being in control enables you to consistently reinforce how employees are expected to treat others and be treated in return.
- Being in control alerts you when customers aren't being properly served, when sales are missed, or when customers are not being followed up on and encouraged to return.
- Being in control enables you to make sure your employees know what's expected of them in terms of their job performance.
- Being in control enables you and your managers to recognize the company's strengths and weaknesses.
- Being in control helps your employees become better at their jobs because by consistently monitoring and evaluating results you can recognize their training needs and provide them.

A company at Level 2, like a company at Level 1, is still largely a mental concept rather than a going concern. In terms of the owner's situation, however, there is a significant difference.

At Level 1, neither ownership nor opportunity has been decided on as yet, while at Level 2 ownership is a given, and an opportunity has been taken or is about to be entered into. And because of that, regardless of whether an owner is opening his or her first business, trying to improve an area of an existing business, expanding or buying a new business, or totally reengineering the business, he or she should know beforehand how they want the business to operate and what controls must be put in place to make sure that it operates that way. Most important, whatever the situation, the owner can never lose sight of the fact that when DNA and control come together they form the backbone of the company, and that the combination shapes the character or personality of the organization.

Control of Information at Level 2

We all know that knowledge is power, but only if that knowledge is based on information that is relevant, timely, and accurate. Otherwise, it's junk. The bottom line is that of all the areas owners can control, information is not only one of the most important but also one of the most underrated. When you think about information regarding your company you probably think first about internal financial information, that is, sales revenue, gross profit, personal expenses, fixed expenses, net profit, and so on. But while it's important for you to gather, understand, and analyze this kind of financial information, it's not the only kind of information you need. It's equally important that you gather information on, among other things, market size and demographics, number of customer contacts versus actual sales, product innovations, competitors' sales, and others. The good news about information is that it's relatively easy to come by. But the bad news about information is also that it's relatively easy to come by.

With so much information available, it's possible that you can be overwhelmed—even paralyzed—by it. That's why it's so important that you make every effort to control it, that is, prioritize it, and focus on the information that will help you meet your success goals. There are basically three ways of doing this. The first is to decide which information will help operate the business on a daily, weekly, monthly, and yearly basis, and make sure that information is provided regularly to those who need it. The second is to continuously check the information for accuracy. Some individual or department has to be assigned the task of seeing to it that any information used for decision making or determining the business's current condition is monitored for accuracy. And the third is to make sure that your employees use the information the way you want it to be used. That means you have to tell them how you want things done and make sure they do it that way. Control is not just about pointing out that something is right or wrong—it's also about what happens next.

Control of Processes at Level 2

As I've mentioned before, creating processes is part of establishing the company's DNA. But no matter how good the actual processes are, without control even the most well-intentioned processes will end up being reinterpreted and redesigned by employees for their own benefit. As an owner, you can't allow that to happen. The way to avoid this is to set up check points within each key process to make sure that what's happening is what you want to happen, that is, that what's happening will work and be of benefit to the company.

It's not enough, though, to simply establish these check points. As an owner, it's imperative that you and your managers continually communicate to your staff why you want things done the way you do. This kind of communication is important because in every company there are individuals who complain about doing things the "company way." Explaining the "why" gives employees a different perspective on what the company is trying to accomplish and opens the discussion to employees who may be able to help develop even better processes.

Control of People at Level 2

There have been literally countless books and articles written about managing employees, as well as thousands of business coaches who teach it. But here's the thing you have to realize as a business owner:

controlling your employees isn't as difficult as many make it seem. All that getting control of your employees requires is understanding and implementing the concept I've already discussed and will discuss again and again: processes operate the business, and employees operate the processes. That's it. That's how successful businesses work. Michael Gerber, in his book *The E-Myth* (Ballinger, 1986), discussed this at length, and there have been others over the years who have said essentially the same thing. But none of these authors have taken the next logical step, which is putting this basic concept into practice. What that means is that, as an owner, you have to determine what you believe is important to the success of the business, develop a step-by-step process for it, and then implement it. If you do this, you will have found the easiest way to gain control over your workforce.

Control of Product at Level 2

As an owner, you must always remember that the sole reason your business exists is to attract customers and keep them. The products you sell are the vehicle through which that's done. At Level 1 you were the product, but now you have to step aside and let what you represent—and the customers come for—be the product. But stepping aside doesn't mean giving up control. In fact, it actually means controlling not just the product but everything in the business that has to do with the product, both before it's sold to the customer and afterward—so you can get the customer to come back.

Controlling a product is not easy but it is essential to survival and success. There are basically three steps to accomplishing it. The first is to recognize there is very little, if anything, as important as product, and because of that, you can afford to leave little, if anything, to chance. The second step is to determine what and how you will exercise control. This step should actually be taken even before you open, expand, or reengineer a business and should be an ongoing project throughout your ownership career. Day 1 is too late to begin figuring out control of the product, and it's a mistake few owners can afford to make. The third step is realizing the extent to which product covers your business. As you will see later on, product is one of the few areas in your business that needs the complete support of all the Facts of Business Life. At this level, however, product control begins with deciding what and how much to order, when to reorder, who to hire to support the product, what the selling price should be, how much gross profit the selling price will leave you, what volume levels you'll need to have to make a reasonable profit, and doing whatever you can to see to it that the customer comes back to make another purchase.

Level 3: From Survival to Success

The objective at Level 3 is obviously for the business to become successful. And it is the point at which many companies do attain that success. But statistics show that it's also the "killing ground" for most entrepreneurs, the point at which most new businesses fail. One of the best weapons you, as an owner, have to avoid this killing ground is installing controls and instilling the discipline to maintain them as core expectations at every level of your company.

Level 3 is where the business begins operating in real time, so it's at this point that all the planning and preparation you did at Levels 1 and 2 has to be put into practice. In order to establish and maintain the controls you determined were necessary at the earlier levels, you have to make sure that four things happen. First, there has to be clear and concise communication between management and staff about what is wanted and expected. Second, there must be constant discipline, from the owner down, to make sure that whatever the controls indicate is not working is corrected. Third, operations and controls must be continually fine-tuned. And, finally, controls must go beyond the normal, everyday financial controls that protect the business's assets. In fact, the controls suggested in this chapter not only cover the financial controls that most owners use, but go beyond that in order to help ensure that you and your company will succeed.

The Benefits of Control at Level 3

- Being in control provides you with an early warning system so you can see what's about to happen before it does.

- Being in control enables you to allow employees to provide input that can lead to streamlined processes as well as improvements in how those processes work and how they are controlled.
- Being in control requires procedures, and procedures give employees guidelines for how to do their jobs and the kind of results that are expected of them.
- Being in control essentially enables you to run your business because Control + Processes = Management.
- Being in control enables you to "inspect what you expect."
- Being in control provides you with early indications of immediate opportunities and threats in the marketplace.
- Being in control requires a tough mental discipline throughout the company, without which good things rarely happen.

Control of Information at Level 3

Level 3 essentially begins at survival and, if managed correctly, ends with success. Control of information is a particular challenge at this level because the business is fluid—that is, it's moving from one end of the spectrum to the other—and the type of information you need changes. For example, when a business is still on the survival end of the spectrum, the most important information an owner needs to have is cash flow, sales, gross profit margins, and expenses, among others, and he or she needs to track them on a daily or weekly basis. But as the business gains some momentum and begins its journey toward the success end of the spectrum, the microfocus on financial issues becomes part of the owner's focus on larger issues, such as business tactics, strategy, how to take advantage of the business's strengths, and shoring up any weaknesses it might have. In other words, as the business matures, what was once key information continues to be important, but new and different kinds of information also have to be generated to help the owner and the company meet its new objectives and goals.

As at every level, though, it is essential to maintain control over information at Level 3 because, as an owner, you can never let up on the relentless pursuit of accurate information. As was the case at Level 2, at this level the best way to do that is to prioritize what information is needed, by whom, and in what time frame; continuously check to determine that the information being used in the company is accurate; and make sure your employees are using the information the way you want them to.

Control of Processes at Level 3

As we've already noted, at Level 2, Creating Your Company's DNA, an owner thinks through how he or she wants the business to operate on a day-to-day, week-to-week basis and devises processes to make sure it works that way. It's at Level 3 that all these processes begin to be implemented, and it's through them that the owner gains and keeps control of his or her business. Again, though, because at this level a company is moving along the spectrum from survival to success, its needs are changing, and implementing processes and their controls is a particular challenge for an owner.

For example, when a company is still on the survival end of the spectrum, processes that involve assets are usually the ones owners pay most attention to, including things like how cash is handled and accounted for, what criteria are used for allowing customers to charge their sales, and how the company decides what products are to be inventoried. But when a company has gotten closer to the success end, the most important thing may not be the processes themselves but the means by which the processes are managed. As I mentioned earlier, developing a process is one thing, but making sure it's working properly may be an even greater challenge. Implementing and fine-tuning processes are, of course, essential, but managing them is just as important and must be an ongoing activity as long as you're in business.

Perhaps the most effective way of controlling processes at the survival end of the spectrum is by micromanaging them. Success is the goal, but first you have to survive. That means you can't afford to let employees make mistakes and learn from them, or discover that a process you thought would work doesn't and hasn't from the beginning. As an owner, you need to be on top of everything and immediately fix whatever isn't working.

Controlling processes at the success end, however, is somewhat different. At that point, the best means of maintaining control is by stepping back and taking more of a macro view of your business. Knowing when to empower employees isn't an exact science, but micromanaging will eventually smother the business, and if you want your company to grow and succeed, you will eventually have to empower your staff. That doesn't mean, of course, that you don't pay attention to what's going on. What it means is that if the company is operating as you want it to, you should leave it alone and get involved only when and if there is a problem that requires your attention.

It's important to note that implementing processes and their controls is far easier if you're starting a new company than if you're reengineering your current business or taking over an existing one. This is primarily because if your employees are used to doing something a particular way, and you want it done differently, there is inevitably going to be some pushback. At the same time, it's never a good idea to overload your staff with changes. It's bad for morale and employee confidence, and it shows up in the results. Because of this, it's particularly important for owners at Level 3 to determine which processes they want to implement first and how they will control each of those processes. Regardless of the challenge, though, the bottom line is that processes have to be implemented or your business will never operate to your standards and will never attain success.

Control of People at Level 3

As I've mentioned before, creating processes and procedures is one thing, but getting people to follow them is another. And no matter how good the processes are, unless they are followed, they will serve no useful purpose. Controlling people at Level 3 is essentially about getting them to follow those procedures, and there are several ways you can do this. First, you can continuously encourage them to follow the procedures and keep explaining why you want them to do it that way. Second, you can try to find a better way by rethinking the procedures and/or encouraging them to do so and implementing improvements. Third, you can tie their following procedures to their compensation. Finally, if you can't do anything else, you can fire them and bring in people who will do it the way you want.

It is very important to remember, though, that control of employees always starts with the company's owners, which is good news for the proactive owner who understands the importance of consistent employee management and control. It's the owner who must set the tone in the business, not just through words but also through actions. If owners want their employees to work hard, be professional, and have a positive attitude, they have to exhibit these characteristics themselves. In addition, as I mentioned earlier, controlling employees doesn't mean becoming a dictator. It does require an owner to be tough when he or she has to be, but it's also important that he or she be fair in dealing with the company's staff.

Control of Product at Level 3

When the subject of controlling a product or service comes up, the first thing many owners think of is quality control. And that's entirely understandable, since maintaining quality is an essential aspect of running a successful business. But controlling quality is only a small fraction of the control needed at Level 3. Since at this point the business has begun operating, there is a lot of activity around your product or service, and this activity has to be well managed, meaning controlled.

In fact, control of product at Level 3 can mean many things. It can mean the way you buy your products for resale, how well you train your employees, how deeply you inventory your products, the price at which you sell your product or service, how well you record which products sell the fastest and which bring in the highest gross profit margin, how you follow up after a sale, how you differentiate your product or service from your competitors, and how you track lost sale opportunities, among many others. Because there are so many areas in which you could exercise control at this level, if you try to control all of them, you are more likely than not to paralyze your company. The real challenge, then, lies in prioritizing, that is, deciding which areas are the most important and, accordingly, which you should concentrate on. This doesn't mean you can ignore the less important areas, but rather that you have to find a balance between those you need to exercise greater control over and those you do not.

It's important to remember that as a company moves across the spectrum from survival to success, as it matures and changes, the areas that are most important are likely to change, and you have to be able to change with them. For example, as the business grows, you will have to invest more money in inventory and accounts receivable. That means you'll have to have more cash to run the business. In a situation like this, it is essential that you exercise control over the expense associated with that extra cash requirement, whether it comes from a bank or from some other area of your business. And it's not easy. This kind of decision, and others like it about product control, account for a lot of the heartburn and sleepless nights that plague owners.

Level 4: Maintaining Success

At Level 4, control is not the most important Fact of Business Life—that role belongs to the fact concerning leadership. However, maintaining control over information, processes, people, and product is still essential, for several reasons. Perhaps the most important of these is that in order to function properly, leadership needs the support internal controls provide. For example, it's hard to lead a charge for improved sales and gross profit without using past performance as a baseline. And if the new sales and gross profit objectives are based on past performance and information that's incorrect, your new forecast will be meaningless because you will have raised the bar either too high or too low and wasted everyone's time and energy. You will also have shot yourself in the foot as far as any momentum you may have made is concerned, and possibly led your employees to begin questioning your leadership.

There are also traps awaiting unsuspecting owners at this level as they attempt to solidify their companies as Level 4 businesses, and without the use of internal controls these traps will be almost impossible to navigate around. For example, it's important that the sales and gross profit figures you get from your sales department balance with those you get from accounting. If they don't and you lose control of the balancing process, you will end up with two different sets of information, with the possibility that neither one is accurate. As a general rule, owners must exercise continuous over-sight and control in order to have accurate financial statements on which to base decisions, as well as continually expand these con-trols as the business grows.

As I've already mentioned, as an owner, it's important to understand that as you move from one level to the next you have to bring the tools and experiences from the previous levels with you. But it's particularly important in making the transition from Level 3 to Level 4 because at this point you don't only have to bring what you've learned with you, you have to improve on it. In fact, if you want to maintain your success and become a strong Level 4 business, you have to take your company to a higher plateau of performance. Unless you do, you will be unable to avoid the traps of success and will never be able to put your company on a continu-ously solid footing. There is an old adage that says it's one thing to win but quite another thing to continue winning, and this is espe-cially true in business. Your competitors want what you have—your customers—and if you don't fight for them, you'll lose them and your business along with them.

The idea of ratcheting up performance is certainly not unique to business. Think, for example, about NFL, NHL, or NBA teams. Hoping to win a championship, they play the entire season to posi-tion themselves to make the playoffs. And then, since only the best-performing teams get into the playoffs, they have to ratchet up their performance in order to win the playoffs and become cham-pions. It's the same in business. Unless you take your company to a higher plateau of performance at Level 4—the equivalent of the playoff games—you will never get any closer to sustained success. There's also another similarity between business and sports at this advanced level of competition—the first rule to continue winning is to not beat yourself. In sports, this means not incurring penalties or making other mental mistakes such as misreading plays or being out of position. In business, it means your company has to be run-ning smoothly on all cylinders, and the only way that can happen is if your company's internal controls are working efficiently and effectively.

How Not to Use Controls

In the 1970s, General Motors (GM) was the world's biggest and most profitable business. A Level 4 company, it dominated the North American market, selling one out of every two new vehicles in the United States and Canada, as well as being a major competitor overseas. By late 2008, though, GM was selling less than one out of every five new vehicles in North America and was warning the financial markets that it was running out of cash. A few months later, it declared bankruptcy. What happened, essentially, was that the company stopped doing what made it a great company and literally beat itself.

The way it did that was by failing to focus on those areas of the business that needed to be controlled. Although the company had controls and knew, for example, that its market share started falling in the late 1970s, instead of addressing this dangerous trend, they made excuses for it. And instead of dealing with it, they focused on other issues and championed other causes, like constant reorganization and buying businesses unrelated to the car business, as well as some that were, which cost them billions before they shut them down or gave them away.

The point is, obviously, that controls are important, as is having the courage to recognize and aggressively address problems until they're fixed. Because GM didn't do this, even though it had at one time been a hugely successful company, over a span of 30 years it fell from being a great car company to being "just another car company." GM's executives were able to walk away and still be well looked after, but most business owners in a situation like this are more likely to walk away bent over from carrying the debt they've accumulated and the money they've lost.

The Benefits of Control at Level 4

- Being in control continuously focuses you on the important areas of your business.
- Being in control helps you improve your company's performance even when the business is already successful.
- Being in control helps you set up your business for long-term success.
- Being in control helps the company improve its performance so that there can be a larger payoff if it's sold or an easier transition if you implement a succession plan.

- Being in control enables you to keep a company fresh and constantly challenged.
- Being in control creates consistency in how the company operates, including how customers are handled, which in turn reinforces customer loyalty.
- Being in controls creates a standard for how employee issues are handled.
- Being in control enables you and your managers to maintain your business's brand message by making sure that it is consistent company-wide.

Control of Information at Level 4

By the time a business gets to Level 4, its owner should have learned about the importance of having relevant, current, and factual information, as well as what a great tool information can be. As I've already mentioned, though, Level 4 calls for improvement over the successes in Level 3, which means improved controls will have to be implemented to attain a higher level of performance. That is, in order to find your best opportunities and meet expectations, new and more detailed information will be needed. This quest for information can lead to a challenge that you, as an owner, may not have experienced before. That is, you have to be particularly careful about what you measure, because measuring the wrong things can promote the wrong activities and lead to a loss of focus within the organization.

For example, if one of your improvement goals is to produce additional gross profit per employee, one possible solution could be adding technology in order to reduce costs. However, while doing so might help your company meet the goal of increased gross profit per employee, it would also add to your overall business expenses, possibly so much so that it would wipe out any projected profit increases. As a result, unless you are sure you are measuring the right thing—in this case, net profit—your decision to add technology may not actually help you reach your goals at all. In other words, at Level 4, the information you gather must not only be accurate, it has to be relevant and must be analyzed in terms of your overall definition of continued success.

Controlling information is a lot harder than it sounds, and it becomes even harder when one of the purposes of doing so is adding value to the overall business, the customer, or both, as it does at Level 4. Adding value can mean finding new revenue streams, increasing gross profit margins, improving internal efficiency, and creating customer benefits, among others. Goals like these can be accomplished by continuously looking for better ways to make use of the information available. For example, similar industries can provide a wealth of information. Automotive dealers can learn a lot from how Harley-Davidson dealers captured their aftermarket accessories business, including clothes, coffee mugs, playing cards, and other items; or how John Deere creates brand awareness by selling toys to kids, like tractors and other machines, that are replicas of what their parents use. Creative information like this is priceless, and it's all around for the taking.

The bottom line, though, is that if you do not control the quality and relevance of the information you use to make decisions, you are likely to find yourself overloaded with it. And information overload usually leads at best to time wasted and an inability to make decisions, and at worst to concentrating on information that takes the focus away from what's important in maintaining success, the same kind of thing that happened to General Motors (GM).

Control of Processes at Level 4

As I've already mentioned, processes are actually the engine that drives the business forward, and those processes need constant attention and maintenance, just like the engine in a car. The reason they do is business is always in a state of motion. Employees, customers, competition, and product innovation are just some of the elements that keep a business in constant motion. And unless internal processes keep up with the changes, they will lose their relevance and become bureaucratic rather than effective. For example, a process that was designed a year ago when sales volume was a third of what it is today won't work without restructuring. And that restructuring can take any of several forms, including eliminating processes, replacing them with new ones, or "retuning" them, that is, adapting them to fit the current reality.

The best way of determining which processes need to be changed is to regularly conduct audits on those processes, and this is particularly important at Level 4. There are a number of ways to do so, ranging from the expensive—hiring consultants to do it for you—to the inexpensive—doing it yourself with your office manager and/or your department managers. Whichever you choose, though, it's essential for you to remember that processes can't be expected to work at more than one level of your business. They can be stretched up to a point, but common sense says if you were selling 200 widgets a month and now you're selling 600, things have to change, and those things are processes. In this instance, that means, for example, that your inventory level will have to increase, which in turn means new ordering and restocking processes will have to be developed, among others.

Control of People at Level 4

Because a company's processes are operated by its employees, understanding the connection between them helps owners at Level 3 in their efforts to move their businesses from survival to success. At Level 4, though, since the primary goal is to solidify a company's position by lifting it to a higher plateau of performance, coordinating processes and people becomes even more important. It also becomes a major challenge for owners, primarily because the kind of problems that arise at this level frequently stem from the owner's effort to improve the company and can be very difficult to solve.

Some of these problems come up because some of your employees may not agree with your decision to take your business to a higher plateau. As a result, as you strive to move the business ahead and make new demands on your staff, you can begin to meet resistance from them, even from some of those at the highest level. And the first place this resistance shows up is through the performance criteria and controls that you've established. This is obviously a very serious problem, and one that won't go away unless you take appropriate action to fix it.

There are several ways you can do this. One way is to watch how frequently your key employees are checking their department controls. If these controls are not being checked often enough, you can step up their frequency by installing more stringent reporting requirements. You can also see how aggressively your managers are developing new controls and processes to match their new volume expectations. And if these new controls are not being developed, you can come down heavily on those responsible, and make it clear to them that unless they start doing so they will be replaced. Problems like this, if not corrected, can take a Level 4 company back to Level 3—and in a hurry. Moreover, in your efforts to fix these problems, it's important for you to realize that others in the company, both those who have and those who haven't committed themselves to improving performance, are watching you very carefully and will view your actions as a test of your commitment. And it's a test you have to pass if you are going to achieve the goal of Level 4.

Control of Product at Level 4

Achieving the goal at this level depends on maintaining control over information, processes, people, and product. However, it's particularly important for an owner to maintain this control over his or her products. In fact, at this level, an owner has to develop a "killer instinct" as far as the product or service is concerned. I talk more about this "killer instinct" in later chapters, but it's important to note that at Level 4 not only do controls have to become more sophisticated, but the discipline that goes with those controls has to be uncompromising. In other words, whenever owners or their key employees see a "red flag" in the product area, they have to deal with it immediately. That's because product issues don't disappear, and unless they're addressed—and the sooner the better—any company can find itself in the same position as GM.

One example of more sophisticated product control is better management of a company's inventory. Most owners know their best-selling merchandise, but they may not know how much or how little these best sellers contribute to gross profit. The goal for inventory, of course, is to stock items that reflect customer demand, sell or turn quickly, and contribute the most to gross profit. But gross profit doesn't always get the same attention as sales does, although it is just as critical. At Level 4, if you want to improve your business, you can "data mine" past sales. That is, instead of looking at your volume leaders, look at your best gross profit leaders. Doing so will allow you to build an inventory that reflects gross profit margins as well as sales. In fact, while the data mining is taking place, you can also track lost sales, seasonality of products, buying practices, and any other critical components in which knowledge might help build inventory that turns quickly, provides an attractive gross profit increase, and increases sales.

It should be obvious by now that products and their controls are extraordinarily important, and without them the chances of becoming a Level 4 owner are slim. But—and this is a big but—controls can never become more important than the product, and can never interfere with why the product is selling in the first place. A lot of products and services sell well not only because of the products or services themselves but also because of the "sizzle" that goes with them. If, for example, a product has some sex appeal, or makes some kind of social statement, the owner has to recognize that fact and never let anything overshadow it. This is something that GM neglected to do with its Cadillac and Oldsmobile brands, and they paid for it. By allowing financial and engineering issues to dominate the product lines, that is, processes rather than the cars themselves, GM forgot that its role was to provide what its customers wanted, and sales plummeted as a result.

There is also another potential trap for owners at this level, and it's a trap that can derail even the strongest company. While it's true that you must have controls if you want to get to Level 4— much less stay there—if you exercise too much control, it will eventually become a negative factor. And that's because, at this level, while strict controls are needed in some areas of the business, relatively little control is needed in others. For example, it is particularly important to maintain strict control over accounts receivables, inventories, equipment, and financial records, among others. Without such controls a company can find itself in serious difficulties. However, it is equally important at this level to not exercise a great deal of control in other areas, including personal management, daily decision making, and training. This is because doing so can have a negative effect on employee satisfaction, company and product innovation, and empowerment.

Too much control can also affect the primary reason a business is successful in the first place—its customers. The vast majority of customers do not want to do business with a company that appears to be robotic and sterile. Customers want to feel appreciated, to enjoy the buying process, to have fun, and to experience a little excitement. And too much internal control interferes with the pleasure they get from doing that. So it's important for owners to take into account what their customers expect and want when they're looking for ways to increase efficiency. Controls are an invaluable tool to attaining and maintaining success, but only when they are used judiciously.

Level 5: Moving on When It's Time to Go

Although every level is different in several ways from every other level, Level 5 is different from all the others in a unique way. It's the only time the owners' goals for themselves and their goals for their businesses do not mirror each other. For the first time since the company began, the owner and the business are no longer joined at the hip as far as the future is concerned. Because the owner will be going one way and the business another, at this level the owner has to control two unrelated issues—his or her exit from the business and keeping the company running as it has been.

Wearing these two hats, and the control issues they create, is a formidable challenge. In fact, it's a lot harder than most people understand, largely because both roles demand time, energy, and patience. In addition, there is a huge emotional issue for most owners at Level 5, one that obviously does not exist at other levels. To overcome these challenges, the first thing an owner must do is recognize the dual nature of what he or she is facing. But it will also require the owner to change how he or she personally oversees the company, and to develop a new set of skills, that is, learn how to understand and control the selling or the succession process.

The Benefits of Control at Level 5

- Being in control helps you decide which of the two major issues you are facing need their attention at any given time.

- Being in control helps you balance your time, energies, and priorities between your two roles.
- Being in control warns you of impending internal problems well before they becomes crises, which is especially important when your attention is divided between the exit process and maintaining the company.
- Being in control enables you to turn oversight over to subordinates and free yourself to deal with exit issues.
- Being in control helps you see quickly where action is needed to refocus and reassure employees when the company has been sold or you are implementing a succession plan.

As I mentioned earlier, there are also two important realities that have to be taken into account at this level. The first reality is that if you don't pick your time to exit, someone or something else will. That is, you could be in a crippling accident or worse, you could develop health issues as you grow older, or your passion and energy for the business may lessen. In fact, there are any number of things that can occur over which you have no control. By the time you've reached Level 5, however, you will have run the race and done it well. So you should finish well, that is, pick your time before someone else does. The second reality is that the best time to sell your business or implement a succession plan is when you don't have to. When your business is doing well, you don't have to sell, and you can afford to wait for your price. And if you are implementing a succession, it's best to do so when the company is doing well, because it makes the transition a great deal easier, on both you and your successor. At Level 5 your goal has changed, and it is in periods of change that control is more important than ever.

Control of Information at Level 5

When you are considering moving on, whatever the reason may be, there are a number of important questions you have to ask yourself, including:

- How much is the business worth?
- How do I calculate the value of the company's goodwill in setting a price?

- Can I live off the sale for the rest of my life?
- What happens after I leave?
- How will my life change?

Answering these questions and many others like it depends on information and, of course, the accuracy of that information. And since it is likely that the answers you arrive at—and the decisions you make based on them—will affect the rest of your life, it is very important to have a good grip on that information, that is, to have control over it.

In fact, controlling the kind of information you use and the accuracy of that information are the two most important factors in making an exit decision. For example, just because an owner feels that his or her business is worth several million dollars does not make it a fact. It just doesn't work that way, even if the buyer is willing to pay the price. In most cases buyers need a bank's support, and a bank won't lend money to a buyer unless it makes sense based on pertinent and accurate information, such as past sales, gross and net profits, current and long-term assets, real estate, and industry and regional multiples, among other factors.

But there are also other benefits of making sure the information you gather is appropriate and correct. For example, doing it provides the substantiated facts you need during any buy/sell negotiation, without which you and the buyer may not be able to come to an agreement. It can also help you determine the best time for your exit in light of possible changes in the tax code that might make it advantageous for you to slow down or speed up the process. If you are passing the company along rather than selling it, having the most up-to-date information about taxes can also play a major role in determining how the transition is completed and over what time frame.

Exercising control over information begins, of course, with making sure that you have all you need and that it's accurate and up to date. But the real value of information lies not in collecting it but in how you use it. If you decide to put your company up for sale, for example, information can be rearranged in new or different ways to present your business in a more positive light, highlight future opportunities, or play down whatever weaknesses it might have. It's really just a matter of understanding the significance of the information and making the best possible use of it. Whatever you do, though, it is essential at this level to maintain control over the information you're using, because during the exit process there is a lot of information being passed back and forth, and it's only by maintaining control that you will be able to guarantee the most successful results for yourself and your business.

Control of Processes at Level 5

I mentioned earlier that at this level, owners have to change how they personally oversee their companies, which means they have to either restructure existing processes or develop new ones to make sure the business will continue to move forward during the exit period. One thing that may change is that, due to time constraints, you will no longer have time to practice management by walking around. Similarly, you may have to delegate responsibility for conducting regularly scheduled daily or weekly meetings to a subordinate and attend yourself only as time permits. You might also turn review of balance sheets over to your comptroller and meet with him or her just a few times a month. Frankly, it's unlikely you will be entirely comfortable with changes like these, because doing these things will probably have become fundamental to your leadership and ownership style. But choices have to be made, and, as the owner, you are the only one who can make them. And there is only so much time to get everything done if you want to exit the right way and with the biggest payoff.

As I also mentioned, exercising control at this level means learning new skills, which means developing new processes that will enable you to successfully sell or pass along your company. Whenever you are selling something, the most important thing to remember is that the road to the sale has to be controlled. And this applies to selling a business as much as it does to anything else. The edge in any sale will go to the party who controls the events. In order to gain control, owners have to understand the selling process and know how to control it. The control process starts, of course, with the exit decision, but there is much more to it. There are, in fact, a number of elements that are part of the selling process, including:

- Deciding whether it's better for you to sell the business as an asset or by selling shares in your business.
- Deciding what is for sale—that is, business assets, real estate, and goodwill—and what isn't, and how the sale price can be justified.
- Determining who the best buyers are, who can afford to pay the most, and who would benefit the most from buying your business.
- Developing a means of upholding confidentiality of discussions and information.
- Deciding, once a buyer has expressed interest, the steps and timing of the sale.
- Determining which elements of the sale will be dealt with first, and in what order the remaining elements will be discussed.
- Deciding on some parameters or framework under which a deal could be made, that is, deciding what you want, what you might be willing to give up, and what would be a deal breaker.

This does not constitute the entire list of issues you must take into account when selling a business, but it's a good start. The key point to keep in mind is that selling a business is a process, and one in which one side or the other will have control. And the one who has that control will be the one who has prepared and developed processes for doing so.

You may, however, want to pass your company along to someone rather than sell it, and this effort also requires a process to be carried out successfully. Among the elements of the succession process are:

- Determining how a successor is chosen based on where the business is today, where it should be in the future, and the skills needed to get it there.
- Determining a means by which tax issues will be considered.
- Deciding how other family members will be handled and rewarded.
- Determining the timing of, and speed with which, you will step aside.

Again, these are just some of the important issues that must be decided during the succession process. One of the other extremely important issues, and one that is often forgotten, is teaching a successor how the business is operated. If you are implementing a succession plan, you need to think about and develop a structured process for explaining to your successor how the company's DNA was created, why processes are the way they are, how they evolved, the importance of expectations and controls, and the owner's role in the process. This is essential because, as we have all seen, many businesses decline or fail after a succession plan has been executed. And since, in many cases, the reason is the new owner's lack of knowledge concerning how the company is operated, it is imperative that a structured process to provide that knowledge be created.

Even if you decide to simply close down your business, you will have to develop a process to accomplish it, because doing so is not as simple as removing the sign and locking the door. In this situation, there are two major control issues, the first of which is timing. When you close a business, you have to select two separate and distinct end points, one being the last day of business, that is, the day you close to customers; and the second being the date by which you want to shut down the company's internal operations. The first date is straightforward, but the second can be more elusive because it takes longer than most people realize to shut down operations and close the books. For example, accounts receivable will have to be collected, assets will have to be disposed of, tax forms will have to be completed for the business and the employees, final financial statements will have to be prepared, the business will have to be legally closed, and so on. Because of this, it is essential that your lawyer and accountant be involved in closing down your company.

The second control issue concerns you—your emotions and your drive. A successful closing means picking the last day you will have customers and then concentrating on sales and profits. And when that day comes, you start doing whatever must be done to wind down the business. Mixing the two is a mistake because it's frustrating and emotionally exhausting to try to do both at the same time, and as a result neither gets done well. When you are closing down a company, the objective is the same as it is when you

are selling one—getting the most money from your business, operations, and assets—and doing that requires a kind of control and
mental discipline that only you can supply.

Control of People at Level 5

By the time you get to this point in your company's life cycle,
you will certainly have figured out the importance of controlling
employees through processes and how to manage those processes.
At Level 5, though, control of people takes on a new and different
significance, because at this level you are essentially embarking on
a new journey, and it's important that the people with whom you
surround yourself on that journey are the ones who will be most
helpful in making it a successful one.

For example, your company's lawyer or accountant may be
a personal friend, but at Level 5 what you need aren't professionals who can help you in the day-to-day aspects of maintaining your
business. What you need are people who are experienced specifically in business law and contracts, tax issues, and estate planning.
Selling a company, implementing a succession plan, or closing a
company is serious business, and unless you have the right kind of
advisers, you could pay heavily in needless taxes, or find out after
the fact that whatever contract you have isn't what you thought it
was. And if you make those kinds of mistakes, you're likely to have
to live with them for a very long time. Conversely, by bringing in
people with the expertise you need, you will build a team that will
be an important asset to you in presenting your business information appropriately, determining strategies and counterstrategies,
doing valuations, considering possible candidates, and even keeping your emotions in check, among others.

The point is that there are people who can help you, and the
quality of their advice and the calming influence they can have is
something you will appreciate long after the sale. In other words, if
you're banking your retirement and legacy on your exit, you should
get quality help, and quality help starts and ends by controlling the
people with whom you surround yourself. There are basically three
ways to surround yourself with solid, experienced people. The first
is to honestly analyze your own weaknesses and find people who are

experts in those areas. The second is to find owners who have done what you want to do and learn from their experience. And the third is to have one or more people ready to help you through the process, however you choose to exit the business. This could be the same group as those above, or new people, or a combination of the two. In the end, the people you surround yourself with should be there not only to advise you but also to keep you, your emotions, and your mouth in check so you don't talk yourself out of a good deal.

Control of Product at Level 5

At Level 5, even though you have made the decision to move on, there is no guarantee it will happen when you want it to, or under what conditions, or if it will happen at all. So even if there were no other reasons, this one should be enough to motivate you to stay focused and control your product or service so that you can keep up with your competition and remain innovative. And, in fact, there are many other powerful reasons to keep your business moving forward during the exit process. Perhaps the most important of these is that, at this point in a company's life, the company itself becomes a product, one that will be sold, transferred to a family member, or closed, and this new product, like any other, needs to be controlled. This is because, also like any other product, a business has value. How much value depends on the demand for the product, the supply, financial conditions, the company's facilities and assets, its past performance and future prospects, business multiples, and the "tickle factor," that, is, how much someone wants to buy or take over the business. Because there is value to a business, controls have to be in place to protect and make sure that value, which is what makes a company attractive to buyers, is maintained.

Controlling a business's value is a priority at Level 5 because no one, especially an owner, likes unpleasant surprises. In order to avoid such surprises, at this point in a company's life, control of the business as a product will focus on:

- The business's customer base and its continued loyalty.
- The functionality and operating life of the business's assets.

- The company's facilities and their flexibility for future expansion and modernization.
- The business's past and current financial results.
- The company's prospects for continued growth in the future.

In making an effort to exercise control over the business as a product, the owner must start by defining for him- or herself how these areas are to be looked after. These definitions must, in turn, be communicated to the company's staff, and controls put in place to make sure the owner's plans are implemented. This is essential because when a buyer takes over a company, he or she expects it to be the company that was presented by the seller, that is, a great asset rather than a sinking ship. So if the business is going to remain an attractive "product," its value must be maintained, and any deviation from the owner's plan must be dealt with immediately.

■ ■ ■

As I mentioned in the opening of this chapter, control essentially is management. That is, the owner gives direction to the business and defines what success will look like, then determines which areas of the business he or she wants controlled and assigns who will be accountable for the results. Once this is done, it becomes the responsibility of those individuals to move the business toward the owner's success definition. As such, control is an important and necessary tool owners must have—and use—on a daily basis, or else the business will be in a state of constant chaos. And a company in such a state will never achieve its owner's expected results.

But, as this chapter has demonstrated, control means something different at every level, and, as an owner, you must be aware of those differences and flexible enough to adapt the controls you've developed to fit whatever the current need may be. By constantly and consistently exercising control at every level over the information your company uses, the processes you've established, the people in your organization, and the product or service you provide, you will have taken an enormous step toward assuring yourself and your company of attaining success.

CHAPTER 5

Fact 3: Protecting Your Company's Assets Should Be Your First Priority

Protecting assets is not usually the first thing that comes to mind when you think about your company's priorities. In fact, if you asked a group of owners what they considered most important to their businesses, the vast majority would most likely say sales and profits. And I'm certainly not suggesting that sales and profits are not important. Rather, I'm saying that they aren't as important to your business as assets. If your sales and/or profits decrease, you have time to regroup, figure out what went wrong, fix it, and make up the difference in the future. But if your assets evaporate, your business is destroyed. Nothing can pull a business down faster than asset destruction, and owners, with their employees' help, have to protect those assets from being mismanaged, stolen, abused, and underappreciated. That's why understanding this Fact of Business Life is critical to your company's success.

It's upsetting to lose a customer, even your biggest customer, but not catastrophic. What is catastrophic is if your product becomes obsolete, your office manager steals a major portion of your cash and "cooks" the books, or your accounts receivables decide not to pay you. To a certain degree, most owners understand the basic principle of protecting their assets. That's why they have lawyers to make sure they and their companies are legally protected, and insurance in case their businesses are destroyed by fire, tornados, earthquakes, or similar disasters. In other words, most owners realize their assets are vulnerable and therefore need protection.

However, owners tend to focus primarily if not entirely on what might be considered *natural* catastrophes. And while protecting your company against such events is certainly essential, it is only partial protection, and leaves your business vulnerable to everyday operational issues like mismanagement, theft, and outright stupidity, to name just a few examples. It doesn't make sense to buy insurance to protect your assets from unusual occurrences and then do little or nothing to protect them from these kinds of everyday business problems. No one would leave $100,000 in cash lying around without making some effort to protect it. But every day, owners essentially do just that when they don't give their assets the care they need, and in the process leave themselves open to some very unpleasant surprises that neither insurance nor lawyers can protect them from.

When you start a company, you inject cash into the business, and for a short time cash may be your only asset. Eventually, though, that cash is used to purchase items to help create whatever you are going to sell, produce, or service, as well as to operate the business on a day-to-day basis. In turn, whatever you use the cash for becomes part of the business's assets, and there are two types of these—tangible and intangible. Tangible assets are physical in nature, something you can usually see and touch, such as plant equipment, computers, desks, supplies, and so on. Intangible assets are things that can't be seen or touched, like customer and employee relationships, your brand in the market, the operating processes you develop as part of your company's DNA, intellectual property, and others. Both of these kinds of assets, however, need to be protected because both have value.

But exactly how do you protect these assets? As already mentioned, some can be protected, at least in part, by making sure that your company is operating legally and that any and all assets that can be insured are covered. Again, though, this kind of protection essentially applies only to the most obvious sort of catastrophes a company may encounter in the course of doing business. It's the other, less obvious problems that need to be accounted for. And the most effective way of protecting those assets is to maximize them, that is, to be aware of what they are, what they are supposed to do, and how to best use them to drive internal efficiency, sales, profits, and customer satisfaction. This is the common-sense part of asset maximization. But there's another aspect of protecting and maximizing assets that is less obvious but equally important. The assets you own were bought or created to capitalize on an opportunity, and if the asset isn't maximized, neither will the opportunity be, and it will be reflected in your company's underperforming in sales and profits.

What that means in practice, for example, is that if your sales rose 40 percent, the sheer volume of the increase would be felt by every other department. One of these would be accounting, which would accordingly have to recreate its internal processes (an intangible asset) because the current ones would in all likelihood be overwhelmed, thereby eliminating any chance of maximizing their efficiency. However, if you have an expensive piece of equipment that you believe is being underutilized, you could sell it, or you could focus on how to fully use it for its original purpose or to create a new opportunity.

The Benefits of Protecting Your Company's Assets

- Protecting your assets can reduce the amount of overall capital needed to operate your business.
- Protecting your assets can enable you to increase output and decrease your operating costs.
- Protecting your assets can help you reduce obsolescence, improve maintenance, and instill in employees an overall appreciation of the importance of both tangible and intangible assets.
- Protecting your assets enables you to minimize potential problems and optimize potential opportunities.
- Protecting your assets helps you and your employees to better match what is produced or inventoried to customer demand.
- Protecting your assets enables you to develop better plans and implement them more efficiently and effectively.

- Protecting your assets helps you develop and focus attention on making the right investments in equipment, systems, and infrastructure that you need to maximize those assets.
- Protecting your assets adds to the overall value of the business because it forces you and your employees to identify what is working well and what isn't, and make whatever changes are necessary.

The Realities of Protecting Your Company's Assets

- Understanding the importance of your company's assets is difficult to make habit forming, and accordingly should be part of every job description and, in some cases, in employees' pay plans.
- Since asset protection lacks the sex appeal and flair of selling or producing a product, your assets' value and the purpose of maximizing them can be easily forgotten in the day-to-day activity of a business.
- You can protect your assets by controlling them through systems and procedures, but you still need to rely on your employees to alert you to problems.
- Asset protection requires discipline on your part and attention to detail by your employees.
- Assets will mean little to your employees if you don't identify the assets and focus your staff on them by connecting performance to rewards or consequences.
- Protecting and maximizing assets must be part of your company's DNA, including processes indicating how well they are being managed and used.

■ ■ ■

The issue of protecting your company's assets encompasses essentially three elements, including the tangible and intangible assets themselves, products or services, and people. These three elements are the ones you need to continuously focus on in order for asset protection to have the most impact on your bottom line and with your customers.

Protecting Tangible and Intangible Assets

As I mentioned earlier, as a rule tangible assets are those you can see and touch, and intangible assets are those that are unseen, like your company's DNA or customer relationships. Both have value, and both should be protected from abuse as well as maximized for the greatest benefit. But in order to do so, you first have to be able to control them and measure their results. I mentioned in the last chapter, on Fact 2: If You Don't Control It, You Don't Own It, that measurement is a key component. For example, if you buy a new piece of equipment, you will want to measure the sales and gross profit it generates over a period of time, as well as keep track of the hours it is used in relationship to the gross profit it generates, and how long it accordingly takes to recoup its cost. The first steps in accomplishing this goal are to (1) list your tangible and intangible assets, (2) describe what they are meant to do, (3) determine if they support the goals and objectives of the company and its current operating plan, and (4) measure the results.

If you've never done this kind of analysis before, or you haven't done it for a long time, you may be surprised by the results. You might, for example, find that your tangible assets are more valuable than you thought, or that they are much less valuable and limiting your potential for growth and reaching your goal. You may also find that the same is true of your intangible assets, that is, that you have more efficient processes in place than you expected, or that the processes you have are too few in number and uncoordinated with each other. This is actually an effort you should make at every one of the five levels, because it helps you analyze the strengths and weaknesses of your assets using realistic and factual data.

Where do you go from here? Depending on which level your business is on at the time you do this analysis, you will have a variety of options available to you. Generally speaking, if you are at Level 1, you can use the information you've gathered to help determine which of the opportunities available to you would be most appropriate in terms of the assets you have at the moment. If you're at Level 2, it would be a perfect time to look at your intangible assets and see how they do, or don't, measure up to the DNA you have created or hope to create for your company. At Levels 3 and 4, you will be able to implement whatever changes the analysis has suggested would be appropriate. And, finally, at Level 5, you can use the analysis to determine the value of the company's assets as you make plans to exit the business.

Protecting Products or Services

Products or services are a tangible asset that requires extra attention for the simple reason that you count on them for so much. Ultimately, your business's success depends on the products or services you sell and how you sell them. And for that reason, they are important elements in every one of the Facts of Business Life, whether the fact concerns leadership, marketing, control, or any other issue. For the most part, these are management issues, but as this particular fact suggests, protecting a product has the same importance as managing one does, and for the same good reason— the business's success depends on it.

Protecting your products or services begins the same way as protecting other assets does, that is, by recognizing that they have life cycles. Manufacturing equipment, for example, lasts longer if it's maintained and used as it's intended to be used. Products or services are similar, except that owners often have very little control over their products' life cycles, and for the most part those life cycles are an unknown. For example, if your business manufactures brake pedals used in farm equipment, the strength of your product depends on the sales of the farm equipment. Similarly, if you own an electronics company, your products' life cycles depend not only on how innovative your suppliers are but, possibly even more important, how innovative your competitors are. In other words, because you don't have control over your products' or services' life cycles, they represent an inherent risk. It's a tough way to do business, but it's the way it is, and it's why protecting your products is so important.

Protecting your products or services is also a proactive activity, both offensively and defensively. From an offensive perspective, you have to anticipate what's coming at you and make plans so you can leverage and excite your current customer base to improve sales and your bottom line. On the defensive side, there are two ways to protect your products or services. First, you can decide which of them will be affected by new products or services and find a way to sell them before the market crumbles or find ways to prolong their life cycle. Second, you can create ways to protect your customer base by developing alternative products or services for those of your customers who are "orphaned" when a product or service is discontinued.

Finally, making proactive efforts to protect your products or services is something that continuously brings you back to each of the five levels of business. For example, in order to determine how long a product or service will last, and to analyze the opportunities new products or services will provide, you have to reach back to Level 1. In addition, when and if you introduce new products into the market, the DNA you developed at Level 2 will in all likelihood have to be adapted. Similarly, if a product comes to the end of its life cycle, or a new product is added, success at Levels 3 and 4 may have to be redefined, and new goals and objectives put in place. And, finally, at Level 5, how and when you choose to exit the company may be affected by your efforts to protect assets. If, for example, your business's market is expanding (an intangible asset), then the value of your business will expand as well. However, if your market is shrinking, you will have to decide if you want to ride it out until another new product or another way is created to grow and stabilize your business, or sell before the impact of the shrinking market erodes the value of your company. In other words, the need to continuously protect your assets affects and is affected by all five levels of business.

Protecting People

When we talk about protecting the "people" element of this fact, we are talking about a group that includes your customers, your employees, and, last but not least, yourself. Although none of these show up as assets on the company's balance sheet, the reality is that without any one of them a business simply can't exist (unless the owner is the only employee). This statement is hardly breaking news, but far too often, businesses become tilted toward one part of this group or another, which is not a healthy situation for any company. For example, if you were to insist that your employees do what you want them to do without regard for them or your customers, you would in all likelihood have a problem going forward. However, if you aren't strong enough and your employees dictate how the business is operated, neither your nor your customers' goals are likely to be satisfied. The point is that, as an owner, it's your responsibility to maintain and protect the balance so all three of these assets are in harmony with each other. Doing so takes both talent and experience, and in my opinion requires a skill set that is underrated in its importance.

Sometimes maintaining that balance means you have to step in and take control of a situation. For example, as important as customers are, the truth is that they are not always right or well behaved. And because of this, at times you may have to protect one or more of your employees from an unreasonable customer. In other words, while customers are valuable assets, employees are, too, and you can't allow either one to abuse the other. Besides being the right thing to do, this kind of action on your part builds morale because it shows employees you are prepared to step in and protect them when necessary.

It's also your responsibility to protect your employees from being bullied or abused by other employees, supervisors, or managers. Unfortunately, this type of behavior is not always noticeable from an owner's standpoint. However, every company has an unofficial internal communication system, and it is up to you to tap into it from time to time by asking informal or apparently innocent questions and carefully listening to the responses. Alternatively, you can encourage your employees to communicate informally with you via e-mail or through other employees.

These are, of course, not the only kinds of difficult situations you might encounter. They do, however, point out that, although these three assets are seldom grouped together in the owner's mind, the way they interact can have a very substantial impact on your business. And that's why, for everyone's benefit, they have to be controlled, managed, and protected.

Level 1: Ownership and Opportunity

One might reasonably ask how asset protection can be an issue at this level when there is technically no business or new opportunity selected, and therefore no assets to protect. And, in fact, if you are just starting to think about becoming an owner, since the only asset you are likely to have at this point is yourself, asset protection doesn't have very much significance. However, as noted earlier, the best way to protect assets is to maximize them, and Level 1 is where you analyze opportunities to determine how they can be maximized. What that means is that when you get to Levels 3, 4, and 5, and want to evaluate opportunities before pursuing them, you will have to come back to Level 1 to do so. In addition, sometimes decisions made at Level 1 require creating processes at Level 2, which means those decisions can have an impact on the development of your company's DNA. In other words, while asset protection does not play a role in determining whether you should become an owner or what kind of business you should be in, it does play a significant supporting role once the business is operating.

The general rule for asset protection can be stated very simply: being proactive protects your assets' value, and being reactive erodes it. That is, you are much more likely to be successful if you make an active effort to seek out and/or create opportunities than if you sit back and allow your business's future to be exposed to threats you could control or minimize. In fact, if you choose to be reactive in asset protection, you are likely to encounter four very serious problems:

- Your business will lose the most lucrative market action at the beginning of your product's life cycle because you reacted slowly to a market opportunity.
- Your customer base will be eroded because your customers will move to businesses that meet their new needs and wants.
- As your competitors offer new products in the market, your products can become worth less than you paid for them because the demand for them has decreased.
- Because of shifts in the market, some of your tangible assets—such as equipment, inventory, and others—may become irrelevant and therefore worthless.

These four situations underscore the importance of asset protection beginning at Level 1. In every case, not only are your assets eroded, which lessens the value of and weakens your business, but your competitors who take advantage of the new opportunities gain strength. In addition, pursuing and/or creating opportunities is likely to be even more important going forward because trends suggest that in the future products will have shorter and shorter life cycles. Just look, for example, at the electronics market, whether it's computers, TVs, or cell phones. What this means is that you will have to be even more zealous in protecting your assets than you are today. It also means owners who don't proactively embrace asset protection could see their businesses suffer and eventually disappear as their assets, including their customer base, continuously erode.

The Benefits of Protecting Your Assets at Level 1

- Understanding the need to protect your assets keeps you on top of the market and alert to where the market is going.
- Understanding the need to protect your assets allows you to develop an understanding of the customer–employee–owner relationship, its limitations and opportunities, and why it must be protected.
- Understanding the need to protect your assets means realizing that the key to doing so is being proactive and using facts to prepare for the future.
- Understanding the need to protect your assets enables you to recognize that adding or changing the use of tangible assets usually affects intangible assets, and vice versa.
- Understanding the need to protect your assets helps you realize that you can't take advantage of every opportunity that's available because both your tangible and intangible assets put limitations on what you can do.

Protecting Tangible and Intangible Assets at Level 1

Level 1 is a preparation level where opportunities are evaluated and risk versus reward decisions are made prior to implementation. The overall goal at Level 1 is to match your assets, both tangible and intangible, to today's market, with an eye on the future. As I mentioned earlier, this is not a one-time activity but, rather, a continuous effort supporting the business at Levels 3, 4, and 5. As I also mentioned, you begin this effort by taking four steps: (1) list your tangible and intangible assets, (2) describe what they are meant to do, (3) determine if they support the goals and objectives of the company and its current operating plan, and (4) measure the results.

Taking these steps will enable you to visualize and realize which assets are being underutilized, which have the capacity to be maximized, and which put limitations on your business. Doing so will also make it possible for you to make better asset decisions because they will be based on facts and current market realities. For example, you might discover that some of your manufacturing equipment is being underutilized and that adding another piece of equipment will eliminate a bottleneck and allow the underutilized machines to operate at their full capacity. Similarly, you might realize that you are getting very little productivity out of a particular piece of equipment, that it has limited potential, and that selling it could create space for a different machine that could be significantly more productive. This is a particularly good example of an ownership–opportunity–asset protection decision, because it highlights the fact that most such decisions should not be made based on a single asset but on what is best for the business overall.

It's important to bear in mind, though, that protecting a business's assets and asset maximization sometimes conflict with each other, such as when an owner wants to invest in something that will maximize assets but doesn't have the cash or credit to pay for it. In a situation like this, you have to balance the potential for increased revenue with the ability of the business to handle increased debt. In fact, it's a rare asset decision that doesn't affect some other asset. And it is always, for better or worse, the owner who has to make those decisions based on what he or she wants for the company. What that means in practice is that a timid owner can substantially undermine a company's ability to grow and prosper, essentially becoming his or her company's worst enemy. The opposite, however, is also true.

Protecting Products or Services at Level 1

Considering how important your products or services are to your business, it is obviously essential that you protect them. Of course, what you are actually protecting is not the products or services themselves but the revenue they generate for your company. And the best way to do that is to make sure that what you are offering is what the marketplace wants. That may sound simple, but it's not that easy to do. It requires you and your key employees to continually revisit Level 1 in search of new opportunities and market trends. That is, you need to watch for anything that might mean an increase in business—one of your products suddenly becomes hot, there is an industry promotion, one of your competitors closes down, and others.

Ultimately, though, what you should be most concerned with protecting is the gross profit provided by your products or services. Sales revenue isn't always a good thing if there isn't sufficient gross profit attached to it. It is, after all, gross profit that pays the expenses of the business, and plays a significant role in making the overall business profitable. Making sure this happens is your responsibility, which means that in weighing opportunities to offer products or services to your customers, you must take the gross profit attached to them into consideration. Understanding this point is important because it also relates to respecting and controlling the costs associated with running your business. That means, for example, if you think it's necessary to offer some loss leaders in order to be competitive, you should do so only if you can balance them with other products or services that provide significant gross profit. At the same time, having too high a gross profit on your products can make you uncompetitive. In the retail business sector, for example, it's best to have fast-moving, low-gross profit products balanced with higher-grossing ones. In other words, as far as opportunity is concerned, all that glitters is not always gold—unless gross profit is attached to it. But when it is, you've got a good chance of being more successful than the majority of your competitors.

Protecting People at Level 1

The customer–employee–owner dynamic is rarely given much attention or considered in the context of asset protection. We all understand why it's necessary to focus on customers when decisions are made, and the importance of employees doing their jobs in a coordinated way and with a positive attitude. We also understand why these two assets must be protected. Seldom, though, is the importance of what the owner wants given much consideration, and some people—mostly owners!—think it is the most important part of the equation.

Every owner, like every other human being, has wants and desires, but exactly because they are owners, what they want can have a very significant impact on a larger number of people—that is, their employees and their customers—and, ultimately, their businesses.

Of all their wants, however, perhaps the most important in terms of its impact on asset protection is how willing—or unwilling—they are to take risks. I spoke of this earlier in the context of tangible and intangible assets, but this issue has an even greater effect on the customer–employee–owner dynamic. This is because, while few owners are willing to admit they are concerned or worried about losing what they have, the fact is—exactly because they are human beings—they do have such concerns, to a greater or lesser extent, and those concerns have an impact on their customers, their employees, and their paychecks.

This is an asset protection issue because the way an owner views an opportunity has a great deal to do with how he or she feels about taking on new risks. Imagine, for example, this scenario. An owner has a key manager who does an adequate job but is content with his position and income and no longer has the drive he once exhibited. In all likelihood it would be in the company's best interests for the owner to replace this manager with someone who understands that standing still in business really means falling behind. In this case, however, the owner is content with protecting what he has and is accordingly willing to retain the manager rather than take the risk of bringing in someone new. On the surface, it would appear that the owner's decision would have an effect only on the manager and himself. In fact, though, the decision would be felt not only in the manager's department but throughout the business.

It would be felt in the manager's department because, as a rule, good employees want to make more money, are willing to work for it, and understand that the best way to do that is to take advantage of opportunities. As a result, if they see opportunities not being pursued, they will become discontented. This discontent will show up in their attitude, which will in turn affect other employees in their own department, and eventually spread throughout the business like the measles. The long-term effects of this are that the better employees leave, usually going to competitors or becoming competitors themselves, and the remaining employees underperform. In addition, when the better employees leave, they are usually replaced by people who have experience but not too much "get up and go." Of course, all of this is eventually passed along to the customers, usually showing up as indifference, which disinclines customers to continue buying whatever the company is selling.

The point is that when an owner is reluctant to take risks, whatever decision he or she arrives at inevitably has consequences, and the result, as in this example, is that everyone loses. The owner loses on opportunity, good employees, and eventually both market share and profit. The employees lose on wage and salary increases and the opportunity to succeed, and the customers lose because of indifference and lack of overall competitiveness—and all because the owner forgot about the importance of protecting all of his assets, in this case the customers and the employees, and focused on preserving his net worth at the expense of his other business. As an owner, then, it is important for you to remember that the customer–employee–owner dynamic is one that requires balance. Focusing too heavily on one at the expense of the others is a slow walk backward on the survival–success spectrum.

Level 2: Creating Your Company's DNA

A company's DNA essentially defines how the business operates. That is, it determines how employees act and react with customers and each other, how competitive it is, how its processes and procedures work, and how all of these things are coordinated so they work smoothly together. As such, it represents the business's character or culture, both in the minds of its staff and customers and in the marketplace. And because it does, it is an asset, albeit an intangible one, and extremely valuable. As with all your company's assets, it needs to be protected, in this case from erosion, incompetence, lack of attention, and all the other ills a company's DNA may be prone to.

The idea of protecting something as important as DNA—along with all of a company's other assets—just makes sense, so it's something every owner should be able to understand. In reality, though, it doesn't get the attention it deserves—except from successful owners, most of whom learned their lesson by not protecting their assets. And yet, DNA plays a vital supporting role in the company by preparing and coordinating the company's activities, so when it moves up to Levels 3, 4, and 5, it's ready to take on the market. And this applies whether you are just starting a business, taking one over, or reengineering an existing one. At this level, then, the most important step an owner can take may very well be to simply realize that DNA has value and needs to be protected.

The reason DNA is so important is that it affects virtually every aspect of the business and vice versa. In fact, DNA is literally at the crossroads of all internal activity—preparation, planning, decision making, and implementation. This is an important point because it makes protecting assets both challenging and critical. Bear in mind, though, that challenging doesn't mean impossible—it just means it's not easy to do. But something being difficult to do is not necessarily a bad thing. The harder something is to do, the less likely your competitors will do it, which means your doing it will provide you with a market advantage they don't have.

It's important to bear in mind that as far as DNA is concerned, your goal should be to create a business that runs flawlessly every day. To be fair, expecting perfection every day may be stretching it a bit—after all, we are human. And, in fact, it's humans who represent the greatest danger to DNA because they're the ones who operate the processes and come in contact with the customers. Your company's DNA must accordingly be protected from the human element, that is, the mistakes people make, whether it's doing sloppy work, being unprofessional, not performing as expected, or any of the other faults people are prone to. Of course, you can't eliminate all such problems, but your goal, as noted, should be to get as close to eliminating them as you can, by focusing in on asset protection.

The Importance of DNA in a Takeover

In the early 1990s, my partners and I purchased a medium-sized business that had been underperforming. We were confident that if we put a fresh face on the business, that is, created proper operating processes and controls; made individuals accountable; and used proper business techniques, the business could improve significantly. We wanted to jump into the market aggressively, but my experience told me to hold back until we could put this new DNA into place so the staff would know what was expected of them. We didn't want to launch a major media campaign and have customers come into our new business only to find that it was being run the same way as the old one. We told our staff that, as far as we were concerned, the past was the past, and that all we were concerned about was going forward.

In order to do accomplish that, I outlined three principles that every employee, including myself and my management team, was to use as a "compass" or guide. They were, in no particular order: (1) we want to win, (2) we want every employee to be satisfied, and (3) we want every customer to be satisfied. These may seem pretty standard and boring, but they weren't, because of the power, passion, and weight I placed behind each one, especially when it came to success or failure. Each of these principles had a clear definition. "We want to win" meant when we set goals or objectives, we did everything we could to make or exceed them. "We want every employee to be satisfied" meant we would treat them with respect; provide a safe, clean environment with up-to-date equipment; provide financial support for their kids' extracurricular activities; and help out where we could in family emergencies. And "we want every customer to be satisfied" meant we would make their buying experience one to which they would return time and time again, and hopefully tell their friends. This didn't mean the customer was always right—it meant we would do whatever we could to correct a mistake, satisfy the customer, and worry about checking out the details later. In other words, it empowered managers to satisfy our customers, and to do it now.

I knew the staff had to understand that things were going to change, and they began to do so immediately. Although most of the staff stayed, a few left, primarily because these three points had sharp teeth. In the end though, everyone knew how they were to treat each other and our customers, and that winning meant making the objectives and learning together from our successes and failures. And it worked. With the help of DNA, we came out swinging day after day, month after month, and took a crippled business and made it a huge success.

The Benefits of Protecting Your Company's Assets at Level 2

- Understanding the need to protect your assets enables you to list, evaluate, and determine the extent to which they will enable you to meet your goals.
- Understanding the need to protect your assets helps you realize that DNA is in every part of the internal machine, and that almost every change the business makes involves DNA in one way or another.
- Understanding the need to protect your assets enables you to realize that any asset can be used to improve the business and to then create a DNA process to do so.
- Understanding the need to protect your assets helps you make better decisions about how to use those you have because you are continuously matching them to the opportunity you have chosen to pursue.
- Understanding the need to protect your assets enables you to anticipate how to protect them and what support will be needed from other assets to maximize their value.

Protecting Tangible and Intangible Assets at Level 2

As I have pointed out, your business is more likely to be successful if you maximize each of your assets and make sure they support each other. But this doesn't just happen by accident—it takes thought, planning, and preparation. And if you don't figure out beforehand what assets you have and how to coordinate and use them, they won't work together efficiently. This is one of the situations in which DNA plays an essential part in your business, regardless of whether you're involved in a start-up, a takeover, or in the process of reengineering your company.

Let's say, for example, that you are planning to open a manufacturing business and will need certain machines to produce what you're selling. You could just go out and buy the machines and have them installed, but doing so wouldn't do you very much good unless you have people to run them. Of course, you could also recruit and hire people, but that won't help much unless you make sure the people you hire either know or can be taught how to operate the machines. And even if they do know how to operate the machines, neither they nor the machines will be of any value unless you develop processes for using the machines, as well as processes to coordinate all the machines so you can manufacture your product. And none of this will happen unless you develop DNA for it, that is, unless you think it out, plan, and prepare for it beforehand.

This connection between tangible and intangible assets—and how they support one another—is, again, one of those underappreciated ideas you need to champion because if you don't do it, no one will. In order to do this, you must focus on two issues. The first concerns protecting all the company's tangible assets from events that could be catastrophic for the business. Your first step obviously would be to get insurance for those assets that can be insured in order to protect your investment and minimize your financial exposure to lawsuits. But is that all you could do? What would happen if your customers just stopped buying from you, or if most of your employees suddenly quit, or if for some reason the demand for your product disappeared. None of these scenarios are very attractive, but they could all happen. How could you protect yourself and your assets if any of these things were to occur? The answer is in your company's DNA.

As long as you have developed your DNA properly, your business should be profitable and operating smoothly, in which case the chances of your employees leaving without any warning would be minimal. In addition, if your business is competitive in price and value, and your customers are satisfied and comfortable with their relationship with you, they would have no reason to leave. And even if there is a problem, your processes would pick up on it, and you would be able to correct it quickly. Your DNA is accordingly one of the best weapons you can have to protect all the business's tangible assets as well as your investment in them.

The second issue concerns protecting both tangible and intangible assets by proactively leveraging, supporting, and coordinating them so they can work together to provide your company with long-term success and profitability. Let's say, again, that you're opening up a manufacturing company, and you've purchased your machines, hired people to run them, set up training for them, and created processes so the machines are all coordinated with each other. That's all well and good, but you will also need managers or supervisors who know how to maximize the use of the equipment and know which parts, supplies, or accessories will be needed to keep them operating efficiently. In addition, you will have to make sure that processes are in place for ordering the required parts, and the accounting department knows when these parts are inventoried, at what cost, and when and how much to pay your suppliers. And that's just the beginning—there could be hundreds of other processes that have to be coordinated, right up to the point at which your customers buy your product, and even after that. The point is that every aspect of your company's DNA has an impact throughout the business, so the best way to manage it all is through the business's DNA.

Protecting Products or Services at Level 2

Since Level 2 is a preparation level, the focus at this point is not on the product's performance in the market, but on how your assets will support the product internally. In this respect, you need to focus on how the product will be delivered to customers, the equipment and personnel that will be required, and the need to educate your staff on the product itself, its pricing, and the processes created to support it. The overall goal here is to avoid sabotaging your own product even before the customer has a chance to buy it. That is, you have to make sure you don't beat yourself with conflicting processes, old rules and beliefs, poor decision making, an uneducated staff, making incorrect assumptions, or ignoring obvious market trends and realities. Of course, no sensible owner would do this intentionally, but it happens when owners don't focus on protecting and maximizing assets.

If, however, your business's DNA focuses on results, success, and internal control, the chances of beating yourself become exponentially lower. This is because an owner who understands DNA and its importance knows the overall goal of the business is to create customers and keep them. And this can happen only if the internal processes match what customers expect from the product and from your business. Of course, in order to accomplish this you have to know exactly what your customers do expect. Among the many things customers expect are getting the product or service when they want it, a competitive price, superior quality, professionalism and courtesy, and a sense that your business cares about them. In some cases, customers might also want to establish an ongoing relationship because they need advice and want to work with people they feel they can trust. And if this is what they want and expect from your company, you can create and deliver it through consistently run DNA processes. Again, this isn't necessarily easy to do, but if you do it and your competitors don't, you will have an advantage over them.

Although none of this actually happens until you reach Levels 3, 4, and 5, it's at Level 2 that you have to make all the necessary preparations. In other words, you have to make sure it works on paper before you ask your employees to implement it in the real world. However, if they are going to deliver what your customers expect, they have to be qualified to do what you want them to, have the training they need, be professional, understand both their responsibilities and their accountability, and know that depending on how they perform there will be either rewards or punishment. And that brings me to the third element—people.

Protecting People at Level 2

One of the more interesting things about the customer–employee–owner dynamic is that while all three represent assets, none of them show up as such on your company's balance sheet. Because of that, they are rarely considered as an important asset group, and even when they are, it's not as a group that needs to be protected. But they do need to be protected because they are all important individually and because, as a group, they need protection from each other. And Level 2 is where you first develop and prepare to implement that protection.

Customers are important because your business needs their money, which they give you because they need or want what you have. As an owner, you need your employees to operate your company's processes and serve your customers. And your business needs you to lead and contribute your expertise and money. Of course, none of this is news, but what may be news is why these three groups need to be protected from each other. The reason is that, outside of the relationships described above, there is no particular reason for there to be synergy among them. What each one wants is essentially incompatible with what the others want. So there are inevitably going to be disagreements and, as a result, conflicts among them. As an owner, it's your responsibility to minimize these conflicts as much as possible, and that can be done largely through the DNA creation process.

The first step in doing so is identifying the major conflicts among these three groups. Customers, the first group, want what you have to sell, but they want to pay as little for it as possible. In addition, they usually want it sooner rather than later, and may feel inconvenienced by having to wait. One of the reasons the Kindle and other e-book products are so successful is certainly because they focus on these two desires and not only give customers a new book in 60 seconds, but do so at a lower price than traditional books.

Regardless of how happy the second group—employees—may be, they would all like to get paid more, know that their future is secure, and have great working conditions (although exactly what that means is difficult, at best, to define). They also frequently perceive of the owner or boss as being in their way, and often see customers as interfering with whatever their superiors want them to do.

Finally, there is you, the owner. You want to charge as much as you can for your products or services so you can make more money, pay off your debts faster, and lessen your exposure and risk. You would also, and let's be honest about this, like to have your payroll on the low side of your competitors because it can give you additional pricing or marketing flexibility, as well as greater profits. In addition, it's these employees who create the problems and situations that give you heartburn, high blood pressure, and sleepless nights.

How do you avoid problems like this? Whether you are starting a business or adjusting the DNA in an existing one, the answer is the same—it's about planning and executing the plan. In other words, you can build things into your company's DNA that can help at least alleviate, if not eliminate, these problems. For example, if your processes are more efficient than your competitors', you can have fewer employees, which in turn enables you to pay them at least the industry norm and still have lower payroll costs, which is to everyone's benefit. Similarly, if your staff is sufficiently trained and follows the processes you've established, it will help eliminate some of their "bad days," as well as the likelihood of their exhibiting a negative attitude when dealing with customers, which will certainly make your customers happier. And as far as your bottom line is concerned, if instead of focusing on just the dollar amount you look at all the variables that go into making it up, and look for ways to increase it without penalizing one group over another, you, your staff, and your customers will all be happy.

As I have said before, none of this happens by accident. Establishing and maintaining a balance among these three assets is more of an art than a science, and it's an effort that requires a healthy dose of ownership skill. You have to not only make sure this balance is built into your company's DNA but, once your business is up and running, make sure it continues working as you intended it to. It's making efforts like these, particularly with intangible assets, that are crucial in protecting your overall assets and making your business successful, which is the greatest asset protection of all.

Level 3: From Survival to Success

Everyone understands that life is a lot easier and more secure when a parent, family member, or trusted friend has his or her back, and it's no different for a business owner or entrepreneur. It's a lot easier to sleep knowing someone or something is looking out for you and that you're not alone. And being human, all owners would like to believe that their employees are looking out for them. The problem, though, is that owners generally don't tell their managers or their staff exactly how they want their backs covered. They tell them their sales and gross profit objectives, and provide policies and procedures manuals, but they rarely talk about exactly how their employees can provide them with the kind of support they'd like to have, that is, how they can help protect the business's assets.

It is, however, important that owners do so because asset erosion can destroy an otherwise successful business. This is especially true when a company is first getting started, when it's expanding or investing in new facilities, and whenever the owner's liquidity and resources are stretched, because it's at those times that the business is most vulnerable. And this is the precarious position owners normally find themselves in when they get to Level 3. Perhaps even more important, while every owner hopes that his or her company will move smoothly and rapidly along the spectrum from survival to success, things don't always happen that way. Sometimes, instead of moving forward, businesses move backward from success to survival. And nothing will move a business backward faster than having its assets disappear or losing a significant amount of its value.

This is because asset erosion reduces the overall net worth, or value, of a business, even if the business is profitable. Assets represent the foundation that successful businesses are built on, and if and when those assets start to crumble the chances for success become much slimmer. Look at lending institutions, like banks or credit unions. They don't base their lending decisions on just the hope of future profits—they rely on the net worth and asset value of the business on the day they're asked to make the loan. In other words, assets represent the value of a business, and without them there will be no business. That's why asset protection has to be foremost in your mind.

Generally speaking, Level 3, the first action level, is where you begin implementing all the plans and processes you developed at Levels 1 and 2. That is, having identified your assets, devised processes to protect them, and satisfied yourself that you understand what and how much those processes should accomplish, you have to put them in place so they are ready to begin operating. In addition, by this time your employees should have received whatever training they need to make sure they know what asset protection is as it relates to them and their jobs, as well as how you want the assets protected. It's important to bear in mind, however, that not all asset protection processes can be rolled out at the same time.

Some processes have to be put in place first because they must be operating in order for other processes to work effectively. The general rule here is the more macro a process, the earlier it has to be in place, and the more micro a process, the longer you can wait before it starts to operate.

There is, however, one additional task that must be performed at this point. That is, you and your key people must continuously watch and exercise control over how these processes are being implemented, how effectively they are working, and what can be done to make them work better. This is essential because, at the end of the day, while asset protection is about protecting or guarding the "machine," that is, your entire operation, including all your tangible and intangible assets, it is also about making sure all those processes are operating in a coordinated way so the final result will be what you want it to be.

Of course, every entrepreneur hopes and believes his or her venture is going to be a successful one. Unfortunately, that's not always the case. In fact, once your business is up and running, there are essentially four possible outcomes—it will be successful, it will be successful initially and then fail, it will be profitable but you will have to struggle before it is, or it will fail. Sometimes which of these scenarios will play out is obvious from the beginning, while sometimes it takes longer to determine what will happen. But regardless of which of these possibilities eventually comes to pass, asset protection inevitably plays an important role.

For example, you can tell early on if you have a good shot at being successful if your sales and net and gross profits are close to what you'd planned. In a situation like this, the best way to protect your assets is to make sure everything continues to operate efficiently and effectively and to look for new ways to maximize your assets. Sometimes, however, an owner can be successful at the start but, after a period of time, see sales and net and gross profit start to slide and losses begin to stack up. In this situation, there are likely to be many problems, but most of them will be centered on the owner's lack of leadership and the company's DNA. To make matters worse, as the business slides backward, the options available to fix it become fewer because the value of your assets and net worth are eroding as the losses pile up. Asset protection in this scenario requires the owner to take quick action to define the major problems and fix them.

However, when a business has a lack of sales, and losses begin to mount right from the start, but the owner still believes firmly in the opportunity, it should be clear that he or she simply executed some important things very badly. The company may have missed the market with its advertising and marketing message, wasn't ready internally to begin operations, was using the wrong pitch to sell the product, or had other problems. Regardless of the exact nature of these problems, in cases like this, cash becomes the issue—that is, whether the company has enough available to wait for the business to turn around—which means that cash will need to be protected above all other assets. Finally, some businesses start out poorly for any number of reasons, and despite the owner's best efforts are never able to be turned around. In situations like this, the best thing to do is to face the facts and bail out as soon as you can. Doing so will enable you to sell whatever assets you have at a higher value than you might at some time in the future, and you will be preserving cash you will need to pay off debt, both of which represent asset protection.

The Benefits of Protecting Your Assets at Level 3

- Understanding the need to protect your assets enables you to realize that you must continuously revisit Levels 1 and 2 in order to find opportunities through which you can maximize those assets.
- Understanding the need to protect your assets helps you appreciate the importance of doing so regardless of your situation.
- Understanding the need to protect your assets enables you to recognize that you cannot focus entirely on sales and profits at the expense of those assets.
- Understanding the need to protect your assets helps you realize that when you begin to maximize their usage, opportunities you may not have considered will present themselves.

- Understanding the need to protect your assets will help if you get off to a bad start by allowing you to hang on longer and either "right the ship" or, at the very least, get the maximum value for those assets if you have to close the business.
- Understanding the need to protect your assets enables you to recognize that changes in the market or changes in your tangible assets will require you to revise your intangible assets if you want to maximize them.
- Understanding the need to protect your assets helps you recognize when you have to change some of the processes by which you operate your business.

Protecting Tangible and Intangible Assets at Level 3

Staying on top of your business at Level 3 is a considerable challenge. You are putting your tangible assets to work, implementing your intangible assets as your customers and employees interact with each other, testing your product, analyzing information, and doing all the other things that must be done when a company is just starting out, expanding, or being reengineered. In other words, there is a lot going on at the same time—some expected and some unexpected—and for a period of time there is no "normal." As the business begins to move along the spectrum from survival to success, staying ahead of the game takes ownership skill, discipline, and leadership. Given everything that's going on, you have to make an effort to keep asset protection in the front of your mind because it can easily get lost in the shuffle. That's largely because, important as it is, it's not as much fun as selling and making money.

Once the business is operating, proactively protecting assets centers on three efforts, all of which ultimately lead owners to reviewing Levels 1 and 2:

- Making sure the tangible assets you have are doing what you want them to do, and finding ways to maximize their capacity.
- Confirming that the tangible assets on your balance sheet are worth what the numbers say they are because it's very hard to manage assets if you don't have accurate information.

- Ensuring that your intangible assets are meeting the customers' expectations, not restricting sales or interfering with the business's internal efficiency, and being used to take advantage of appropriate market opportunities.

Where protecting tangible assets is concerned, your company's balance sheet and cash flow statements are the best friends you can have, as long as they are accurate. Cash flow statements are particularly useful tools for owners whose businesses are new, growing, or being reengineered. Cash availability is always important, but knowing how much there is, and how it has been used, is a critical tool when making decisions. For example, even if your business is successful and meeting your objectives you can still go broke by spending more money than your net profits. If, however, you check your cash flow statement, you can avoid taking too much money out of the business or spending it on things that don't produce immediate profits.

Intangible assets—such as the processes you developed at Level 2—can also play an important role in asset protection. If, for example, you have a customer who hasn't paid you for 60 days when he was supposed to pay you within 30, a properly designed process would let you know about it before you sold him anything else and exposed yourself to additional risk. Similarly, you can set up a process in which any cash received is counted twice at day's end, once in the department and then again in the office to confirm it's correct, and take action if it isn't. Because intangible assets like these protect the tangible assets and alert owners and key employees to potential problems, it's particularly important at Level 3 that they be continuously inspected for accuracy and to make sure they are doing what they were designed to do.

Protecting Products or Services at Level 3

Neither the importance of products or services nor the importance of protecting them can be understated. However, at Level 3, product protection isn't necessarily what most people would think it is—that is, making sure the product is available and ready when a customer wants it and that it's never exposed to theft. Rather, protecting products and services is primarily offensive in that it centers and focuses the owner on protecting the product or service's market share and enlarging it. In other words, the best way to protect your product or service is to sell it and then protect its market position. This is essentially a proactive effort based on the concept that the best defense is a good offense, which is consistent with overall asset protection.

Since whatever you sell is integral to your company's success, your business as well as your products or services have to stake a claim in the market and then defend it. For example, if you own a family restaurant, the neighborhood it's in is your primary market because of its location. And if you want to become successful and continue to be, you have to have a strong market presence there. Then, if you want to expand your sales and profits, using your base you can begin to widen your turf to draw more customers from neighboring areas. If, however, a direct competitor were to open a restaurant close to yours, you would not be able to ignore the challenge. You would have to attack, drawing on your creative skills of marketing and advertising, and developing a very aggressive war zone mentality to compete with this new restaurant on every possible level. This could include things like hiring their best cook or waiters, providing larger portions, developing specials, and on and on. Assuming you are successful in defending your turf, you will eventually reach a point where your location is a concern for only some of your customers, while others will make the trip to the restaurant regardless of where it is. If and when that happens, you will have maximized your product and more than likely a lot of your assets, which is a good thing, as long as it meets your profit and career goals.

So at Level 3, product protection begins with defining a market turf, owning it, expanding it, and then protecting it from those who want to take it from you. Some of the battles that take place as a business expands are harder than others to win. But when it comes to market battles, the one you cannot lose is the battle for your turf. Losing this, or letting a competitor overpower you and take some of your market away, weakens you and your business. The bottom line for product protection is that once you establish a market that makes the business profitable, you can't give it up because it's too hard to get back.

Protecting People at Level 3

As with the earlier levels, it's important at this level to maintain a balance in the customer–owner–employee relationship, because its impact on the business can be very considerable. For example, when your customers aren't happy, you can see it immediately because sales slow down, repeat customers come less frequently, and customer complaints increase. This in turn makes employees start to worry about their future as well as question your intelligence and decision-making ability. In a situation like this, you would also probably become frustrated because sales and profits aren't what you need them to be, and upset with your employees because it looks like they don't care about the business or the possibility of its going broke. Obviously, this is not a very good situation; unfortunately, it is not a particularly uncommon one, especially at Level 3.

Conversely, if the business is going well and your customers are coming back time after time, your employees are busy and feel they are part of a winning team. In this kind of situation, you can give out small raises as well as cash bonuses to further motivate your employees and insert some fun and competitiveness into the business. In addition, since you will see the business as a success and be excited about it, your excitement will spread to your staff and in turn be transferred to the customers. As a result, because all of the people assets are satisfied, these assets are being protected.

But how do you make sure all of this happens? The best way to do it is to rely on the ultimate asset protection weapon—gross profit. It may not seem at first that gross profit has anything to do with people assets, but it does. This is because, since gross profit is a major component in net profit, it gives you options for how to operate your business. And without a strong gross profit, there will in all likelihood be an imbalance in the people equation because there will be too many negative forces at play, such as those in the first example. Fixing this obviously requires both leadership skills and overall ownership talent, but if you can do it, it will give you hope, which can be transferred to your employees through bonuses, better working conditions, and higher salaries, which will improve their attitudes. And their improved attitudes will in turn be transferred to your customers in the form of improved service. And all of this puts the balance back into the customer–owner–employee relationship.

Level 4: Maintaining Success

Business owners can essentially operate their businesses any way they want, provided they continue to make a profit. That's because profit is not only the essence of becoming successful but also of remaining successful. What that means, however, is that even after your business has achieved success, the pressure to deliver acceptable profits year after year never decreases. The reason for this continued pressure is that when your business is viewed as a success, your aggressive competitors will all want to take a shot at you. And it's not just your customers and the gross profit attached to them they're after. They're also after your better employees, your systems, and anything else that will help them improve their businesses at your expense. And what that means is, in order to maintain your success, you have to protect your assets—all your assets—from your competitors.

Becoming successful—that is, moving up the survival–success spectrum—is primarily a result of your own efforts. Remaining successful, however, requires you to lead the business through your key employees. You can do this by empowering your employees and delegating both responsibility and authority to them. In fact, empowerment and delegation are especially important for asset protection at Level 4 because, at least in some instances, owners have to protect themselves from themselves. There are basically two reasons for this.

First, asset protection eventually becomes boring for owners, and at times frustrating to manage. Because of this, they tend to put it off and spend their time doing things they find more exciting and interesting, such as creating opportunities and working toward resolving problems. But rather than ignore asset protection, it's far better for owners to develop processes that others can manage and take responsibility for while they continuing to exercise general oversight. Alternatively, owners can delegate some asset protection responsibilities and continue to maintain control over assets that are vital to the company's existence—like products or services or customer retention and satisfaction.

Second, as a business grows, unless its owner empowers its employees, its growth will actually be stunted because by exercising so much control the owner is not maximizing the employee asset. That is, he or she is not enabling employees to do all they can, which conflicts with the overall goal of asset management. One area in which responsibility can be delegated, for example, is in inventory control and ordering. If, as an owner, you put dollar amounts on total inventory based on previous sales, inventory turns, days in inventory, and other factors, it not only frees your employees to make daily decisions and react quickly to trends and opportunities, it also gives them the opportunity to learn from experience, all of which maximizes your company's assets.

However, in order for your employees to take responsibility for asset protection, it is necessary that you educate them on the rules of asset protection, that is, teach them how to do it. As with virtually everything else, there are many different ways of accomplishing this. One, for example, is to explain the purpose of asset protection in terms of what could happen if assets aren't protected and what happens when they are. Another is to ask whichever employee you're considering giving more responsibility to how he or she thinks the company's assets can be protected, and see if his or her ideas line up with yours. And a third might be to simply hand over what you have been doing and show the employee, by example, how it works. It's important to note, however, that passing an important responsibility like asset protection to your employees does not mean you are giving up control of your company. It simply means that while you continue to oversee the entire business, they will have the opportunity to exercise their talents and abilities and, of course, grow their portion of the business as much as they can.

Perhaps the most important thing to remember at this point is that maintaining success is not the same thing as "resting on your laurels." You can't succumb to the myth that once you've become successful you can sit back, relax, and spend the rest of your days playing golf and counting your money. That isn't the way it works. Proactive management, as it applies to asset protection, means continuously challenging the market because, in business, remaining the same means falling behind. Whether you want them to or not, your competitors will change their market tactics, your customers will change their expectations (even if the product remains the same), and your business and employees will change—all of which adds to the challenge of Level Four.

The Benefits of Protecting Your Assets at Level 4

- Understanding the need to protect your assets enables you to help key employees understand it, which in turn helps develop a team focused on assets and their importance.
- Understanding the need to protect your assets enables you to allow proactive employees to find new ways of maximizing assets, as well as discover which assets are expendable and should be replaced by newer technologies.
- Understanding the need to protect your assets helps you and your employees find new ways to use both tangible and intangible assets, and, if appropriate, restructure the company and its processes to meet the challenges of tomorrow.
- Understanding the need to protect your assets helps you and your employees grow closer together, which in turn positively impacts on the customer–employee–owner dynamic.
- Understanding the need to protect your assets enables you delegate asset protection, which not only provides employees with new challenges but helps eliminate the apathy that success can engender.
- Understanding the need to protect your assets enables you to continue watching over your company while you start to think about the future and the possibility of your eventual exit from the business.

Protecting Tangible and Intangible Assets at Level 4

The only real change in moving from Level 3 to Level 4 as far as your company's assets are concerned is that you give up day-to-day control over their protection. In fact, sometimes this delegation and empowerment takes place even before the business reaches Level 4. This is because some departments grow faster or become successful sooner than other departments, usually because they are led by an employee or group of employees who demonstrate leadership and a capacity to achieve results. Your overall goal, however, should be to turn asset protection over to your staff by no later than Level 4.

While the individuals taking responsibility for asset protection may change, the way assets are protected should remain the same. This is important because when people take over new assignments, they often like to show their authority immediately. As far as asset protection is concerned, however, you can't let this happen. Whatever is working should be allowed to continue working until everyone has become comfortable with the changes in responsibility, particularly you.

Imagine, for example, that you've given your comptroller the authority to protect the cash transactions in your business and make sure the cash is all deposited into the business's bank account. However, once she takes on the responsibility, she decides to change the asset protection process of having two separate cash counts and reduces it to just the one office count. On the surface this may sound efficient, but in reality it opens the door for internal theft by someone in the office—including your trusted comptroller, who can easily cook the books. This example brings up another important point in asset protection. The unfortunate reality is that when you empower someone to take on this kind of responsibility you may choose the wrong person to trust. This is one of the reasons you have to continuously make sure for yourself that everything is operating the way it's supposed to be.

Whenever the transfer of asset management takes place, you have to make sure those who become responsible for it continue to fulfill the three tasks I mentioned at Level 3:

- Making sure the tangible assets you have are doing what you want them to do, and finding ways to maximize their capacity.

- Confirming that the tangible assets on your balance sheet are worth what the numbers say they are because it's very hard to manage assets if you don't have accurate information.
- Ensuring that your intangible assets are meeting the customers' expectations, not restricting sales or interfering with the business's internal efficiency, and being used to take advantage of appropriate market opportunities.

The balance sheet, the income statement, and other financial documents will continue to be great management tools for you in overseeing the business, but other management tools will also have to be created so problems can be easily identified. For example, intangible assets, such as processes, have to be constantly managed for relevancy and accuracy. You can't just delegate responsibility for them to someone else and simply walk away. This means you have to develop ways to ensure that what you believe to be happening actually is happening. This can be accomplished as easily as by walking around asking questions, talking to your employees and customers, or just watching what takes place. Some businesses record all telephone conversations and use them for training purposes, and some have cameras running wherever cash is handled. There are still others in which the owner conducts management training classes every month, or every quarter, to make sure the right message is getting through to all levels of the company. In other words, there are any number of tools that can be developed for this purpose.

Your handing over day-to-day responsibility for asset protection also has an additional benefit. That is, it gives you time to develop another aspect of protection—looking for additional opportunities, including some that might be considered outside of normal business. These might include investing in land with an eye toward relocation or speculation, public speaking to draw attention to your business, buying a competitor, or providing financial backing to help some promising individual start his or her own business with you as a partner. You will be able to do this because successful businesses accumulate cash, and this accumulation of cash and added net worth will provide you with the means of pursuing opportunities that were previously unavailable. With this cash you will be able to consider—or reconsider—expansion, new facilities, or new locations, as well as the potential profits and added risks that accompany them.

The point is that the availability of capital opens up new avenues of possibilities for you, and you should investigate those possibilities that interest you because doing so can lead to even greater asset maximization. In fact, as your exit from the business gets closer, these other capital opportunities can also have a powerful effect on your exit decision because they can start filling up your time and providing you with income that could enable you to stay connected to business and your community even after you leave the company. For example, a home builder who sells his or her business might take the profits and invest them in property management or purchase a construction supply business. You can, of course, simply leave business altogether with a big bank account and no responsibilities and get on with the rest of your life.

Protecting Products or Services at Level 4

As I noted earlier, at Level 3, asset protection means concentrating on a segment of the market, staking an ownership claim, and then protecting it at all costs. In other words, protecting earned market share is a major consideration at that level, and any expansion comes through pushing out the boundaries of your turf. Turf protection is still a key component at Level 4, but at this level there are two additional strategies that can be implemented to protect your products or services and increase your gross profit.

The first of these is reaching out to your customers with items that provide some convenience to them, even if it's not directly related to your business. Truck stops along interstate and main highways are particularly good examples of this. Drivers stop for fuel, but they stay for the food that's served by national chains like Subway, Arby's, Burger King, and McDonald's. They can also buy caps, T-shirts, sweatshirts, audio books, magazines, sunglasses, coffee mugs, and on and on. In other words, these businesses know their customers. The need for fuel brings them in, and the truck stops take full advantage of that by marketing related and unrelated products that drivers need or want. In effect, these truck stops make conquest impulse sales at the expense of other retailers like Walmart, Target, and the like, because if they didn't sell convenience items like these to their fuel customers, those customers would in all likelihood go to other retailers when they needed them. There are few rules telling retailers what they can and can't sell, and depending on your circumstances, there may be some gross profit available if you're creative. For fuel businesses like Flying J and Love's, this expansion of their product lines pays a lot of the bills, even though it's unrelated to fuel.

Another strategy is developing a competitive advantage. Doing so not only provides you with the ultimate weapon as far as product dominance is concerned, it's also a great way to protect your business and the products you sell. Price and uniqueness are usually the two main drivers of competitive advantage. For example, if you can find a way to sell a product cheaper because of your lower expense structure, or to make more gross profit than your competitors because you pay less for the product, you will have provided yourself with an advantage. Amazon is a good example of this because it not only sells products for less but also provides conveniences that other sellers cannot. However, the kind of cross-marketing truck stops do doesn't really provide them with a competitive advantage. This is because while the first business to cross-market does have an advantage, it can maintain it only for a short time before its competitors copy what it does.

Microsoft had, and to large extent still has, a competitive advantage with its operating system, which they continue to exploit despite the increasing popularity of Apple's products. Microsoft still powers a large percentage of new computers, and the great many people who don't want to bother with learning another operating system continue to use Microsoft. This is true despite the fact that Apple's system is considered easier to use and less likely to be attacked by computer viruses. Microsoft has a competitive advantage that cannot be duplicated, only challenged, and it has made its owners among the wealthiest people in the world. This is the power of competitive advantage. It's a goal worthy of achievement in any industry, and the only downside is the time it takes to create it. It is, however, a worthwhile goal for any Level 4 business.

Protecting People at Level 4

The customer–employee–owner dynamic is tested time and time again in regard to asset protection at Level 4, but it's actually the employee–owner dynamic that represents the largest challenge at this point. This is because the business is changing internally as the owner moves away from the company's day-to-day operations and takes on what is largely an oversight position. The objective at this level is accordingly to make the transition as seamless as possible for customers, and to keep the business operating as it has been through employee skill and commitment. But no matter how you draw it up on paper or how good it sounds in theory, an owner who has a dynamic personality inevitably leaves a void that no employee can fill. As a general rule, employees understand the reason for these changes, but since they have by now learned to trust the owner, at first they are uncomfortable when they see other employees taking on the owner's responsibility for their general well-being and working conditions.

Assuming that you have a positive relationship with your employees, maintaining that relationship will depend on how you handle the changes that take place at this level. One of the most important factors is how you deal with delegating authority. Because there are several human emotions at work here, in order to implement this change efficiently and effectively, you have to be sensitive to your employees, including those you promote or move into new positions, as they work through these changes.

The first thing you have to bear in mind in this situation is that those you are turning responsibility over to are not you. In some cases this may be good news for your employees, but, as a rule, successful owners don't have many employee problems at this level. Most of their employees respect them, like them, and trust them. But that's a hard combination to replace, and having to start putting their trust in someone else may make some employees feel they've been abandoned. This in turn will make it hard for those you have designated to take charge to maximize your employees' performance. Keeping this problem from arising—or eliminating it if it does—is your responsibility, and there are several ways you can do this. For example, being visible and communicative is extremely important. So, too, is recognizing employees for doing something particularly well and letting them know you are still on top of what is going on. Saying a kind word, asking about their families, or asking for their input on something doesn't hurt, either.

It's also important that you be very careful in selecting those you put into positions of responsibility, and oversee them to make sure they are upholding the company's values as well as maintaining the business's DNA. When the people you pick are a good fit—that is, have the talent and personality to handle the job—the transition can go very easily. Unfortunately, that's not always the case, and it can make things very difficult for everyone. In situations like this, the most prevalent school of thought among owners is to let the new manager or supervisor get a feel for the job and settle in, but I don't agree. There is too much at stake—for you, your customers, and your employees—to allow a poor choice on your part to disrupt what you and your employees have built. I believe if there is any doubt whatsoever about anyone who is taking over even part of your job, it's your responsibility to take immediate steps to fix it before it causes any more damage.

What you want, ultimately, is a replacement who is essentially an extension of yourself, only better, and to make sure this happens you may have to rein the new manager in and control and teach him or her how you expect things to be done and why. I don't believe in the sink-or-swim theory when it comes to others filling any of your responsibilities. You have to guide them, coach them, hold their hand, do whatever, but you can't let the business slide backward. Your job, and your replacement's, is to move it forward, do whatever is necessary to make the transition seamless, and keep the customer–employee–owner relationship in perfect harmony. Finally, you must remember that until you're gone. it's still your business, your employees, and your customers, and it's up to you to protect those assets from any negative fallout from your bad decisions.

Level 5: Moving on When It's Time to Go

The company's focus on maintaining success—and protecting assets—at Level 4 carries over to Level 5, and continues through to the owner's eventual exit from the business. This is because the business's goals don't change, even if the owner's personal goals do. In other words, it's the owner—when he or she is ready to make a change—who dictates the move from Level 4 to Level 5. This change essentially takes place when owners become more serious about leaving the business and begin thinking about its monetary value and whether selling it will provide them with enough to live on. It's essentially at this point, when the owners' goals and interests begin to separate from those of the company, that the business begins to move to Level 5.

As an owner, it is essential that you be aware of this paradigm shift in your thinking and take appropriate action to make sure the business's assets are protected and the company continues to be successful until your exit. Exactly what constitutes appropriate action, of course, depends on the condition of the company. It can be as extensive as restructuring the business or as minimal as having a few key personnel take over some oversight responsibility so you can devote more time to planning your exit. This is true whether you are selling the business, turning it over to a successor, or closing it down.

If you have taken asset management seriously throughout your career as an owner, there will be a huge dividend waiting for you when you exit. This dividend can take several different forms, but the most important may well be goodwill. This is a misunderstood term, and some buyers are unwilling to pay it because they don't understand what it is. Goodwill, in this sense, is the amount sellers ask buyers to pay above and beyond the value of the company's assets to compensate them for the future profits they will be giving up by selling the company now. The amount is usually calculated based on a number of years. For example, if the business averages $400,000 a year in profits, the owner may feel he or she can ask for three years' worth of goodwill, or $1,200,000. Knowledgeable buyers would probably consider this reasonable because they are buying a proven business, particularly if they believe they can improve on the profits.

Another dividend of protecting assets lies in the advantage it provides a seller in his or her selling presentation to a buyer. It's one thing to show a buyer past profits, but it's quite another to show that those profits will remain at the same level and why. By explaining how you protected your assets and their value, you will be able to demonstrate that your success was not a fluke but the result of instilling skills throughout the business that won't disappear when you're gone. For you, this is a great way to capitalize financially on the company's value through goodwill. For your buyer, a story like this—one that's backed up by facts—is hard to ignore or argue against, and not only builds confidence but also enables him or her to develop a better of understanding of what you are actually offering for sale. This is true in succession as well because your successor will want an accurate picture of what he or she is taking over or buying, and other family members will want to know the value or what they are giving up—an important point where family harmony is concerned.

The bottom line, then, is that since both your business's tangible and intangible assets have value, they can not only help you tell the business's story, they can help you sell it. And if you have taken asset protection seriously, and your company has profited by it year after year, these added dividends will be your well-deserved reward.

The Benefits of Protecting Your Assets at Level 5

- Understanding the need to protect your assets enables you to realize that you have a new customer at Level 5—a buyer or a successor.
- Understanding the need to protect your assets helps you accurately explain your business, including its tangible and intangible assets, and choose a buyer or successor who understands the value of the business.
- Understanding the need to protect your assets means you will have seen to it that they are working and producing

income, and can accordingly be used by the buyer or successor as soon as he or she takes over the business.

- Understanding the need to protect yours assets means when you exit the business there will be limited write-offs for obsolete inventory and nonexistent or nonfunctioning equipment.
- Understanding the need to protect your assets enables you to demonstrate to buyers or successors how you maximized assets and in doing so produced or created opportunities that will benefit them in the future.
- Understanding the need to protect your assets gives you a clear understanding of how all the assets tie together and helps you give the potential buyer or successor a clear picture of what he or she is buying or taking over.
- Understanding the need to protect your assets, and demonstrating that you have done so, gives both buyers and successors confidence in the internal structure of your business, as well as a "playbook" of its inner workings.

Protecting Tangible and Intangible Assets at Level 5

Protecting both tangible and intangible assets at Level 5 is as important—and works the same way—as at Level 4. In fact, some argue that it's even more important that you pay attention to it at this point because, as you prepare to leave, it is easier to become distracted and forget about it. And Level 5 is definitely not the time for you to back off asset protection. It's the time to make sure it continues so you can show a buyer the added value it provides him or her in the way the business is operated, or pass on to your successor a great business with no surprises.

Ultimately, every business has three types of assets—real estate, goodwill or blue sky, and tangible and intangible assets. Regardless of how you choose to exit the business, at Level 5 it is your responsibility to determine the value of those assets. The most important thing to remember in doing so is that the value must be justifiable and connected to reason. This is an important part of the exit for several reasons. First, the value placed on assets will determine the qualifications of potential buyers as well as potential successors. Second, asset values have to be justified not only to a buyer but also to a buyer's lender. Third, in a succession, if a member of the family is picked to operate and own the business, a reasonable value has to be established on behalf of the family. That is, if the owner wants his or her successor to buy the business, the value established for it must be fair and justifiable to the other members of the family who will want their fair share of the pie. And, finally, the determined value of the assets will give you your "cash-out" financial position, which will indicate if you will have enough money to live well after your exit or you need more time to build up the business to a specific profit level before you can leave.

Determining the value of your assets can be something of a balancing act because your goal is to maximize your assets' value while your buyer or successor wants to know that the value you've placed on those assets is supported by the business. For example, if there is real estate involved, the usual way its value is determined is by the owner, buyer, or successor having the land and/or the building appraised. However, even though such an appraisal might seem to be very straightforward, as with most things in business, it isn't always so. If, for example, the value of the property has increased over the years and is now greater than the ability of the business to cover its cost, it creates a problem for the buyer or successor. This is a problem the owner has to solve, possibly by leasing the property to the new owner, selling the operating company and having the buyer/successor find other property, or finding a way to make up the difference in goodwill or operating asset values. That's where the balancing act comes in.

But the balancing act doesn't apply only to real estate. Since goodwill and other tangible and intangible assets have to be taken into consideration in establishing the total value of a business, exactly how an owner and buyer or successor get to that number is invariably a result of negotiations. But if you've made asset protection a part of your business, you will have an advantage over those who haven't because you will know the value of your assets—all your assets—and will know the best way to structure your payout to minimize the tax effect. For example, capital gains may be taxed differently than goodwill, and if this is the case more money can be allocated to whichever category is taxed the least, thus maximizing your payout. Similarly, the buyer's lending source may be reluctant to lend too much money on goodwill but comfortable doing so on tangible assets. In this situation, the buyer can pay more than you've agreed to for tangible assets and an equally smaller amount for goodwill. The overall goal is to maximize the monetary value of your tangible and intangible assets, and knowing what they are enables you to structure the deal so you can take home as much of the sales price for your business as possible.

Protecting Products or Services at Level 5

At Level 5 you have a new product—the business itself. And like any product, its value has to be explained and justified. Price, quality, the business's longevity, the employees, the customer base, and past profits are all factors in the business's valuation. How well you can explain all these aspects of the business to a potential buyer directly affects the overall price. However, when you are selling this particular product, you have to do more than simply explain what it is. As I mentioned earlier, your explanation should also include a value-added presentation that enables the potential buyer to picture him- or herself at the helm of your business and points out all the great things the new owner will be able to accomplish with the business in the future. And no one knows the future possibilities of a business better than an owner who has been able to forecast market changes and successfully adapt the company to those changes.

So if you can help your potential buyer see not just what the business is now but also what it can be after you've gone and he or she has taken over, you will be able to paint a picture of the future showing where the opportunities lie and how those opportunities can be used to grow and expand the business, which in turn gets the buyer excited and gives him or her confidence in the business's moving forward. This is always a good strategy, but when talking about the future and its opportunities you should always follow it up with a statement like, "I only wish I were young enough to keep growing the company," or something similar. This is because, after you've painted such a positive picture of the future, not only may the buyer wonder why you're selling, someone along the line is bound to ask him or her, so you might as well provide an answer to the question before it's asked and reinforce it if it's already been discussed.

Protecting People at Level 5

Level 5 is a particularly difficult one in terms of the customer–employee–owner dynamic. By the time a business has successfully gone through Levels 1 through 4, the owner, his or her managers, and the employees will have developed a relationship based on mutual respect and trust. In fact, if that trust hadn't been developed, it's unlikely the company would have ever attained—much less maintained—its success. One of the reasons this trust develops is that over the course of the business's history the owner has discussed most of the important decisions with his or her trusted employees. At Level 5, though, the situation is different because, in thinking about leaving, he or she is essentially breaking that bond of trust with the company's employees, and it puts an understandable strain on the relationship. What's worse, the more drawn out the decision or the negotiation process is, the more difficult the situation becomes.

As noted earlier, it's essentially the owner's decision to make a change that moves the business from Level 4 to Level 5, and few owners discuss it with their employees. Of course, if a current employee will be succeeding the owner, or one or more of the employees are buying the company, they will be involved. But if the decision is to sell the business, turn it over to a family member, or close it down, employees are usually left in the dark about the owner's intentions. There are basically two reasons for this. The first is that the owner doesn't want the business operation to be jeopardized or disrupted in any way. The second is that, even if the owner wants to sell or close the company, it may not be happening for years, and he or she doesn't want to erode the shared trust, or lose the momentum, focus on results, or excitement of moving the business forward.

Both of these reasons are entirely legitimate and justifiable, but it's always hard to keep a secret, and you can be sure that rumors will begin circulating almost as soon as you start working toward leaving. Obviously, rumors like these won't help the business, but what's even more important is that it rattles the confidence of those who trust you. Eventually, someone will ask you about the rumors, and you'll need an acceptable answer, because dodging the question or giving a vague answer will only generate more anxiety and add fuel to the fire. Perhaps the best way to deal with this situation is to acknowledge the rumors, say that you will be exiting at some time in the future, but not today, and then ask the questioner about his or her department or area. You must be careful, though, because the last months are important for both the buyer and the seller, and you don't want unnecessary gossip or chatter getting in the way of focusing on objectives and results.

Of course, you also have to keep in mind that not every negotiation works out, and you don't want to get excited—or get your employees excited—about selling the business only to see the deal evaporate at the bargaining table for any one of a hundred different reasons. If negotiations break down, it will be hard enough for you to refocus on business, but it will be even harder for your employees because the trust you will have accumulated over the years may have been damaged or broken in the process. And once that trust is broken, it's hard to earn back. Unfortunately, there is no way to entirely keep something like this from happening, but there are things you can do to minimize the damage and rebuild the trust.

One way to do this is to put some fun back in the business by challenging your staff's competitive nature with short-term objectives that have substantial financial rewards attached to them. This in turn will refocus your employees on the business at hand. The problem is also likely to be less severe if you have a meeting with your managers and key employees and tell them that the rumors were true but you were bound by a confidentiality clause, but that in the end it wasn't what you wanted. At that point you can pick up the pieces by refocusing the staff on what needs to be done going forward.

On a positive note, if the sale becomes a reality, one benefit of maintaining a positive relationship with your employees at Level 5 is that it provides your buyer or successor with a big advantage as he or she takes over as owner. If the customer–employee–owner dynamic is in balance, the buyer or successor will have a clear understanding of what his or her ownership role is and know what the employee and the customer expect. This can help make the transition as seamless as possible while the new owner or successor and employees get used to each other. It can also give the person replacing you not only added confidence but also a direction in which to move the business forward right from the beginning.

■ ■ ■

Although asset protection is rarely discussed as an important element in business, to the entrepreneur or owner who has suffered through continued asset write-downs it is not only a major concern but an effort that pays dividends when selling. Focusing on assets and their performance through management accountability and improved processes may not make asset write-downs completely disappear, but it can severely limit them. As this fact makes clear, owners have to focus on and gain control over their products or services, the business's tangible and intangible assets, and the customer–employee–owner dynamic if true asset protection is to be achieved.

Asset protection is not easy, and even after you feel you have it under control you have to not only continually work on it yourself but also challenge your employees to focus on and improve it. However, once asset protection becomes part of your business's DNA, it is a strong market weapon because it enables you and your employees to get the maximum out of every asset the business owns or controls, which in turn focuses the business on the opportunity the asset was bought or created for in the first place. And all of this adds up to a stronger market presence, more success, and more profits, and it does it by using a valuable weapon that only the most successful owners use.

Fact 4: Planning Is About Preparing for the Future, Not Predicting It

Imagine that you're standing in the middle of an intersection with cars coming at you from every direction. It's obvious that you're in danger and that moving from the intersection is your only option. The problem, though, is that the landscape looks the same no matter which way you turn, so it's impossible to tell which road will take you where you want to go. That's what planning is about—it points the owner and the business in the right direction.

Every owner stands at this dangerous intersection, not once but many times. Some of them never make a choice, stay at the intersection, and watch their businesses die. Some guess which road to take and only find out they are on the wrong one when it's too late. And some guess right, have some initial success, and then lose their way. But there are still others who anticipate the intersection and determine beforehand which road to take, what to expect along the way, how to avoid the dangers and capitalize on the opportunities, and how to recognize and correct errors. This last group is the planners, the ones who realize that planning is one of ownership's best tools, as well as one of the best ways to put the odds of success in their favor.

Of course, most businesspeople realize that they should plan. However, the majority of owners don't do it, primarily because it's hard to do, because they don't want to put themselves in a position in which they are accountable, or because they don't want to have to force others to be accountable. These owners discount planning's importance by telling themselves there is little point in planning because, since they can't predict the future, there's no reason to plan for it. But this is a trap—and a costly one—because it puts the owner in the middle of that intersection. It's true, of course, that you can't predict the future, but you can prepare for it, and that's what planning is about.

■ ■ ■

Planning is both a science and an art. The "science" is in determining what information is needed in order to build a strong factual foundation for analysis and decision making. Such information might include, for example, what's happening in the market today, what the historical trends have been, how large the market is, who has the largest shares of it, and which businesses have been winners and losers. Gathering this kind of data will enable you to better understand the market and determine not only why the best companies are where they are but also what the less successful companies are doing, or not doing. Planning, then, is about facts and realities, not assumptions, and that means that the questions you ask are as important as the answers.

The "art" of planning is in how an owner sees the facts the "science" has uncovered and uses them to develop a plan. But that's easier said than done. And it's an effort in which experience counts. We know, for example, that economists and scientists can look at the same facts and reach conclusions that are diametrically opposed to each other. The difference in conclusions occurs because of personal bias, because some facts are ignored to prove a point, or because of a narrow focus that impacts on how the facts are interpreted. But, as an owner, you can't afford to fall into this trap because incorrect decisions have costly personal consequences. In fact, one of the main reasons businesses have boards of directors or mentors is to tap into the experience of those who have mastered the "art" of planning. Further complicating this art is the fact that the goal of planning is not to find the correct answer but rather to choose the best answer for your circumstances and your tolerance for risk.

Of course, the first step in planning is always to determine where the business is headed and what it will look like when it gets there. Once that determination has been made, planning is essentially about getting the business from where it is today to where you want it to be. Planning can be immediate, short-term, or long-term. Immediate plans are for today, this week, this month, or this quarter. Short-term plans, which are very specific, define what needs to be accomplished in anywhere between six months and three years, depending on the industry and what needs to be done. Long-term plans are less specific, and more flexible, than short-term ones. The key to planning, though, whether it's immediate or short- or long-term, is that the sum of all the parts has to add up to the long-term destination you have set.

The Benefits of Planning

- Planning forces you to choose a destination and a direction for your company, without which it is impossible to establish criteria for success and, accordingly, determine whether the activities the staff is involved in are productive or efficient.
- Planning helps you optimize the company's future. Because profit is the lifeblood of business, when planning focuses on profit, efficiencies are created, as is a scorecard for success and failure.
- Planning gives your company a purpose and directs its focus toward customers and the revenue/profit they generate.
- Planning generates factual information you can use to evaluate immediate and short- and long-term plans. It also exposes both the immediate realities of the market and possible future market trends.
- Planning gives you a marketplace advantage over your competitors who don't plan at all or don't plan well because you can use the strategic and tactical ideas that are developed to expand or protect your company's market position in both the short and the long term.

The Realities of Planning

- Planning relies on the other Facts of Business Life for support and implementation. Even if, for example, your company has the best-developed plan, it won't work if you don't provide leadership (Fact 1) or understand the importance of accountability and control (Fact 2). More than any other management discipline, planning exemplifies the reality that to succeed you have to be proficient in numerous leadership and management disciplines.
- Planning is one of the things that successful owners have in common, and the way to become successful is to do what they do.
- Planning means keeping up with marketplace changes, which may lead to internal changes and the employee resistance that usually goes with it.
- Planning can be successful only if your company has accountability and internal discipline. If you aren't prepared to captain your own ship, you may not have what it takes to be an owner.
- Planning, especially in the beginning, is always hard because every step is a new adventure, but it becomes easier with experience.
- Planning is about eliminating excuses and creating an atmosphere in which employees and the business can succeed.
- Planning is less about developing a plan than it is about implementing the plan and reaching the goal. The real battle doesn't start until after the plans have been made, and it's a battle that has to be fought—and won—if ownership success is to be achieved.
- Planning is not just something that takes place once a month, once a quarter, or once a year. Making plans and implementing them is an everyday blocking and tackling event. In other words, when it comes to planning, every day is game day.

The Elements of a Proper Business Plan

Few owners have the same definition of success, the same market, the same available capital, the same opportunities, and so on. And just as every owner's situation is different, every business plan is different. However, all effective plans do have commonalities of structure and framework, including the following:

- *Destination or vision.* Where the business is going, what it will look like when it gets there, and how long it's expected to take.
- *Mission statement (company culture/DNA).* What the business's purpose is and the kind of conduct that's expected of the employees in their interactions with each other and with the company's customers—that is, the atmosphere of the company in regard to expectations, accountability, and professionalism.
- *Goals.* What the company is expected to achieve, which in turn determines the kind of objectives and strategies that must be developed.
- *Analysis.* What the company's status is, both externally and internally, including the size of the market, trends, competition, and market share for the former, and financial strength, employee processes, and management strength for the latter.
- *Strategies.* The best way to exploit and protect the business based on the external and internal analyses, including the positive and negative consequences of the strategies and the extent to which they align with the company's goals.
- *Objectives.* Based on the goals and strategies, practical plans for the company's future that are exact, easily measurable, have a short timeline, and provide for individual accountability.
- *Summary and communication.* Sharing the plans with those who will be responsible for implementing it.
- *Implementation.* The orderly execution of the strategy.
- *Review.* The constant review and revision of strategies and objectives, while never losing sight of the goals.

In order to plan successfully, all of these elements must move and work in unison with each other. Hard work, patience, and an understanding of the other pertinent Facts of Business Life will also help you in reaching your owner's overall goals.

Level 1: Ownership and Opportunity

Planning is important at every level, but perhaps nowhere more important than at this one. If you get planning wrong at Level 1, the result is likely to be, at best, an unpleasant surprise, if not a series of them. Proper planning will show, among other things, if the market niche is too small, if there are too many competitors, if the industry is shrinking or growing, and if the profits are likely to be slim or very good. In other words, planning enables you to make intelligent, well-thought-out risk and investment decisions.

At this level, though, there is a step you must take even before beginning to develop a plan. That step is to ask yourself a series of questions that will enable you to determine whether you should even be thinking about going into business for yourself, specifically:

- Do I like this business?
- Am I good at doing what has to be done to make the company successful?
- Do I understand the industry and the marketplace sufficiently to competently analyze it?
- Is ownership really what I want?
- Do I have the talent, the discipline, and the experience to make this opportunity work?
- What would happen, personally and professionally, if the business failed?
- Do I have access to enough capital to enter this market, and is the potential net profit sufficient to make this a good investment?

If you can't answer "yes" to all these questions, it would be advisable for you to give some more thought to whether owning a business or taking this opportunity is something you are really ready to do.

The Benefits of Planning at Level 1
- Planning shows how much profit you are expecting and provides a timeline for that profit.

- Planning shows how much cash and credit you will need to operate the business successfully.
- Planning provides banks and other business lenders with a blueprint by which they can analyze the opportunity you are presenting and determine how much money they will lend you, their pricing structure, and the conditions under which they will make the loan.
- Planning forces you to analyze your own ability, the level of skill you need to lead and operate the business, and the policies, procedures, and processes you will have to implement to reach your objectives and goals.
- Planning makes you focus on the type of talent you will have to recruit.
- Planning enables you to show your mentors or advisers what you expect to happen and test the reality of these expectations with them.

Gathering Information at Level 1

As it is at every level, at Level 1, collecting information is an essential part of the planning process. At this level, the most important area in which you need to gather information is the financial one. This is because fundamental financial questions should be answered before too much time and money is spent on an opportunity that may actually have very little profit potential. You must determine how much personal investment will be required, how profitable the venture can become, and how long it will take to repay the investment. And it's not only important for you to know this yourself—these are questions that bankers and investors will want answered as well. The specific areas in which information must be gathered at this level include:

- The size of the market, market demographics, competitors' strengths and weaknesses, and so on.
- The stability of the overall market, potential for growth, possible threats and opportunities, and how you can exploit them.
- Hard facts that will prove or disprove market assumptions and help you to make better decisions.

- Industry financials that show composite revenues, average industry gross profit margins, net profit, cash flow, and the like.
- How the income statement and balance sheet work, their importance, and how to interpret them.

Analysis, Planning, and Implementation at Level 1

As noted earlier, planning means gathering facts (science) and forming an opinion based on these facts (art) in order to determine what steps must be taken to get the company to where you want it to be. Once you have done a financial analysis at this level, you will be able to understand the profit potential, opportunities, threats, investment needed, and potential return on that investment, and make appropriate plans. Let's say, for example, the results of your financial analysis indicate that, based on previous profit history, your investment could be paid back in three years from profits, and there is also considerable new business available. You might then develop a short-term plan that would enable you to pay off the debt sooner than expected by bringing sales up, expanding gross profit margins, and increasing the business's internal efficiency. The long-term plan might then be for you to borrow additional money (after the initial debt was paid off) to buy equipment and inventory, and hire new employees to take advantage of the additional business that the market study showed was available. Once the initial debt was paid off, the long-term plan would become the short-term one, and the new long-term plan might be one of expanding the company's facilities to handle the increase in employees and customers.

If, however, the analysis suggests that the market is strong but the business is not as well run as it might be, your short-term plan could be designed to make the company more profitable by improving sales. You might do this by developing processes to capture and retain new business, and by training and educating your employees on the importance of the customer, future expectations, and accountability. The long-term plan might then be one of market domination through conquest sales and buying some of the competitors' weakened businesses.

Of course, creating a plan is only part of the process. The real issue is whether you can do what you thought you could— that is, implement the plan. That's why it's necessary to develop objectives that will lead to the goals you've established. For example, in the preceding scenario, the company's internal efficiency could be improved by establishing objectives such as reducing some expenses, training employees, creating incentive pay plans, refocusing the marketing plan, and buying products more competitively—all of which would help pay off the debt faster. Then, as the short-term plans are being implemented, you could focus on the long-term plan, deciding which market niche has the greatest opportunity, what new equipment you would need to increase business, how many new employees would be needed to service the extra customers, and what your strategy should be to attract new customers.

Planning isn't easy, but even though it may not seem like it, that's actually good news. If it were easy, all your competitors would do it, so if you do it and they don't, you have an advantage. In addition, simply because they've never done it before, new owners tend to be surprised by events—both good and bad. But for those who plan at Level 1 and do the due diligence required, the surprises tend to be much more pleasant than for those who don't.

Level 2: Creating Your Company's DNA

At Level 1, planning is about developing a plan that has reasonable expectations and will deliver profits. At Level 2, planning is about designing processes that will help you achieve the planned-for results. These processes are essentially the DNA that will run your company, and it's the company's DNA, or culture, that turns strategies into reality. Such processes include things like determining how cash sales are handled and accounted for, how inventory is replaced after a sale, and how customers are treated. They are in turn supported by job performance, job accountability, the expectation of results, and employees' attitudes.

Developing these processes is an extremely important step toward success, but, unfortunately, many businesspeople aren't aware of its importance until it's too late. The fact is, as I mentioned earlier, processes operate the business, and employees operate the processes. This is the owner's reality, and the sooner you understand this, the better off you will be. Planning and DNA creation are each other's yin and yang—they need each other. You can create a great plan for your company, but you can't implement it without the help of your employees. And your employees can't implement a plan without workable processes showing them how to do their jobs. It's as simple as that.

The Benefits of Planning at Level 2

- Planning provides your employees with a "playbook" on how to interact with each other and with customers, and what is expected of them.
- Planning makes it possible to enforce expectations and disciplines company-wide.
- Planning enables your employees to understand what success is—and isn't.
- Planning shows your employees what processes they have to follow, what their jobs are, and what has to be managed.
- Planning enables your employees to understand the ethics and style of the company they work for.
- Planning guarantees that you define responsibility and accountability and clarify their boundaries.
- Planning provides you with parameters around which you can lead, manage, and communicate.
- Planning enables you and your employees to more easily determine and solve problems.

Gathering Information at Level 2

At this level, there are two types of information that must be gathered. The first is external information that will be used to determine management strategies to succeed in the marketplace. The second is internal information that will enable you to devise processes to achieve that success. The type of internal information needed varies by industry and by customer type, but there are some commonalities.

Virtually every owner has to ask him- or herself the following questions regarding the company's interactions with customers:

- Was the customer satisfied? Will he or she return? How will we know if he or she does or does not?
- Were the employees knowledgeable and professional?
- Did we have the required services or inventory available for immediate sale? Did we lose a sale? Did we save a sale by postponing the transaction until we were ready for that customer? How could we have been more responsive to the customer?

It's also important, though, for every owner to ask him- or herself questions that deal with the larger issues than go beyond individual customers. Among such questions are:

- Was this a profitable activity for us? Do we want to expand this activity?
- What services or products give the company the best profits? Can we expand our market share in these profitable segments? Can we do something new or different to improve our sales and profits?
- Did we reach our objectives and goals? Why or why not?
- Can we improve our processes to create efficiency internally and at the same time improve our customer loyalty? (Note that improvement of efficiency must always be considered at the same time as increased customer satisfaction, and vice versa.)

In other words, the purpose of DNA analysis is to enable an owner to understand what is working well, what isn't, what can use improvement, and why. And the only way to do that right is to dissect the internal operations of the company and focus on processes and personnel.

Analysis, Planning, and Implementation at Level 2

The creation of your company's DNA at this level is the foundation on which you can build a successful business. At Level 1, you determined what the sales and gross profit levels must be to break even, the sales potential of the opportunity, the profit those sales will bring in, and so on. The big question now is "How will the company and its employees do what I think can be done?" The second, although seldom-asked, question is "How can I be sure that my employees will look after my customers and my assets the same way I would every time?"

Processes are designed with these questions in mind, and on the basis of those processes, expectations are determined and responsibility given to employees. Successful owners explain through designed processes how they want their employees to act, grow the business, and protect the business from unpleasant surprises. Far too many business failures can be traced to owners who did not dictate how they wanted their employees to execute their jobs and protect the company. That's why DNA creation at Level 2 is so important.

For example, let's say that you've done an analysis and determined that there has been a very high level of inventory write-offs after inventory counts. You've also discovered that a considerable portion of the write-offs are of common inventory transactions, a large percentage of which are cash sales, and that only one person counts and balances both the sales slips and the cash from sales. The obvious question you have to ask yourself, then, would be "Are the write-offs mismanagement, theft, or both?" And since write-offs are both a cash drain and a net profit issue, not only do these questions have to be answered, but a process must be designed to put in checks and balances so that theft can be ruled out. A simple plan that could be implemented immediately would be to have the cash counted at least twice, by different people, one of whom is outside of the selling department, and both of whom are spot checked for accuracy. You could also balance the sales slips against inventory by spot checks and more frequent inventory counts.

Your analysis might, however, show that inventory write-offs are due to inventory aging and having far too much money tied up in inventory based on current sales. A situation like this would obviously be a result of mismanagement, and the immediate plan would be to identify the aged and overstocked inventory and find a way to turn it into cash within a certain time frame. At the same time, though, you would be working to develop an inventory process that would include capping the dollar amount in inventory based on current, 30-, 60-, or 90-day sales revenue; inventorying products based on past sales history; and keeping track of what your competitors are selling at your expense, as well as the products you're experimenting with to see if there is a market for them.

The important thing to remember is that, when it comes to information and its analysis, it's one owner's talent against the other owner's talent. And the owner who understands the importance of analysis and how it affects DNA usually comes out on top. That's because DNA creation—its processes, disciplines, and accountability—is what make a business run all day, every day. DNA enables employees to understand what they have been hired to do and how they're supposed to do it. Just as important, though, it also enables them to understand what they're not supposed to do, and why they're not supposed to do it.

Level 3: From Survival to Success

In the beginning, every entrepreneur's objective is to survive. And because of that, the first months of any new business are driven by adrenalin, fear of failure, optimism, and the nagging question, "What the hell have I done?" In fact, as long as a business is in the survival mode, managing the company is largely about controlling the chaos. However, as the company makes gains and matures, it begins to go through a transition from one level to the next, that is, from survival to success.

Perhaps not surprisingly, it's been proven time and time again that owners who have planned at Levels 1 and 2 are not only more likely to attain Level 3, but also to attain it sooner. And there are good reasons for that. For example, owners who have done sales and profit forecasts at Level 1 and understand their expense parameters know what they need to achieve to be successful and are able to measure their results against forecast. That means they will know if they are heading into trouble and be able to pinpoint it immediately. But it also means that if business is better than expected, they will know why and be able to quickly take advantage of the situation. Similarly, at Level 2, owners who have planned, that is, developed the business's DNA, have established processes, job accountability, expectations, and a solid base on which to make decisions. If you were to compare this to an owner who has ignored planning at Levels 1 and 2 and is "winging it," the advantages of planning should be obvious. And although planning at this level is different than on the earlier levels, it's no less important.

The Benefits of Planning at Level 3

- Planning enables you to understand the path you're on, where you are headed, and what you need to do to get there.
- Planning gives you added confidence in your decisions because you know they are based on facts.
- Planning makes it possible for you to better identify and fix whatever is not working.
- Planning helps you recognize opportunities.
- Planning enables you to better determine key job functions, the skill levels needed by your employees, and which employees can handle responsibility and accountability.
- Planning helps you develop an understanding of the leadership style you have to adopt, and determine the training and motivating that needs to be done.
- Planning makes it possible for you to prioritize information, which keeps you and their staff from being overrun with it.

Gathering Information at Level 3

Once your business becomes "live," that is, once it gets going, internal information starts to flow, and it's up to you to make sure that processes are in place so the necessary information can be captured. There are, however, two basic facts about information at this level that apply to every company. The first is that during the survival period the information you need is broader in nature. Examples of this kind of information include actual sales dollars versus forecast, gross profit as a dollar amount and as a percentage versus forecast, actual expenses versus forecast, net profit versus forecast, and cash usage and cash in the bank versus forecast. This key information will give you some tools to accurately judge how your company is performing, and where problems or opportunities may be.

The second fact is that as the business starts moving toward success, the kind of information you need becomes more detailed and focused. At this point, it's no longer just about expenses being too high but about pinpointing exactly which expenses are too high and which are not. In other words, as your business moves toward success, your focus has to be on the inner workings of the company. In order to accomplish this, you might, for example, reclassify your expenses into three categories—personnel expenses, fixed expenses, and semifixed expenses. Doing this would help you determine which expense groups need attention. You might also break down sales and gross profits into subaccounts for every product and service category, which would make it easier for you to identify exactly where your sales are coming from, how to improve them, and how to expand your gross profit margins.

Of course, the financial area is not the only one in which you need to gather information. When you are planning at this level, it's also necessary for you to review such things as inventory ordering and stocking processes, customer credit policies, scheduling or dispatching the workflow, customer contacts versus actual sales, employees not performing up to expectations, lost sales opportunities, and others. And in each case, problems have to be investigated, analyzed, and dealt with.

Analysis, Planning, and Implementation at Level 3

As always, once you've identified the key information, the next step is to analyze and then act on it. If, for example, you discover that sales are above forecast but cash is significantly lower than expected, it should be clear that there is a problem that needs correction right away. It could have been that more inventory was ordered than was sold, or that the majority of the sales were charged rather than paid in cash, which created a cash flow problem. In this situation, it may be necessary to redesign the ordering process so that ordering too much, too soon doesn't happen again. You may also have to review your credit policy and start putting immediate emphasis on collecting those receivables. The point is that regardless of what the analysis reveals, you will be able to respond to the problem or opportunity.

Unfortunately, very few plans go exactly as expected, which makes implementation challenging, although not impossible. As mentioned earlier, a short-term plan essentially consists of a series of steps, all of which add up to a long-term plan. What that means in most cases is that the two plans are joined at the hip. This is particularly important to understand when designing or implementing a plan at this level. For example, in the survival mode, an owner's lack of confidence in his or her decision-making ability might lead to a reluctance to put in processes that might result in push-back from employees. But if those processes aren't implemented it can put the entire short-term plan in jeopardy, which in turn can impact on the long-term plan and put the transition from survival to success very much into question.

It's very difficult for most owners to pinpoint exactly when their businesses have made the transformation from survival to success, primarily because it's more of a gradual transition than a single event. However, if you have been planning appropriately at each level, it's a lot easier to recognize the transition when it happens. That's because when you establish plans and monitor your success, you always know where you are, where you're going, how far you have to go, and when you've gotten there.

Level 4: Maintaining Success

What makes a business successful? Who decides whether a business has achieved success? Is success the point at which the owner's fear of going broke disappears? Can an owner ever relax and take it easy? These are common questions most owners ask themselves, and planning can help answer them. The answers you get may not be the ones you want or expect, but they will bring reality into sharper focus, as well as destroy the long-believed myth that once a business becomes successful it can run on its own.

Having this sharper focus is important because at Level 4 there is a cruel trap awaiting the unsuspecting owner: success today does not guarantee success tomorrow. Owning a successful business and not actively watching over it, or not operating it with the same vigor you did to make it successful, can be the initial step on the road to failure. This reality is all around us. If you need any proof, as I mentioned earlier, look at General Motors and Fannie Mae. If large and successful businesses like these can collapse, as both did in the late 2000s, the same thing can certainly happen to any smaller, privately owned company. Planning can play a vital role in keeping that from happening.

The Benefits of Planning at Level 4

- Planning reenergizes you and focuses you on new challenges, possibilities, and threats.
- Planning protects your company from the overconfidence and apathy that sometimes comes with success.
- Planning keeps the company fresh, aggressive, and on the hunt for opportunities.
- Planning forces the company to improve and reinvent processes that enable it to continue being a dominant competitor.
- Planning starts you thinking about succession or developing a personal exit strategy that coincides with and complements the business's future goals.
- Planning helps you begin thinking about adding value to the business so that it will become more attractive to a potential buyer or make it easier for your succession candidate.

Gathering Information at Level 4

Of course, if you're successful, competitors will run at your customers and try to take what you've earned. Giving it back without a fight is not only bad business, it also shows you didn't deserve those customers in the first place. To avoid this, owners need to create and design processes that will enable them to answer questions in four critical areas:

- Customers:
  - How can we keep all our customers?
  - How can the business attract new customers, and what do we have to do to keep them?

- Which of our competitors are weak and how can we take advantage of that?
- Will the market continue to expand and attract new customers, and how can we capture the majority of these new customers?
- Product, process, and people:
  - Are our competitors offering any new products or services?
  - Are there any new products or services on the horizon in our industry, and how can we dominate the market with these new products or services?
  - Which processes are fully mature and can be reworked for even better results?
  - Which processes are outdated and need to be replaced with new ones?
  - What new training methods will we need to keep our employees' product knowledge and professionalism at a high level?
  - Will the quality of our employees have to be improved?
- Conquering the competition:
  - Can we acquire any of our competitors, and would such an acquisition put our company into a dominant market position?
  - How can we create an "unfair" competitive advantage that would drive customers to our business?
- Added value:
  - What can we do to make our business more attractive and worth more to a possible buyer?
  - What are the positive aspects of our business, and what can we do to improve on them?
  - What aspects of our business represent negatives to someone considering buying our business, and how can we eliminate them?

Analysis, Planning, and Implementation at Level 4

When you're a success, everybody wants a piece of you. This is true in sports, in life, and in business. It's also true that competitors tend to get better, so you must get better, too, if you are going to maintain that success. There's little time to relax, and you need to find an edge. One way of finding that edge is to work "smarter" than you have in the past. Smarter, in this instance, can mean two things. First, you can become a student of business as well as an industry expert. Doing so will enable you to learn how the best owners—particularly those within your industry—operate their businesses, and then implement their best practices. Second, you can become the best at understanding how customers; product, process, and people; conquering the competition; and added worth connect and support each other, and use this knowledge in your analyzing, planning, and implementation. This in turn makes your business better, and even further out of reach of your competitors.

In the customer area, one of the best ways to keep your current customers is to provide them with more value or, as some say, "overdeliver." For example, if your business is selling computers, you might give free seminars to your customers to help them maximize their use of computers and the Internet. Similarly, if you own a restaurant, you can give regular customers free samples of new food or desserts, showing them you appreciate their business and giving them additional reasons to come back and to tell their friends about you. This kind of "overdelivering" comes in many forms, and is limited only by your imagination. If conquest sales is your goal, you can go after your weaker competitors' customers by giving them something—such as lower prices or added service—that your competitors can't afford to give. You can also find a location that you're not penetrating and plan and implement strategies to increase sales in that area. An additional strategy to attract customers is to determine what the future growth in the market and industry will be, and try to capture this market before your competitors.

In regard to product, process, and people, it's important to remember that customers come to you in the first place because of the *product or service* you provide. However, they come back to you because of the *processes* that deliver what they want and when they want it, and because of their relationship with the *people* who deliver it. Most important, customers want all of these things to go right every time. The only way to guarantee that happening is to plan what you're going to do and how you're going to do it, and then implement the plan efficiently.

Taking market share, or conquering your competition, requires good strategies as well as good tactics, both of which are key elements of planning. An excellent example of this is Walmart and how they created a competitive advantage over their competitors. Walmart claims they have the lowest prices, but their pricing strategy depends not on what they *sell* items for, but on how they *buy* and *inventory* them. Sam Walton understood planning and competitive advantage, and he recognized that he could use computers to be more efficient than his competitors at purchasing and inventorying what customers wanted. And he did it so well that, to date, the Walton family has made more money from the invention of the computer than anyone else—more than Steve Jobs and more than Bill Gates.

As noted above, the fourth critical area at this level is added value. Added value is important because every owner eventually has to deal with his or her exit from the business. Whether it's selling the business, executing a succession plan, or simply closing the business down, doing it right takes time and proper planning. There are essentially two aspects to doing this, the first and arguably most important of which is timing. If you're talking about a sale, timing means figuring out when the business will be worth the most, balanced against your personal situation and finances. If you're talking about succession, however, determining the best time to turn over the business depends on the successor and his or her experience and maturity level, balanced against your personal situation and the current state of the business and the industry. The point here, though, is that you have to be constantly planning and monitoring your situation so that you don't let a good exit opportunity—much less a great one—pass you by.

The second aspect is that you must consider what you can do to make your business more attractive to buyers. Improving the attractiveness of the facility is something that virtually all owners do, but it's not the only thing that can be done. Trained personal, a large repeat customer base, accurate financial statements, and continued "fine-tuning" of products, processes, and services, are all important to buyers. If these things are done well, buyers will pay more money, and if you are planning a succession, it will be easier for your successor to step in. Conversely, if there are things that would turn off a buyer, they should be identified and eliminated. Added value is about making the business attractive to others and preparing for both the expected and unexpected, which is ultimately what planning is all about.

Level 5: Moving on When It's Time to Go

Whether you want to believe it or not, there will come a time when you are going to move on. The prospect of leaving the business you've nurtured and made a success of may not be a pleasant one, but at some point in time you are going to have to face it. And, as I mentioned earlier, the reality is that if you don't pick the time to do it, someone or something else will. Of course, every owner's situation is different, but as I also mentioned earlier, it's always important to remember that the best time to sell a business is when you don't have to. Efficiently transferring your business to a family member, or capping your career with a big payday when you've sold your company, is always tremendously satisfying. But whether you decide to implement a succession plan or you sell the business, as long as you do it *on your own terms*, you've beaten the odds and won the game.

The Benefits of Planning at Level 5

- Planning enables you to identify possible buyers and determine which the best ones are, that is, which have the capacity to pay and would benefit the most from buying your business.
- Planning helps educate you on the market value of your business by comparing how like businesses have sold, what criteria are used for setting valuations, and how these compare and relate to your own circumstances.
- Planning provides you with a time frame for improving your business's performance before selling and gives you a time horizon for accomplishing your goals.
- Planning helps you develop guidelines for making and executing decisions that will add value to the business.

- Planning enables you to recognize that selling a business is a *process* and to understand the various issues of that process.
- Planning makes it possible for you to "cherry pick" their selling team, including mentors, lawyers, accountants, and bankers.
- Planning helps you select the timing of the sale as well as the conditions of the sale, which provides you with more control over the process.

First Sale versus Last Sale

The first time I sold a business it was because an ownership opportunity in Texas that I couldn't pass up had presented itself, and buying the new company meant I had to sell the business I owned in Canada. It was a good business (and my first one) with good employees and good prospects. Unfortunately, I had no idea what to sell, how to sell it, who to sell it to, or how much to sell it for. I also underestimated the emotions involved. In other words, I was clueless about selling a business, and I knew it. To make matters worse, the buyer knew it, too. The result was confusion, surprises, and lots of stress. After the sale, I pledged to myself I would never be in that position again.

Many years later, when my partner, Bill Sterett, and I sold our group of businesses in Texas, the situation was the exact opposite. Bill and I had started talking about our exit five years before we actually sold the business. We identified who the most likely buyers would be and prioritized which ones would be the best (i.e., who would pay us the most money and have the capacity to pay). We knew what these buyers liked about our business, and what they didn't like, eliminated the negatives, and worked to improve the positives. We approached our best buyer, set the expectation level, determined an orderly selling process to follow, negotiated hard, and closed the deal with few regrets.

We knew where we wanted to go, planned for it, found what we believed was our company's "sweet spot," and sold the business on our own terms. I would classify us as successful entrepreneurs, not just because we were able to accomplish what we had set out to do, but because we sold when it was right for us.

Gathering Information at Level 5

Planning at this level requires learning about the pros and cons of selling and succession, and how to determine the best time to exit the business. There's a lot of information to be gathered, but it all falls into three categories.

The first category is market information, including such things as sales trends, market and industry expansion, common conditions in buy/sell agreements, current selling prices, industry goodwill (national, regional, and local), who the buyers are, bank-lending constraints on buyers, and others. You must have this kind of information if you're selling the business. Without it you'd be exiting "blind," which is a situation no owner wants to be in. All active owners usually have this information, but it's always best to verify that what you think you know is correct. Where succession is the choice, family members will usually be more supportive knowing decisions have been made on current market facts and valuations.

The second category is internal financial information. Having accurate financial statements, and being able to show how financial statements are prepared and internal processes work, is a huge plus for any seller. Doing so enables you to comment confidently on the market and the business, and have these statements supported by market and financial facts. In fact, nothing slows the momentum of a sale more than misinformation and the uncertainty of inaccurate financial statements. Accurate financial information helps you determine the selling price, its justification, the type of sale preferred—asset or share sale—and selling strategies. For buyers, knowing they are making risk and opportunity decisions based on accurate facts and information usually translates into higher selling prices, and makes it easier for a bank to lend them the money. Critical as this information is for selling, though, it's equally critical for succession. Family members will want to know what's in it for them, and it's always hard to argue against facts. When this financial information is added to the market information, a complete picture of the business is presented, and, again, it becomes clear to everyone that your decisions are based on factual information and sound reasoning.

The third category comes into play only if you are planning on succession rather than a sale. Succession is a widely used exit strategy for family businesses, but if it's not thought out and planned in advance it can be like walking through a never-ending mine field.

If you are planning a succession, then, it's essential that you select a lawyer and an accountant who have experience in succession issues and can provide you with information and suggestions on how to accomplish your goals efficiently and eliminate any possible future ramifications that can disrupt a family.

Analysis, Planning, and Implementation at Level 5

As with all the other levels, at Level 5, once you have gathered the information you need, the next step is to analyze, plan, and act on it. In doing so, however, it is extremely important that you bear in mind the four realities that every business owner must face when he or she has decided to move on.

- If you don't pick and plan the time to move on, someone or something else will.
- The best time to sell a business is when you don't have to, and if you don't do it then, you will have missed a golden opportunity.
- Not properly determining the market value of your business and the many tax and legal implications of passing on ownership will put you at a distinct disadvantage.
- Emotion, personal goals, and your own biases and ego can have a huge impact on the entire selling or succession process, and it's important that you guard against it.

There is no escaping these realities, and the cost of trying to do so can be extremely high. If, however, you recognize them, and take them into account, you're much more likely to be satisfied when the process has been completed and you've successfully turned your business over to someone else.

Let's say, then, that you've done your analysis and determined that both the market and the business have been growing at a steady rate over the last number of years. But you've also recognized that you have, to some extent, lost your enthusiasm for the work required to continue growing the business. This lack of enthusiasm, which is very common, can unfortunately mean a decline in sales and profits. This in turn can make it difficult to get as much money as you might from selling the business or to arrange a successful succession. The old saying that "a skunk stinks from the head down" is true for the skunk and true for the owner.

In a situation like this, the best course of action would be for you to hire someone to help you lead and operate the business, someone who will bring added enthusiasm to the company and who will work toward meeting the goals and objectives you have set for the business. An additional benefit of doing this is that it would give you the time to learn the business-selling process and address the value-added issues to achieve maximum payout. Alternatively, you can continue operating the company yourself but redouble your efforts to maintain the success you've already achieved. Both of these choices are easier to say than to do, but in most cases either choice is a better option than not maximizing your business exit.

However, your analysis might have shown that your business's sales and profits have remained flat while the market and industry have continued to grow and prosper.

In this situation, knowing that you'd like to sell the business within a few years, the best solution for a maximum payout would be to improve the business's performance through a short-term plan. This usually means that you would have to solve the problems that have kept the company from growing along with the market. These problems usually include personal issues (including the role of the owner), process issues, product issues, and finding ways to attract new customers and keeping them.

The only alternative you would have in such a situation (besides hiring someone to do the job if you can't do it yourself) would be to attempt to sell the business based on what the sales and profits *could be* rather than what *they are*. The problem with this option is that it's hard to convince buyers to pay more money for a business than it's currently worth. And even if you can convince someone to "pay all the money," getting a bank to lend him or her the money is likely to be very difficult. Even though this option is hard to do, it's not impossible, which means that you and the buyer would have to get creative when negotiating the deal. Being creative could mean your participating in some of the buyer's future profits, leasing the building or equipment rather than selling it outright, entering into some type of management buyout agreement, or changing the sale from an asset purchase to a share purchase. Deals like this take place much more often than most people realize, and doing it this way can get you the price you want and give your buyer the business he or she wants.

Good things rarely come to those who sit and wait. Hoping that a great candidate to whom you can turn over or sell your business will come along just isn't realistic. As with every other stage in your business's life, in order to get what you want, when you want it, you have to make plans. You have to gather the appropriate information, analyze it, develop a plan, and then implement that plan. In a sense, the plan you develop at Level 5 will be the most important one you'll ever make for your business because it will determine whether all the work you put into the company, and all the time and effort you expended to build it into a successful business, was worth it.

■ ■ ■

At the beginning of this chapter, I suggested that you imagine you are standing at an intersection with cars coming at you from every direction. You know you're in danger where you are and that you have to move, but since all the roads look the same, you can't tell which one will get you where you want to go. Planning—as I said and have now shown—is what enables you to determine which road is the right one for you and your business. Regardless of which of the five levels your business is on, it is only by determining where you want to go and making plans for how you're going to get there that you will be able to achieve success. Most important, as I've demonstrated, you don't need a crystal ball to do it: planning is about preparing for the future, not predicting it.

Fact 5: If You Don't Market Your Business, You Won't Have One

We have all heard marketing experts tell us not to think of marketing as an expense, but rather, as an investment. And what they say is certainly true. But instead of proclaiming the obvious, these so-called experts should be explaining to owners the two most important—and frequently forgotten—macro concepts regarding marketing. First, marketing is not a department. Marketing, in all its many aspects, is about capturing customers and doing all you can to keep them coming back, and achieving that is not just the responsibility of one department. It must be, either directly or indirectly, the responsibility of every employee in the organization. Second, marketing is ultimately about making more money—gross profit, to be precise. And that won't happen if the overall gross profit is not sufficient to cover costs and expenses. This might seem like a very elementary idea, but business failures occur far more often than business successes, and lack of gross profit is one of the main causes of those failures. One thing you can be sure of is that successful owners understand the importance of gross profits, and they battle hard, through pricing and product offering, to preserve them.

There is nothing pretty about marketing—it can be a blood sport. And its function is fairly straightforward—attract them, sell them, and keep them. That's the simple reality of marketing.

Unfortunately, that definition is the only simple thing about it, because attracting customers isn't easy to do, and the ones you do attract won't all become loyal customers, even if you do everything right. That is, it takes marketing to bring customers in, but it also takes marketing—through businesses processes, selling skills, and employees' interactions with customers—to keep them. Having the right product, at the right time, at the right price is one thing, but delivering it to customers in a way that provides acceptable gross profits is something altogether different.

In other words, marketing is not one specific thing, like telling customers you exist, but a whole series of things, from offering products the public wants, to presenting and selling them profitably, to following up on sales, to making sure your employees are always knowledgeable and professional, just to name a few. Marketing is the vehicle that connects your products to the customer. What that means is that if it affects your customers, marketing is involved in some way. And it's this kind of customer focus that owners have to instill at every level of their companies.

As essential as marketing is, though, it's important to remember that no matter how good your marketing may be, unless you also have a good product, you may not be successful in the long term. General Motors and Coca-Cola are two well-known companies that forgot this and paid dearly for it. In the late 1970s and early 1980s, when GM redesigned their midsize, full-size, and some of their luxury vehicles as "look-alikes," it became hard to tell a Chevrolet from a Pontiac or an Oldsmobile from a Buick. GM was a good marketing company, but as good as they were, customers revolted and moved to other companies because GM's cars were no longer distinctive, especially when compared to each other and some of their competitors' cars. Coca-Cola was another great marketing company, and its flagship product, Coke, was the undisputed heavyweight of all colas. But then they developed a product called New Coke to replace the original, and although they spent an enormous amount of money marketing it, their customers didn't like it and didn't buy it. Eventually, the company went back to its original product and New Coke disappeared from the shelves. The point here is that marketing is a powerful tool, but it can only do so much. Marketing needs a good product and a good product needs marketing.

Nike and Apple are two good examples of this. Both companies have great products, but so do their competitors. Both became successful by establishing strong brand awareness backed by solid products. Nike used the "swoosh" as its symbol, and its marketing showed creative, colorful, and attractive Nike running shoes, clothes, and other accessories just like the pros used, pitched by famous sports figures like Michael Jordan and Tiger Woods. In fact, the "swoosh" became a product of its own, getting customers to buy Nike's products just because of the symbol and the statement it made about them. Apple, of course, created the symbol of an apple with a bite taken out of it. They also strove to market products that were unique in some way, making them easy to identify as Apple products, and clearly differentiating them from their competitors' products, which appeared to be out of date by comparison. Apple's uniqueness of design and style, constant upgrading of products, cutting-edge technology, and willingness to not just create new products but completely new product categories all added to the company's mystique—and to its success.

The Benefits of Marketing

- Marketing lets prospective customers know that your company exists and what you do.
- Marketing allows you to shape customer perception of your company.
- Marketing differentiates your business from your competitors.
- Marketing allows a business to deliver your "why buy here" and "why buy now" message.
- Marketing helps your company capture market share and maintain success.
- Marketing enables you to develop brand recognition and expand your product lines.
- Marketing can help reinforce, or shore up, your business's reputation.

- Marketing enables your company to protect itself from competitors by promoting a competitive edge or advantage they can't duplicate.

The Realities of Marketing

- Everyone in the company has to have marketing in his or her job description in one form or another and be able to deliver on the business's marketing promise, one customer at a time, and every time.
- All the various elements of marketing—advertising, public relations, community activities, and others—are useful tools, but they must be coordinated if your marketing is to be as effective as possible.
- As an owner, you have to make sure your company's marketing efforts, message, and—especially—money are clearly aimed at your target market.
- It is essential for you to keep up with the market, if not be on its leading edge, as well as be able to "read the tea leaves" to predict which products will be "hot" and which will cool off in the future.
- Everything you do in marketing must be designed to attract the customer, sell the customer, or keep the customer—that's why your business exists.

The Elements of Marketing

Marketing is an enormous challenge for many people. It often seems like the more you learn about it, the more you need to know. But like anything that's complicated, the easiest way to understand it and gain confidence in dealing with it is to break it down into manageable elements. And marketing can be easily broken down into three such elements: attracting the customer, selling the customer, and keeping the customer. These three elements have remained largely unchanged since people started marketing products and services, and they form the backbone of any marketing activity.

Attracting customers means getting their attention, and the first step in doing so is finding out where they are. This is not always easy to do, and often requires some trial and error. Pfizer, one of the world's leading biopharmaceutical companies, does not advertise Viagra on MTV, because the people who watch rock videos are not concerned about erectile dysfunction. However, they do advertise it on cable TV sports shows and in health magazines that cater to older men, among other places. They do this because they know their target market, which consists largely of aging baby boomers who are interested in any product that will help their flagging libidos.

Once you have the customers' attention, the next step is to hit them with a powerful message that will motivate them into action. Marketers know they have very little time for their messages to hit home, and that the message can be quickly forgotten, even by those who are interested. That's why they repeat advertisements again and again—it's through repetition that the message makes an impact and prompts a prospective customer to go out and buy whatever it is you're selling.

It's at this point that the process shifts to selling the customers. However, those responsible for attracting customers still have one more task to perform—analyzing which message attracted the most customer interest, which media generated the most traffic, and which message and media produced the most actual sales. These and other analyses are a major part of finding out what works and what doesn't in terms of media and message, and are essential in developing appropriate advertisements and choosing appropriate media in the future.

Selling the customer, the second element, is paradoxically something that owners sometimes forget is the main purpose of marketing. They spend a lot of time, effort, and money on trying to attract customers, but once they have their attention, they neglect to close the sale. That is, they don't pay sufficient attention to how customers are handled—from the time they come into the store, open the Web page, or start talking on the phone to a staff member, to the time they leave, log off, or hang up. When your company has an opportunity to sell, your employees have to be ready to do that—sell. And it won't happen unless you train your staff to do it and make sure there are appropriate sales processes in place.

The third element, keeping the customer, is similar to selling the customer, in that it's also something owners don't pay as much attention to as they should. In fact, developing a tracking system so you can contact customers or potential customers after they leave your business is an essential part of effective marketing. Creating loyal customers is important because they cost so much to get, and they are a limited resource. Moreover, once they have bought something from you, they are far less expensive to connect with, as well as easier to market and sell to. They already know who you are, where you are, and what you sell, and if your staff has done a good job attracting and selling them, a bond is formed. It's a fragile bond at first, but one that grows stronger with every purchase. Developing these kinds of repeat customers not only enables you to build a solid foundation for your business and provides you with a strong competitive edge, it may even be a game changer for your company.

Level 1: Ownership and Opportunity

At first glance, common sense would seem to suggest that marketing would have little impact on the decision process regarding ownership or opportunity. And this is true for ownership. But as far as helping distinguish a good opportunity from a bad one is concerned, marketing—particularly marketing research and analysis—can be extremely helpful. In fact, the research that goes into developing a marketing plan can provide a wealth of knowledge about the market, its strengths and weaknesses, its complexities, its challenges, its competitiveness, and how much money will have to be invested in marketing to have an impact in the marketplace. Each of these elements can have a significant effect on which opportunity you choose to pursue, so they should all be researched thoroughly. There is also, however, an additional item prospective owners, owners who are expanding their businesses, and owners who are reengineering their companies often tend to forget: how much gross profit can be generated. Gross profit has to be at the core of any marketing analysis, because ultimately, the reason your business markets and sells its product or services is to generate gross profit. Marketing always seems to concentrate on sales, but the fact is that sales are important only in terms of the gross profit they bring in.

Unfortunately, most owners don't begin their research or start to develop marketing plans until after they have chosen which opportunity to pursue because they think doing so prior to making that decision is a waste of time. This is a big mistake, because at this level, making the right decision is the goal, and you are going to have a problem if you commit to an opportunity only to discover, for example, that the market has a huge appetite for what your business offers but not at a price at which you can make adequate profits. It doesn't matter how smart or talented a marketer you are, if you get the opportunity decision wrong, very little will go right. So whether you are starting a new business, buying one, or expanding your current one, researching the market and developing a marketing plan can bring clarity not only to the opportunity decision but also to the challenges of attracting customers, selling them, keeping them, and managing the gross profit they generate.

In order to help you decide which opportunity would be best for you, there are several questions you should ask yourself about each of those you are considering. The purpose of these questions is to help you focus on making an accurate assessment of the various opportunities, and they must be answered with facts rather than assumptions. These questions include:

- How large is the market? That is, does everyone need this product or service or just a small number of people?
- Is the market already overcrowded, and is it one that's easy for new competitors to enter?
- Is the product or service I'll be offering in the early stages of its life cycle or nearing the end?
- Who are my potential customers, why do they need the product, and how large is the demand for it?
- What will my gross profit margin be, and how will it hold up to aggressive market pricing?
- How much money can I reasonably make in this business, and is it proportionate to the investment in effort and money it will require?
- Why will customers buy from me, and how will my competitors defend their positions when I come into the market?

These are not the only questions you have to ask, but they do represent some of the most important ones. You will, hopefully, have noticed that in one way or another all of these questions revolve around profit and product, and the reason for that is simple: it's profit and product that make everything worthwhile. If there's no profit, there's no business. This may not sound politically correct, but it's true. It's equally true that profit is what's important to bankers or other investors, because it represents the sustainability of your business, and that's ultimately all they are really concerned about. There are, of course, other reasons for going into business—because you enjoy the challenge of it, because of your "love" of the business, or because you like the lifestyle. But none of this will matter if your company can't make enough money to be self-sustaining. As a matter of fact, if the business can't be self-sustaining, then all your investment will have done is buy you a job, and you could end up becoming a slave to your business.

The Benefits of Marketing Research at Level 1

- Marketing research enables you to determine the competitiveness of the market and forecast how far other owners will go to protect their turf.
- Marketing research provides you with a clear understanding of the pricing matrix and the gross profit opportunity.
- Marketing research enables you to analyze and determine the strengths and weaknesses of your potential competitors.
- Marketing research provides you with information you can draw on to work out estimated marketing costs and develop preliminary marketing strategies.
- Marketing research helps you recognize the challenges of selling the customer even before you make the opportunity decision.
- Marketing research provides you with a good overall view of the opportunities you are considering before you choose which to pursue.
- Marketing research draws attention to the important marketing realities and variables that are factors in the opportunity decision-making process.

- Marketing research provides support for the research conducted for the other Facts of Business Life.

Attracting the Customer at Level 1

Since at this level there is no business yet, you obviously can't start to implement any effort to attract customers. And because of that, the majority of businesspeople don't even think about how to attract customers at this point. If you do think about it, though, you will have a head start on the process. That is, if you do the appropriate market research, you will know the size of the market, your target market, who your customers are, and how the marketplace prices its products, as well as have a good idea of how you will attack the market. And you can learn all this by answering the questions suggested above, in effect killing two birds with one stone—gathering the information you need to make an informed opportunity decision, and preparing yourself to start attracting customers even before you open your doors. Attracting customers is where marketing starts, and where successful owners shine. The lesson at Level 1 is that if you want to shine at marketing, you have to do the kind of research that will enable you to understand your market. This "digging for details" not only helps you determine which opportunity would be best for you but also provides you with a means to attract, sell, and keep your customers.

Low-Hanging Fruit

Every business I have owned or mentored has had what I refer to as "low-hanging fruit," that is, the customers who are the easiest to attract. Low-hanging fruit customers generally come in three types: (1) those who buy from you only when you offer deep discounts or special pricing; (2) those who buy from you because your business has some particular advantage over other competitors, usually location or convenience; and (3) those who have been customers in the past or are current customers.

When I moved to Texas and purchased an existing business, our marketing and advertising efforts began by targeting these low-hanging fruit customers. Although we used a shotgun approach announcing our presence to the

(continued)

entire market, we also offered grand opening specials to attract the deep discount customer. We then launched a more targeted campaign aimed at potential
customers in the neighborhoods where we had a location and convenience
advantage. At the same time, we marketed hard to the previous owner's
past and current customers. Although we appreciated those who came just
for the discounted pricing, we knew these were customers who only appreciated price and would buy from whoever offered the deepest discounts. We
put most of our effort behind marketing to the other two groups—those with
whom we had an advantage and past and present customers—because we
knew they could serve as a foundation on which we could build our business.

Selling the Customer at Level 1

At Level 1, selling the customer is still a long way off. After all, at
this point, you're still trying to figure out if you're ready for ownership and, if so, what kind of business you want to own. Developing
a sales system—that is, determining how you are going to sell the
customer—is always a good idea. But whether you're ready to do
it at this level will depend on how much importance you put on
marketing overall. You can't put enough emphasis on marketing
because, as this Fact of Business Life says, "If you don't market your
business, you won't have one." And since everything you do is ultimately measured in sales and the gross profit those sales produce,
it doesn't make sense to not think about how your business will sell
the customer—even before you have any customers to sell.

Again, at this level, there is nothing to implement, but there
are efforts you can make that will stand you in good stead when
the time comes to start doing it. One of these is to learn what your
competitors are doing to sell their customers. Find out who the
best marketers and sellers in your industry are, and learn how they
do what they do. This is easier to do than most people believe and
more important than new owners realize. To begin, talk to industry-
related national or regional organizations, tell them what you're
thinking about doing, and ask who they would recommend you talk
to. The vast majority of owners will be candid about their businesses
and give you their opinion of what you present to them, as long as

they don't perceive you as a threat. Besides, you never know—an opportunity may appear that you didn't even know existed. It happened to me, and it could happen to you as well. This can, in any case, be extremely helpful to you, and you should think very seriously about doing it.

Another step you can take is to determine how aggressive those companies are in their efforts to sell their customers. In fact, finding the answer to this question speaks to both ownership and opportunity. If the market is full of competitors with the "killer instinct," you have to determine if you will feel comfortable and be able to function effectively in such an environment. But even if the market is full of sharks, it doesn't necessarily mean that the opportunity isn't big enough for more passive owners to thrive. Lawyers provide a good example of this. Every market seems to have some lawyers who advertise themselves as so "bad" that they will destroy their opponents. But every market also has a place for lawyers who don't portray themselves as killers, and both seem to survive. So if your market is like that, even if you don't consider yourself to be a "killer," you can still have a very successful business. One way or the other, though, this is something it's important for you to think about even before you start your business.

Understanding how you want to sell into a market is an important issue to consider, and ignoring it could lead to an irreversible mistake. Knowing the selling climate speaks to both your specific ownership philosophy and your competitiveness. Doing so will enable you to find the opportunity that will most closely match the way you want your business to be recognized and the reputation you want your business to develop. In other words, as far as marketing and selling goes, it's essential that you be comfortable with the way it's done, and that you know even before going in whether you want to compete with the "killers" or will be satisfied making a good living by selling less aggressively.

Keeping the Customer at Level 1

Part of the formula for keeping your customers is being smart, creative, and copying what great companies do to keep their customers; that is, finding out the best practices and trying to duplicate them. But that's a lot easier said than done. And there's not much point in even trying unless you know you have the determination and passion to enforce the discipline necessary to keep customers. In this regard, keeping customers is more about ownership than opportunity. By this point, the opportunity has been achieved—you've created a customer by making a sale—so now you have to make the most out of that sale by doing whatever you can to make sure the customer comes back. The fact that someone bought from you once doesn't mean he or she will do it again. Your business has to not only treat customers right—as you define it—the first time but also work continuously to earn their business.

In order to illustrate the best way to keep a customer, in his book *The Seven Habits of Successful People* (Free Press, 1990), Steven Covey talks about the difference between shearing sheep and skinning them. He suggests—and successful owners will certainly agree—that it's much better to shear the sheep time and time again than to skin it once. It's the same with customers. You might be able to "tag" them once, but if you do you will never see them again. This is the way you need to start thinking about keeping customers at Level 1, and the way you will have to get your employees to think about them at later levels. But it requires effort, and unless you're strong enough to make that effort, to make sure your employees are sufficiently disciplined and professional to treat your customers "right" so they keep coming back, competing and winning will not only be difficult, it may be impossible.

Level 2: Creating Your Company's DNA

In the discussion of marketing at Level 1, I said the kind of marketing an owner chooses to do reflects both his or her personality and competitiveness. This is equally true at Level 2, but at this level, marketing also reflects the owner's character. This is because the way an owner chooses to sell the company's products says a great deal about the kind of person he or she is. For, example, owners who advertise a product at a particularly low price even though they only have one or two items at that price are likely to have a somewhat questionable character. However, owners who are honest with their customers are unlikely to engage in such deceptive practices, and will accordingly be able to earn the customers' trust. In other words, marketing is not only about driving traffic to your business, it's also about building and displaying an attitude that's reflected in how you market your business, how you operate it, the type of people you hire to serve your customers, and the way your customers are treated. In other words, it's about your company's DNA.

Having decided to become an owner and selected an opportunity at Level 1, at Level 2 you have to begin to match your company's marketing to the opportunities available. That is, you have to make sure your marketing goes where the customers and the opportunities are. If, for example, you determined there was a market opportunity in the automotive supply industry for low-priced tires and batteries, you would stock such items, hire and train your staff to help your customers, and then let those customers know that you have what they are looking for. Similarly, if your research indicated that there was a demand for quality automobile body work, you would hire experienced repair people, get the most up-to-date equipment, and start advertising to your target market. The point is that the opportunity defines the market, marketing attracts the customers, and your business's DNA has to support the image your marketing projects. In order to accomplish this, it is necessary that you essentially develop both internal and external marketing programs.

Internal Marketing

The internal program is the means by which you implement the first macro concept concerning marketing—that is, marketing is not the responsibility of one department but, rather, the responsibility of every employee in the company. Customers want their presence recognized and their expectations met, and the only way to make that happen is for every one of your employees to have some responsibility for marketing included in his or her job description. And that means everyone—from your most junior part-time clerk to your most highly paid executive. It might mean as little as saying hello and smiling to a customer, answering a phone no one else is picking up, or replying quickly to a customer's e-mail inquiry, but it's important, and it's all part of the internal DNA you have to instill in the company.

The goal of internal marketing is essentially to deliver on the promise of the external marketing, that is, what you tell prospective customers about your company and the products or services you provide. At this level, though, the internal marketing program actually needs to be developed before the external one. This is because external marketing must be backed by substance, and if you don't know exactly what your company can provide its customers, or the way in which your employees will provide it, it will be pretty difficult to sell your business's differences and skills. What ultimately separates successful owners from the also-rans is not the size of the external marketing and advertising budget but the internal effort to make sure the staff meets the owner's expectations for the way customers are handled. It's one thing to attract a customer to a business, but it's another to make the sale and to keep the customer coming back.

Put yourself in your customer's place. Imagine that a business has attracted your attention, but when you try to purchase something, the company's employees treat you with a lack of respect or an "I could care less attitude." You might still buy something from the company, but it's not likely you would go back. Your customers are no different than you are. They don't like being ill-treated either. And what's even worse, if they don't like the way they're treated by your employees, they're likely to tell others about their experience. So in the process you don't only lose one potential customer, you lose any number of them. This is why implementing an internal marketing program as part of creating your company's DNA is so important.

Internal marketing is not, however, just about how the customer is treated. It's also about creating and controlling internal processes that support the sale, that is, making sure the business can deliver on the marketing and advertising promise. If, for example, one of your selling points is quality, you have to set up a quality control process to make sure you can deliver quality. You don't want a customer to come in to pick up his car after you've supposedly repaired his front bumper only to find that it's still full of dents. Similarly, if your marketing projects an image of professionalism, you have to develop a training program to ensure not only that your staff has the most up-to-date product knowledge but also that they know how to sell the benefits of your business and your products. You don't want a customer asking one of your staff about the latest version of a product only to have him or her stammer out an incoherent answer. In other words, the image you project externally has to be backed up by internal action, and if it isn't, the disconnect will cost your business sales.

External Marketing

The external program is the means by which you develop the message you want to send to your target market about your products or services, and about the company itself.

The primary goal of this program is to match your marketing and advertising to the opportunity, that is, to make sure your marketing is focused on your target audience and delivering a message that not only gets their attention but also moves them to action. Eventually, the way to do this will be to develop a process that will track your customer traffic and sales so you can see if your message is reaching them, and make adjustments if it isn't.

At this level, however, in order to get the program started, you have to make three important decisions. First, you have to decide how you want to attack the market, that is, how you will price your items, what kind of selection you will have, and other factors that will enable you to exploit the opportunity. The second is to decide what media and message will attract your target audience, that is, whether you will use print, radio, television, social media, or some other means of reaching those who should be interested in what you have to offer. And, third, you have to decide how you want your customers to be able to contact your business—such as through a web site, e-mail, or telephone—and how you will greet them and make a positive impression. In other words, you have to develop an external marketing program that will drive customers to your business, where they will be met with an internal marketing program that fulfills the promises the external program made. And the sooner you do that, the sooner success will come, and the sooner you will be able to make the most out of the opportunity you have discovered.

Understanding the various aspects of marketing and how they impact on each other is not an easy task. But like so many other things in business, as in life in general, if you first concentrate on the basics the rest will eventually come to you. In marketing, those basics begin with understanding the difference between internal and external marketing, recognizing their importance, defining what you want your company to represent, and then mastering the three elements of marketing—attracting, selling, and keeping customers.

The Benefits of Marketing at Level 2

- Understanding marketing enables you to recognize that it must be aimed at the audience that matches the opportunity you've selected.
- Understanding marketing enables you to see that it has two macro elements, internal and external, and that they must be connected and coordinated if your business is to be successful.
- Understanding marketing helps you develop transparent processes that will ensure what you want to happen does happen.
- Understanding marketing makes it easier for you to make critical decisions because you will recognize that it must be appropriate to the opportunity.
- Understanding marketing enables you to not only direct traffic to your business with a "buy here" message but also to brand the business in a way that customers can identify with it.

Attracting the Customer at Level 2

Attracting customers is a continuous activity regardless of what level your business is operating on, simply because attracting more customers means increased sales, increased profits, and usually a greater market share. It's often thought that attracting customers is limited to external marketing, but the fact is that internal marketing plays an important role as well. The reason for this is that customers talk to other people about their buying experiences, and often recommend businesses where they have been looked after and treated well. So once your business is live, whatever you and your employees can do to make the sales process more enjoyable for your customers, the more they will tell their friends and neighbors about it, and the more customers you will have. It's as simple as that.

Of course, first you have to let them know that your business exists, and the way to do that is through advertising. The issue here is making sure that you are advertising in the media that your target audience uses. You may have a great message and a wonderful product, and spend a lot of money on advertising, but if your customers aren't where those dollars are spent, you're wasting your money. It's at Level 2 that you must research where your target market goes to get its information and entertainment. It's also at Level 2 that you set up a process so that when customers start contacting your business you will be able to track how they found out about you, which will not only sharpen your media buying but also enable you to more effectively match messages to the various media.

It's very important, though, that you recognize the difference between attracting traffic and attracting buyers. There are lots of media that brag about the campaigns they run that can get a lot of people to your door or your web site. More traffic is obviously a good thing, but traffic has to eventually translate into sales. And the sooner you can find out where your buyers are and how to attract them, the sooner your business will become successful. At Level 2, there are several ways you can do this. Perhaps the most obvious is to research how your successful competitors market and advertise their products. However, what's even better is going to other markets and talking to successful owners about how they do it. This will not only give you fresh ideas, it will also give you ideas about how to collect the information and how to design processes that will provide you with solid data you can use to your advantage.

Selling the Customer at Level 2

Making the sale is ultimately "where the rubber meets the road." It's what all of your hard work is about. So when you are creating your company's DNA, one of the first questions you have to ask yourself is "What can I do to give my employees the best chance of making a sale?" That is, how will we handle the web site contact, the phone call, or the customer who comes into the business? And the answer is to make sure your employees know to ask for the business, the steps to take in making a sale, and how to close—that is, the sales process. Addressing this issue is essentially what creating the DNA for your marketing program is about.

An example of a simple but effective process that can work, with modifications, whether you are selling products or services is one in which the salesperson:

- Welcomes the customer, introduces him- or herself, and thanks the customer for coming in, phoning, or visiting the web site.
- Begins building rapport by asking questions to determine exactly what the customer either needs or wants.
- Restates what the customer has said to confirm his or her understanding.
- Explains how your products or services match up to the customer's needs, possibly even suggesting options the customer may have not known were available, in turn reinforcing why doing business with your company is his or her best alternative.
- Begins to start closing the sale by asking for the business, that is, saying, for example, "Can we make the appointment to perform the service tomorrow, or would Thursday be better?"
- If the customer has objections, slowly starts working through the objections, continuing to sell the benefits of your business, and ends by asking for their business again.
- If he or she can't make the sale today, finds out when it might be done, asks for the best time to contact the customer, and requests his or her contact information.

As you can see, selling processes are simple to design. More important, they are easily adaptable, so depending on your preference and your company's DNA, they can range from being very passive to being extremely aggressive. Regardless of what kind of selling process you create, however, the fact is that if you want your business to do well and be consistently successful you will not only need to have a selling process but one that is sufficiently transparent that, if there is a problem, it can be readily identified and corrected.

Keeping the Customer at Level 2

Generally speaking, businesses today have to do more to impress and keep their customers. This is due more to competition than to any other factor, because more and more industries and businesses have made customer retention an extension of their marketing efforts. As a result, companies are being creative in keeping their businesses in front of their customers long after a sale has been made. Technology has made customer contact and retention relatively easy and inexpensive to do, which has leveled the playing field for small business owners who are going up against large public companies like Walmart, Home Depot, or Macy's. In fact, you can pick up generic customer retention software programs at stores like Office Depot or Best Buy, as well as have a program designed specifically for your business.

Amazon's program is a good example. They not only thank you for your purchase, they keep track of the authors and types of books you like, then keep you up to date on new books by the same authors as well as books that are similar to those you've bought in the past. In fact, Amazon's customer retention program has essentially become a marketing department in itself. For example, by keeping its business in the customers' "mind's eye," letting customers know in advance when new books by their favorite authors are being released, and giving them the opportunity to preorder them, Amazon effectively takes its customers out of the market for any other business. Similarly, automobile companies have begun monitoring their customers' driving mileage and vehicle performance, then contacting the customer regarding upcoming or suggested maintenance to drive them into their dealerships, where they are likely to purchase some of the company's after-sale maintenance products.

As with Amazon, there are two basic elements to every customer retention program. The first is thanking customers for their business and providing them with contact information so they'll know where to go if they have any questions or concerns. This is fairly easy to accomplish because all it means is setting up a process to send out a "thank you" within so many minutes, hours, or days after the purchase. The second basic element is sending customers timely reminders concerning specials, new products, or other information they might find to be of interest. Thanks to technology, setting up this kind of process is also very easy. Once you have these two processes in place, the rest is up to your creativity and imagination. It is important to remember, though, that you don't want to upset your customers by being too aggressive, especially if you communicate with them electronically. That means you have to give them a way to "turn you off" if they want to. It's all right if they do, but if they do, you should find another way to keep in contact with them, either by mail or phone, so you can continue to keep your company in their minds.

Level 3: From Survival to Success

Level 3 could be referred to as the "killing ground" because that's where most business closures and foreclosures occur. But the reality is that while it's at Level 3 that companies go out of business, many of these failures actually begin at Levels 1 and 2. That is, by not doing the kind of preparation that should be done at the earlier levels, or by doing it poorly, owners put themselves on the road to ruin, even if they don't get there until they reach Level 3. Unfortunately, despite owners being told that preparation is essential if they want to succeed, this same scenario is played out day after day.

This is particularly true for marketing. The day you open for business is not the time to start thinking about where your target market is, where to place advertisements, how competitively you should price your product or service, who the easiest customers to attract are, or what your marketing and advertising budget should be. This would be like an NFL team going into their first game of the year without any set plays on either offense or defense. The outcome of the game would be a foregone conclusion—an embarrassing loss. Even if the team had some of the best players in the league, without preparation, it wouldn't be able to exploit its talents or attack the other team's weaknesses. It's the same in business. If an owner doesn't know how to attack the market or where opportunities lie, the outcome will be equally inevitable—and equally unpleasant.

One of the major goals for marketing at Level 3 is to make it an integral part of moving the business along the spectrum from survival to success. In order to accomplish this goal, you have to implement the marketing programs, both internal and external, you developed at Levels 1 and 2. By the time you begin Level 3, you will need to know where the "low-hanging fruit" is and be prepared to attack that part of the market. You also should have defined additional market opportunities, set up your product offering and priced it accordingly, and designed a message that will resonate with customers and move them to action. In addition, you should have trained your employees in their marketing role by teaching them to sell the way you want them to, to be knowledgeable about the product or service, and to work at developing relationships with your customers. You also should have developed internal processes to support sales both before and after the sale is made, including customer retention.

Perhaps the most important thing to bear in mind is that, as an owner, the better you know your market—how to reach potential customers, what "hot buttons" to push, what customers like to buy, and the gross profits they can generate—the faster your business will move along the spectrum from survival to success. But there is another very important point to be made, which is that doing all these things, and doing them right, is just the price of admission. In order to consistently succeed, your knowledge of the audience and the best way to market and advertise to it will have been at least equal to that of your competitors. If this isn't the case, your business will get off to a slow and probably rocky beginning.

The Benefits of Marketing at Level 3

- Understanding marketing enables you to recognize the importance of the preparation done at Levels 1 and 2 and how valuable it is in making marketing decisions at Level 3.

- Understanding marketing gives you an appreciation of how important it is to develop hard data by measuring your customer traffic and sales penetration.
- Understanding marketing helps you save money by keeping the marketing and advertising focused on your market rather than learning what does and doesn't work as you go along, and in the process miss potential valuable opportunities.
- Understanding marketing enables you to fine-tune what works so you can keep your business on the forefront of the market and on top of any market shifts.
- Understanding marketing enables you to recognize that it is essentially a process whose many aspects must be coordinated in order to effectively attract the customer, sell the customer, and retain the customer.

Attracting the Customer at Level 3

As I noted earlier, the first thing you have to do in marketing is attract your customers' attention, let them know your business exists and where it is, and deliver a message that will move them to action, that is, to buy whatever it is you're selling. How you do this depends a great deal on the kind of customer you're attempting to attract, your creativity, and your DNA. A good example of this is the television commercials with the baby who talks about how E*TRADE's pricing and market tools are all you need to trade stocks on the Internet. What makes these commercials great is, first, they grab your attention with the talking baby, which cuts through the clutter of the other commercials they are competing against. Second, once they have your attention, they entertain you, which means you will continue to listen to they are being said. And while you're listening, they deliver their message and brand the business as a fun company that will meet your trading needs. Not surprisingly, these commercials have been very effective for the company.

Another good example is the television commercial for the "Gears of War" video game that features a machine gun chainsaw. The commercial is obviously aimed at gamers, and its graphics and the violence they display—along with the audio—draw the gamers' attention. One of the things that's particularly interesting about this ad is that it tells viewers only when the game will be available, not where it can be found. The company that makes the game can do this because they know their customers already know where to find it, and they don't have to waste time and money giving them information they don't need. Instead, they use the time to whet their audience's appetite and let them know when the game will be available.

As these examples show, marketing and advertising are not, or at least should not be, based on guesswork and assumptions. They should be based on facts about your product and your customers. One of the ways of making sure this happens is to measure the effectiveness of your marketing, that is, determine if you have made good decisions about your message and the media you selected. You do this, first, by determining exactly what you want to measure, such as sales and gross profits, gross profit per sale, same period year-over-year increases, number of customer contacts, and the like. Then, after you have launched a marketing program, you continuously ask yourself questions like these to monitor your results:

- Was the goal we set realized? Why or why not?
- What was the traffic like? Did it attract buyers? Did everyone buy? Did some buy? Did just a few buy?
- Did our internal processes work? Could they be improved?
- Did we do particularly well in selling some products and services? Did we miss the mark on others?

In marketing, knowledge is king, and knowing the answers to questions like these gives you the kind of information you can use to your advantage in helping move your company faster along the survival–success spectrum. It also enables you to avoid wasting time and money by focusing your message on what the customer cares about and what works best for your business.

Selling the Customer at Level 3

Selling the customer is something that can never be left to chance. Of course, nothing you do can ever entirely guarantee a sale, but the way your company presents itself and the processes you develop for your employees to follow can make the difference between staying on the survival end of the spectrum and becoming successful. It's particularly important to remember that, whether you're selling a product or a service, selling begins with your customers' first impressions—what they see, how they feel about what they see, and how they feel about the way they are welcomed to your business.

Let's say, for example, that you own a furniture store. If customers come in and find a dark, unorganized display with a week's worth of dust on the furniture, they are not likely to have a very positive impression. Nor are they likely to be pleased if the person who greets them is unkempt or uncooperative. But the opposite is also true. If customers come into your store and find it neat and clean, and your salespeople friendly and helpful, they will be much more inclined to buy something from you because what they see is a business they feel they can trust. For example, Ashley Furniture and Dillard's Department Stores are all well lit and well organized and have knowledgeable, professional salespeople, so customers get the impression the salespeople know what they're talking about and, accordingly, have confidence in what the salespeople tell them.

Keeping the Customer at Level 3

Customer retention is essentially making sure that the customer comes back for more of whatever you're selling. But if you asked 10 different entrepreneurs how to keep customers, you would in all likelihood get 10 different answers. That's because, in at least some respects, every type of business is different, and every type of customer is different. If, for example, you owned a business that catered primarily to the older generation, you would probably find that what they respond to best is competitive prices and a place where they are remembered and appreciated. However, if your clientele is made up mostly of college students and recent graduates, you would likely discover that they are attracted to places where they are made to feel comfortable and can be with liked-minded people. The television show *Cheers* featured a bar "where everybody knows your name," where Sam, Woody, Diane, Carla, and Coach all added to the experience of having a beer, which in turn kept Norm and Cliff coming back. That's customer retention.

Ray Kroc, the brains behind McDonald's, understood customer retention well before almost everyone else, and he defined it in his own way. He believed that if his customers could have the same experience regardless of which McDonald's they visited—that is, if they could have the same burgers, the same fries, and the same milkshakes—they would keep coming back. And, needless to say, he was right. Kroc was the process "King." He didn't rely on people, he relied on people following processes, and it's because of these processes that people have bought billions of meals from McDonald's all around the world. The point is that you have to define exactly what customer retention means to you in order to make sure that it fits your business's demographics and what you're offering your customers.

Although there has been more attention paid to customer retention over the past decade than ever before, keeping your customers isn't anything new. In fact, successful owners have always known the value of retaining customers—it's one of the reasons they are successful. What has changed, though, is that because of today's increased competition, the bar for after-sales contact has risen substantially. One of the most obvious examples of the increased interest in retaining customers, and one of the most successful, is the airline industry. Concentrating on their best customers, airlines offer programs that enable customers to earn miles toward future travel, as well as enjoy other benefits. Other industries have followed suit, offering reward programs that provide cash back or credit, including credit card companies, drugstore chains, department stores, and other kinds of businesses. Of course, maintaining contact and thanking your customers for their business is always smart. But the goal for these companies isn't just to stay in touch with customers—it's to have customers return time and time again rather than going to one of their competitors.

It's important to remember that customer retention doesn't begin when you sell a customer, it begins when you start to market to them. That means that the goal of marketing at Level 3 is not just selling a customer but selling him or her again and again. It's this understanding of marketing that has always separated those who remain at the survival end of the spectrum from those who reach the success end. The way you attract your customers; your business's DNA; the sales processes; and the courtesy, professionalism, and knowledge of your employees should all add up to customer retention. As I mentioned, however, since every business is different, it is essential that you find the most appropriate ways to keep customers for your company, and no one can do that better than you.

Level 4: Maintaining Success

By the time a company has reached Level 4, the success goals the owner defined years before will have been reached, the business will be firmly planted on a solid foundation, and it will in all likelihood be a force in the marketplace. The goal at Level 4, then, is not to become a successful company, as it was at Level 3, but to become even more successful, and thereby maintain and secure the business throughout the owner's tenure. But Level 4 contains a trap for the unwary owner, one in which past success can become the enemy of future success. This happens for a variety of reasons. Sometimes the owner becomes tired, bored, or both. Sometimes he or she becomes satisfied with the status quo of sales and profits. And sometimes the owner fails to define the new destination for success that Level 4 demands. Regardless of why it occurs, when it does, the company's competitiveness begins to fade, it begins to lose its competitive edge, and company-wide apathy slowly sets in, led, at least in part, by the owner.

Because of its prominent role in any successful business, marketing is far from immune to this apathy. The aggressiveness the owner and the company's employees once exhibited in finding new opportunities or increased market share begins to fade. Internal improvement of employees and processes becomes less important than it was in the past. Marketing and the money spent on it become routine decisions, especially when compared to what it was like when the business was starting up and every dollar spent was well thought out. As a result, marketing and its many components go on cruise control, and the company begins to rely on what has worked in the past. The problem, though, is that what worked in the past won't necessarily work in the future.

All of this happens because once apathy sets in, you essentially create a void in the market, and that void will be quickly filled either by your more aggressive competitors or new competitors who see an opportunity where you have stopped looking. When this happens, your marketing dollars stop generating the business they once did, usually because your marketing isn't keeping up with the market. Your first reaction is likely to be frustration, because even though you're spending the same amount of money, you're getting a smaller return and your market share is being reduced. But that isn't really the big expense. The big expense is in losing your customers and your connection to them.

As bad as this sounds, however, there is some good news. First, when your sales and profits decline at Level 4, getting back on track lies, for the most part, in your control. So as long as you recognize the signs of apathy and take steps to overcome it, you have an excellent chance of meeting the challenge. Second, as far as marketing is concerned, you're not starting out, as you did at Level 3, at the survival end of the spectrum but closer to the success end. Your business has customers, is well known in the market, and has been a consistent performer. You've also gained valuable market experience and intelligence. So if you rework your marketing model, that is, go back to using market facts and your experience to attract new customers and keep the ones you have, you will be able to regain your marketing momentum, capture lost market share, keep up the attack on the overall market, create market opportunities, and, hopefully, become an even stronger competitor.

The Benefits of Marketing at Level 4

- Understanding marketing enables you to refocus your efforts and recreate the competitive edge the company had before the apathy of success worked its way into the company.
- Understanding marketing helps you recognize that you have to define a new destination, with various success points along the way, and develop a new marketing model to help the company meet its new goals.
- Understanding marketing will enable you to realize that you have to become more creative than your competitors and that

this creativity will entail taking ideas from other industries or competitors outside the local market and experimenting with them in order to improve your company's internal and external competitiveness.

- Understanding marketing will help you recognize the need to revisit Level 1 to look for new opportunities in the market or expand old ones by feeding off your competitors.

- Understanding marketing will help you become more competitive internally by revisiting Level 2 and developing new and more effective process.

- Understanding marketing will enable you to recognize that some of the employees who helped you become successful at Level 3 may not be the right ones to help you remain that way at Level 4.

Attracting the Customer at Level 4

The overall challenge of attracting customers at Level 4 is essentially the same as at Level 3—you have to get your customers' attention and then deliver a message that moves them to action. The process is also essentially the same, meaning you start by identifying the low-hanging fruit that, at Level 4, will more than likely be the customers you have lost. To accomplish this you may have to reconfigure your internal processes in order to define exactly what constitutes a lost customer, such as someone who hasn't purchased anything within a specific amount of time, and then identify those who fit the criteria.

These customers are not necessarily easy to attract, but they are easier than others because you know who they are, and can target them individually through the Internet, mailers, or personal follow-up. Of course, simply contacting them is not enough. You also have to give them a reason to come back, such as a special offer, an event, or some new personal service. Regardless of how you contact this group, what you promise them, or how you identify them after they've indicated renewed interest in your products or services, it's important to remember that reacquiring former customers is an important first step in reestablishing your marketing preeminence and, ultimately, in maintaining your success.

Another way of attracting customers and increasing your market share at Level 4 is focusing on new customers. Most markets have a finite number of customers, which means any new customers will have to come from a competitor. One particularly effective strategy at Level 4 is cannibalizing, or feeding off, some of your new or weaker competitors. Since your business is one of the more successful ones, you can offer amenities that your newer or less successful competitors can't afford to offer. For example, you can provide additional customer service such as e-mail alerts about new products or services, updates on the status of items customers have already ordered, or expert advice on questions they may have about your products or services. The point is that if you can do something your competitors can't because of your strong financial position, you have a good chance of taking customers away from them.

Another effective way to get a Level 4 company back on track is niche marketing. The positive aspect of niche marketing is that these kinds of markets are usually smaller in size and therefore easier to control and "own." The negative aspect, however, is that, because these markets are small, the cost of catering to them is usually higher, and the profit potential usually lower, when compared to other market opportunities. This is why niche marketing isn't particularly advantageous at Level 3. At Level 4, however, any incremental business usually means added profits because the company's cost per customer is lower since it can spread costs over a much larger customer base. If your Level 4 company picks the right niche, then, you will have the ability to own the market, and owning a market others have given up on opens the door to eventual added gross profit, which can make the niche financially attractive.

Reacquiring old customers and getting customers away from your competitors, as well as niche marketing, are time-tested ways Level 4 businesses can get back in the game, or stay in it by pushing past the goals they've already achieved and working toward becoming even more successful. But Level 4 owners shouldn't ignore the power of attracting customers, both old and new, through social media. If, like most of today's Level 4 owners, you attained your success before the various social media were even invented, much less being used for marketing purposes, you are probably not very familiar with them or their potential. Marketing is, though, about going where your customers are, and social media is where your customers are today and where they're going to be in the future. And since they can present enormous opportunities to attract customers and deliver a message, it is essential that you learn how use them, and sooner rather than later.

Selling the Customer at Level 4

Since the goal at Level 4 is to make your business a more success-ful and financially stable company than at Level Three, marketing in general, and sales in particular, clearly have a major part to play. At the same time, it's important to remember that while improvements can always be made, significant improvements in your selling process may be difficult. The good news, though, is that it's not just one thing that propels your business forward. It is, rather, a series of marketing improvements that, when added together, have a strong impact on your company's bottom line. For example, if you were to improve your closing ratio slightly, sales would go up, but probably not enough to give you a substantially larger market share or signif-icantly higher profits. If, however, you could improve your closing ratio and at the same time attract more customers, you would prob-ably see a considerably larger increase in both market share and profits. And if you were to add a new niche market, the impact of all of these things added together could be very significant. In other words, when improvements in your external marketing are supplemented by improvements in your internal marketing, the dif-ference can be dramatic.

These are all, of course, traditional means of improving sales. But as is the case with attracting customers, in order to success-fully sell customers today it is essential that you make use of the new technologies. The Internet has given selling a new twist over the past 10 years, and there is more change to come, so unless you stay ahead of this new surge you will risk taking a step backward. In most industries, if you are not on the Web, don't have employees who are comfortable communicating and selling over it, or aren't using new technologies as an aid to selling, you're already behind the curve. But you're likely to fall even farther behind if you don't recognize the impact the Internet will have on sales in the future. There is a generation growing up that has never known a world without the Internet, and this is just the beginning.

So if you want to prosper in this environment, your company will have to be flexible, fast, and smart. In fact, it's companies within striking distance of Level 4, and those that have already attained it, that could be the most vulnerable to the coming changes. This is because as a business becomes more successful, the company's structure becomes more cumbersome compared to a new, aggressive, flexible business that can adapt quickly when it recognizes an opportunity. This will be one of the bigger challenges successful businesses will face in the coming years, and if you want to continue to be a leader at Level 4, you will have to become as flexible to change as you were in the past.

Keeping the Customer at Level 4

If a company has reached Level 4, it is in all likelihood because its owner and his or her staff are already concentrating on their customer base and understand the value of their customers. So it's probable that by the time your company has attained this level, you will have long since defined what customer retention means to you, and are already maintaining some control over the customer experience, as well as some form of continuous contact with your customers. However, because at Level 4 the goal is not just to keep your customers coming back when they need to, but to get them to return on a more controlled basis, it is necessary for you to rethink exactly what customer retention means. In other words, while keeping customers is still a philosophy that starts with first contact and continues beyond the purchase, the goal now is a more aggressive and sophisticated one, requiring you to think outside the box to find ways of increasing your company's revenues.

A good example of this is the automotive market. For decades, the car business took a backseat to Christmas shopping every December, making it one of the slowest months of the year. Today, it's one of the better—if not best—selling seasons for cars and trucks. What changed it was, about 30 years ago, the automotive companies began making almost unbelievable offers of low interest rates, no payments for 90 days, and large customer rebates, and sometimes all of them combined. The net result was that customers jumped all over the offers, and now, because buyers recognize it's one of the best times of the year to buy new vehicles, they wait for Christmas.

Programs like these can be established in service industries as well. For example, air conditioners are, not surprisingly, a tough sell in the winter, as is servicing them. In order to remedy this, some aggressive air conditioning companies have begun offering their customers specials on maintenance and checking overall air conditioning systems during the winter months. These specials help customers because they save money on something they know they will need soon anyway, and it helps the air conditioning companies because it provides them with needed work and the opportunity to replace air conditioners that didn't work well during the previous summer.

Creating business in the slower or offseason has proven successful for other industries as well as for many astute business owners. And the fact is that if you want to keep operating successfully at Level 4, it's something you really need to do. This is because the way to maintain success at this level is to be aggressive in the market and increase profits, which is something you will find hard to do if you don't visualize or create opportunities throughout the year. There's an old saying that "you go fishing when the fish are biting." That may or may not be true when it comes to fishing, but in business, at Level 4, you have to market whatever you sell during your traditional busy time as well as at those times that the fish aren't necessarily biting. That is, you have to create and/or find ways to attract them to your hook.

Level 5: Moving On When It's Time to Go

When your business gets to Level 5, that is, when you have decided for whatever reason that you're ready to move on, you have to choose whether you want to close the business down, turn it over to a family member, or sell it. If you decide to close it down, from a marketing perspective there is obviously nothing to be done. If you want to turn it over to a family member, the most important thing to do is continue what you've been doing all along, that is, market, lead, control, plan, and implement all the other Facts of Business Life, so the company you turn over to your successor will be in the best shape possible. If selling the business is your preferred option, you also have to continue operating it as you have in order to maximize your return. In that case, though, from a marketing perspective, there is a new dynamic you have to understand, which is that at this point the business itself becomes your product. That means that until the sale is concluded, you will effectively have two different—and potentially conflicting—jobs to do.

Marketing at Level 5 takes a bit of courage. Not only are you moving your life in a new direction, you're also putting your business on display for your peers or family to judge you by showing them your financial secrets and statements, and that can be unnerving. Not surprisingly, some owners falter or procrastinate at this point, and some even become paralyzed and unable to do anything. But the hard reality is that the longer you hold off taking this step, the less time you will have to fix any issues that may be problematic for buyers, family members, or yourself. And the fact is that it takes a fair amount of time to dress up the product and get your personal and business affairs in order.

However, even though the business itself has become your product at this point, your marketing mind-set shouldn't be all that different than it's been all along. Since the marketing process is essentially the same, you have to keep doing exactly what you've always done. That is, you have to research the market, price the product, identify your target audience, create value in the product, attract promising buyers, and sell it. The fact that it's your business you are selling can be daunting, but if you've gotten to this point you already know how to sell a product successfully, and there's no reason for you to stop doing it now.

Of course, a business is a different kind of product, so you have to package it differently.

That means you have to decide exactly what it is that's for sale, the terms of selling (such as selling your assets and goodwill but leasing the facility), the preferred time frame for the sale, how much time you'll give prospective buyers to decide if they are interested, and what kind of assurances you are willing to offer potential buyers. In other words, just as with any other product, you have to demonstrate how it works, why it will continue to work, list the ingredients (in this case the assets), and wrap it up in an attention-getting package in order to maximize your business's value and attract the best buyers.

The Benefits of Marketing Research at Level 5

- Marketing research provides you with the information you need to identify your best buyers and the value of businesses like yours.
- Marketing research enables you to determine the competitive environment in terms of supply and demand, the number of buyers vs. sellers, and other factors.
- Marketing research helps you determine how to present your company's operations and facilities in the way that will be most appealing to potential buyers.
- Marketing research enables you to recognize a problem or an opportunity that may not have been apparent before and to take action on it.
- Marketing research helps you determine which buyers will be able to pay the most and which can benefit the most from buying what you have.
- Marketing research enables you to find past sales of businesses in general, and in your industry in particular, and uncover facts on which to make marketing decisions (e.g., pricing, terms if facility is bought or leased, industry multiples, equipment pricing).
- Marketing research allows you to discover, approach, and market to buyers who may not have realized the significance of buying your business.

Attracting the Customer at Level 5

The fact is that if you have a good business, people will want to buy it. Actually, even if you don't have much of a business, someone might be willing to buy it, depending on the price and terms.

In other words, at any given time there are likely to be a number of people who might be interested in buying what you have to sell. The problem, then, is finding and attracting them. However, the last thing you want is for every prospect, be they rich or poor, experienced or inexperienced, to come banging on your door. If you have a less-than-successful business or are asking too much money, it may come down to that, but this is not how you begin attracting customers for your business. You begin by drawing up a list of potential buyers based on three criteria:

- Who can afford to buy my business?
- Which of my competitors would benefit most from buying my business and will therefore be willing to pay the most?
- Who will be put at a market disadvantage by my selling the business to someone else?

Putting together a list based on who can afford to buy your business is an essential first step. Of course, when you're selling a business, you want to find, or create, more than one buyer, but you don't want to waste time with those who can't afford your price or terms of sale. Paradoxically, your most motivated buyer, someone who desperately wants what you have, might be someone who can't afford your business, and there's no benefit to you in pursuing such a prospect. The best way to determine what companies are likely to have the kind of money you're looking for is to use common sense. New owners are likely to be highly leveraged, while owners who have had successful businesses for a number of years probably have substantial net worth, such as Level 4 owners or owners at the success end of Level 3. In considering possible buyers, though, you should not limit yourself to your local market, because there may be an owner in a neighboring market who wants to expand, or an owner in the supply chain who would be interested in your business, such as a distributor who wants to buy an end-users' business, or vice versa.

When you're considering who would benefit most from buying your business, it's a good idea to try thinking a bit outside the box. For example, there may be a candidate for your business in another city who has children ready to take over a company and is looking for an opportunity to put one of them into business. There may also be a competitor who would automatically gain a significant share of the market by buying your company, and through economies of scale create a competitive advantage for his or her business. In both of these cases, as well as in others, your company can have value beyond the pure, financial mathematics of a business purchase, and that additional value can motivate those potential buyers to pay more for your company than others might. If you are considering selling to other companies like this, however, it's up to you to make sure they know your business is for sale.

As noted earlier, it's also important to take into consideration those potential buyers who might be disadvantaged by your selling to someone else. For example, some of them might not be overjoyed at the prospect of buying your company at the moment, but believe they can't afford to have you sell to a competitor because it would give the acquiring owner too much of a market advantage. Others might feel compelled to buy your company because they feel that allowing you to sell to someone else would result in their losing the opportunity to have a broader product line. The bottom line, so to speak, is that any company that can't afford to let a competitor acquire what you have is a willing and motivated buyer. And it would be to your advantage to determine, as best you can, which companies these might be.

Regardless of the circumstances, you will invariably have a better group of buyer candidates if you become proactive and pick out and plan who you want to attract as buyers. Your most willing buyers will be easier to recognize once you have taken the time to understand your specific exit goals, the market for businesses, and the rules of engagement, as well as defined your business well enough to give buyers a clear understanding of what they're buying and what a great opportunity you are presenting them.

Selling the Customer at Level 5

As far as selling is concerned, there are only two ways to sell a business—an asset sale or a share sale. An asset sale is one in which you sell the assets associated with the business, including goodwill, but the seller retains responsibility for all the liabilities associated with those assets. A share sale is one in which you sell the company's assets and the buyer assumes all the liabilities associated with the business. The more knowledge you have about the differences between an asset and a share sale, the better and more informed a decision you will be able to make, and the better your chances of maximizing your business's value. If you are unfamiliar with the difference, you should have an accountant explain them to you.

When you are first beginning to enter into negotiations with potential buyers, price is usually their primary concern, and they are likely to want to know what it is sooner rather than later. At this point, though, your primary concern should be to develop a presentation that provides those buyers with the information they need in order to make an informed decision. There are essentially three elements to this presentation. The first is explaining to them exactly what it is you are selling; that is, which assets will be included in the sale and their book value and replacement cost. The second concerns whether the real estate is to be part of the total sale price, if you would consider leasing your facilities, or if you would be passing on a third-party lease and how you attach a value to it. And the third is telling the prospective buyer about your past profits and why these profits will have to be taken into consideration in the overall purchase price.

So regardless of whether you are offering an asset or a share sale, the first step in the selling process is to provide the potential buyer with your sales and value story; that is, to do your sales presentation. After you've made your presentation, if there is still interest on the buyer's part, you should work together to draw up a plan so you will both know what will happen at each step of the process. For example, you may want to start with a confidentiality agreement, after which you could begin to explain the specifics of your business. Next, assuming the buyer likes what he or she has heard, the buyer would be expected to provide some sort of assurance that he or she is in a strong enough financial position to buy what you have to sell. Once this has been done, the next step might be for you to release your business's financial information. Regardless of what kind of process you set up, it is important that there be one.

A selling process gives you control, helps both of you focus, and, if the negotiations stall, enables you to go back to your last item of agreement and use it as a new starting point to look for common ground.

Regardless of the type of business, at the core of almost all business sales, there are essentially three things for sale: goodwill, assets, and real estate. Goodwill, as I mentioned earlier, is the amount sellers ask buyers to pay above and beyond the value of the company's assets to compensate them for the future profits they will be giving up by selling the company. This amount is usually calculated based on a number of years. For example, if your business averaged $1 million a year in profits over the previous three years, you might ask for a goodwill payment of $3 million. However, goodwill is difficult to negotiate because of its subjective nature. That is, although the company's profits represent actual figures, how much the seller is entitled to receive to compensate him for selling the company is obviously open to debate.

Nevertheless, the question of goodwill is a good place to start the negotiation process, because if you are going to insist on receiving goodwill, it should be put on the table up front. That way if the prospective buyer is unwilling or unable to pay goodwill, you will know that he or she is the wrong buyer, and it's best to know that sooner rather than later. However, if you do start the negotiations with a discussion of goodwill, it may not be advantageous for you to get down to the final goodwill number right away. Instead, you would be better served by spending some time selling the concept of goodwill and what it covers, such as your customer base, internal processes, experienced employees, and future profits. This is important because your buyers may not know what goodwill actually includes, and it's your job to tell them so you can be sure you're talking about the same thing.

After goodwill, the next item to be taken into account in a sale is the company's assets. Assets, in this sense, are the physical items the company owns; that is, machinery, vehicles, computers and office equipment, inventory, and anything else that should be listed on your company's balance sheet. So if you and your potential buyer can come to some sort of understanding regarding goodwill, the discussion about assets should be considerably easier. You provide a list of assets and negotiate a price based on either their replacement value or their book value, or somewhere in between.

The final element of the sale is the real estate. In most cases, an outside appraiser is brought in to determine the price, which makes the real estate transaction fairly straightforward. However, as I've alluded to elsewhere, in business, even things that look routine often are not. For example, in a fair number of cases, even after both parties have agreed on an appraisal valuation, they discover that the lending institution's terms and conditions drive up the anticipated operating costs so the buyer needs more cash than expected. That is, the down payment he or she has to make turns out to be larger than anticipated, which leaves the buyer with less cash to pay for goodwill and assets. This situation presents a problem for both parties, and it would accordingly be in both of their interests to find a solution. One way of dealing with it might be to work out a leasing agreement. Making such a deal can actually be beneficial for both sides, because it can lower the buyer's costs and free up down payment cash that the buyer can then use to pay for goodwill and the company's assets.

In the end, no matter how you look at it, the stakes are always high when you're selling a business, and negotiations are never easy. Ultimately, how successful you will be in selling your business comes down to attracting the right qualified buyers, developing a strong value story, being flexible and creative, and having good negotiating skills.

Keeping the Customer at Level 5

At this level, keeping the customer means something different than at all the other levels. At Levels 1 through 4, it means getting them to come back after an initial purchase and buying from you again. At Level 5, it means keeping all your potential buyers interested in what you have to sell—your company—until either they or someone else buys it. Accomplishing this is tricky at best, particularly since the time frame can be so long. It is necessary, though, because until the sale goes through you can never be sure who the ultimate buyer will be.

Eventually, of course, you will have to choose someone to take to the dance; that is, you will have to get serious about a particular buyer. Unfortunately, that means the other potential buyers are going to feel left out in the cold. And while you don't want to burn any bridges, stringing potential buyers along is never a good strategy, because they are likely to know far more about what is going on than you think they do. The problem, then, is how to move forward with the buyer you are most interested in selling to while, at the same time, keeping other potential buyers from giving up. At this point, you have several options. One is to tell potential buyers that you have another interested party and need to evaluate their competitiveness. Another is asking all your potential buyers to put up a significant deposit to demonstrate their interest in buying your business. And a third is drawing up a negotiation schedule that will allow you to negotiate with several buyers at once. Each of these options has its obvious downside, but they have a common upside, which is that one of the potential buyer may not want any other competitors to be considered, and accordingly surprise you with an offer you may not be able to refuse. At the very least, though, it is essential that throughout the process you stay on respectful terms with all your potential buyers.

Finally, not every negotiation works out. It could be because the buyer decided for some reason that he or she wasn't interested in the deal after all. It also could be because you realized that the buyer you'd been pursuing wasn't going to be able to provide you with what you wanted. Regardless of the reason, you may well have to go back to one of your previous candidates to re-present the opportunity. Unfortunately, in a situation like that, you're likely to have to do some damage control, and that's hardly the strongest position to be in. If you should find yourself in this position, the best strategy is to say that you simply picked the wrong candidate for whatever reason. It's important to give a reason, though, because the potential buyer will otherwise think it was about price, which may not be the case. Of course, no one likes to have to start all over again, but if you have to, there's no reason why a second—or even a third—negotiation shouldn't be successful.

■ ■ ■

There are essentially three marketing concepts that you, as an owner, must keep uppermost in your mind. The first, of course, is that if you don't market your business, you won't have one. The second is that the more effective and well thought out your marketing is, the quicker your business will realize its goals. And the third is that the best marketers are not the ones who spend the most money, but rather the ones who get the most out of the money they spend.

As I have shown, these three concepts must be applied, as appropriate, at each of the five levels of business, that is, on the planning levels as well as on the action levels. What that means is that if you want to achieve success, maintain that success, and get the kind of reward at the end of your business career that you are entitled to, it is essential that you learn everything you can about your market, design both internal and external processes to facilitate sales, plan and execute sensible internal and external marketing programs, and make sure you and all your employees know how to attract the customer, sell the customer, and keep the customer.

Marketing represents one of the highest costs your business is likely to incur, but it's even more expensive if you do it wrong or don't do it at all. This is why the facts you learn during your research at Level 1 have to be matched to the processes you develop at Level 2, and then implemented at Levels 3, 4, and 5. And it's this orderly sequence that provides you with a valuable tool with which you can compete, succeed, and maximize the opportunity you have decided is right for you.

Fact 6: The Marketplace Is a War Zone

The Marquis of Queensbury Rules do not apply in free markets. Competition for customers and their disposable income, that is, their money, is the order of the day—every day. So if you're an owner of a small or large business, an entrepreneur, or an investor in any of these enterprises, the law of the jungle applies. And that means you have to be strong, smart, and agile, or die. The reason it's this way is that the marketplace is finite, meaning there is a limited number of customers and money to be spent. And it's these customers, and their money, who will determine your fate. It's not a friendly battle, the stakes are high, and the difference between success and failure is as distinct as night and day. If you don't understand this concept, or don't like the idea of it, business ownership is in all likelihood not for you. That's just the way it is. The marketplace is a war zone, and the battle never ends.

If you think I'm overstating the situation, think about the last recession. As of this writing, the economy seems to be starting slowly back on the road to recovery, but there's been a lot of damage done. Home builders, car dealers, banks, financial brokerages, real estate brokers, and other businesses have had to close. Literally every industry has been affected in one way or another. Because potential customers have limited disposable income, businesses find themselves competing for sales not only within their own industries but with other industries as well. Credit for businesses and consumers is harder to get, and unemployment is high. And fewer people working means fewer customers and less business for everyone. In addition, because of the economic uncertainty, those fewer consumers have slowed down their spending. As a result, the competition has become fierce, which has led to all-out warfare based on price, giveaways, rebates, extended hours, and all kinds of event-type marketing. If this isn't a war zone, I don't know what is.

One of the things that makes competition difficult—not just in downturns but all the time—is that your competitors don't all compete the same way. Some companies are aggressive, some are lazy and unmotivated, and others are moderately successful and content with their market positions. Moreover, there are some companies that compete on price, while some compete on location or convenience. Others compete on service or the quality of their products, while still others compete on depth of selection or on the basis of their market reputations. And these are just some of the more common competitive niches owners develop. This presents a problem because, being so diverse, your competitors are hard to pin down. Since they all have different perspectives, they all have different tactics, so the best you can do is try to anticipate what they're going to do. And that's not easy, and it's not going to get any easier.

But there's also another important difference in the ways companies compete that makes the war zone such a difficult place to do business. Some businesses fight hard and cleanly, while others, frankly, cheat in a variety of ways, and still others operate in a gray area by using half-truths, innuendoes, and misleading statements. As difficult as it is to compete against companies that fight fairly, it's even harder to compete against those that don't. While knowing this is true doesn't make competing any easier, one thing you can do is encourage customers who have had bad experiences to report these businesses to your local Better Business Bureau. Thankfully, while there are certainly companies that operate this way, there are still more honest competitors than dishonest ones, and eventually these questionable businesses close down. In addition, with today's social media, it's hard for a bad business to hide, which means they won't survive for as long as they might have 10 years ago. The point is that from time to time your business may lose customers to these shady operators, and as upsetting as it may be, you can take comfort from the fact that they won't exist for long and the customers you lose to them will be back, especially if you keep track of them.

The bottom line is that, whether you like it or not, all these competitive realities are continually in play. They are also always in a state of flux. That is, you never know when one or more of your competitors is going to make a decision to change direction or tactics, and that makes an already volatile marketplace an even more volatile one. Ultimately, there are only two possibilities in the marketplace war zone—you win or you lose. If you win, you make money. If you lose, you not only don't make money, you lose your investment. In fact, if you lose, you not only get your butt handed to you, you pay for the privilege—and in front of your friends and family.

The Benefits of Understanding the Marketplace War Zone

- Understanding the marketplace war zone helps you evaluate the competitiveness of the market, consider how others compete, and determine if it's a marketplace you can survive in.
- Understanding the marketplace war zone enables you to choose a competitive niche and clearly market to it.
- Understanding the marketplace war zone helps you recognize lazy and incompetent competitors that are vulnerable to attack, and shows you how to attack them successfully.
- Understanding the marketplace war zone helps you recognize competitors that have become complacent and lost their competitive edge, and how you can take advantage of it to increase your market share

The Realities of the Marketplace War Zone

- The marketplace is not always fair; someone is always looking for an advantage.
- If one or more of your competitors crosses an ethical line, it doesn't mean you have to go there yourself.
- Price as a competitive weapon is not as important as many people believe—it should be only one of the many weapons in your arsenal.

- Keeping up with your customers' wants and needs is a challenge, but keeping up with your competitors' changes and tactics is equally important, and something that all successful businesses do.
- Winning is a serious business for every successful business, so if you try to take one of your competitors' customers away, you should expect them to fight back.
- Competing in the war zone means if you find a competitive edge, you should go at it hard because your successful competitors will do the same.
- New innovations in products and technology constantly change the competitive landscape, so in order to compete successfully you must stay up to date.

■ ■ ■

There are three major elements that are critical to success in the marketplace war zone: the products or services you sell, how well your business operates, and how your business competes. Although these elements are extremely different, they are connected, and understanding this connection is important to a business's long-term success. Exactly how they are connected will become clear as you learn more about each of the elements.

The Products or Services You Sell

Not all products or services are viewed equally by consumers. Some companies have inherent advantages over others in the marketplace. Rolex watches and Mercedes-Benz automobiles, for example, have a reputation for quality. Similarly, a company that's been around for a long time has an advantage over a start-up simply because of its longevity. Newly opened big box stores such as Best Buy are also likely to take customers away from even thriving local businesses. Having advantages like these leads, not surprisingly, to greater sales, and greater sales lead to higher gross profits, which is the reason you sell things in the first place.

In the 1960s, for example, if you owned one of the four "C" franchises—Caterpillar, Cadillac, Coke, or Chevrolet—you were most likely a millionaire. Ironically, these brands were so strong at the time that even if you were only a mediocre owner-operator, you could still be very successful. Customers want what they want, which in a competitive market means some products are far easier to sell than others. So if you have one of these "A-list" products, owning a business and competing in the marketplace is going to be considerably easier. Current examples of products like this include Pepsi and Coke in the soft-drink market, Harley-Davidson motorcycles, and Nike in sports equipment and apparel, among others. Perhaps most important, selling products or services that already have a strong presence in the market can serve as a foundation on which to build an aggressive and highly successful business.

But whether or not you offer a dominant product or service, it's always appropriate for you to be both concerned and optimistic. That's because the market is constantly changing, and what was true yesterday isn't necessarily going to be true tomorrow. Look, for example, at the "C" franchises mentioned earlier. Of the four, only Caterpillar has remained basically the same. Coke is still dominant, but the rules have changed. The company has bought back most of its franchises and distributorships, so while the brand is still strong, a lot of the owner-operators are gone. And neither Chevrolet nor Cadillac dominates the marketplace anymore. In other words, three quarters of the most dominant brands in the world have shifted over less than one lifetime.

Will Google exist in 20 years? It's hard to think what would replace it today, but tomorrow, who knows? RCA Victor and Capitol Records, Oldsmobile and Plymouth, AIG and Bear Sterns, AOL and Exxon, and many more, have disappeared or are only remnants of what they once were. The point is that having a successful product today is no guarantee of success tomorrow, and it's important that you, as an owner, be aware of that. This is true for the service industry as well. At one time there were blacksmiths everywhere, but today they mostly ply their trade in restored eighteenth- and nineteenth-century villages. Nor are there any more electronic or appliance repair shops because the prices of these products have fallen so dramatically, it's usually better—and cheaper—to buy a new one than fix the old one.

The realities of the marketplace, then, are that customers first have to want or need what you're offering, there will always be preferred brands to compete with, and both your competitors and the market itself change over time. And if that doesn't look like a war zone to you, you might want to take another look.

How Your Business Operates

In the marketplace war zone, the best operators are not necessarily those who make the most money. At first glance this may not seem to make sense, but it makes a lot of sense when you factor in product inequities. As I mentioned earlier, some companies have a very strong market presence, which in turn enables those who sell their products to make more gross profit on what they sell. Nike, for example, is able to command a higher price than a "no name" brand for its sportswear, even if the two are of equal quality. The Nike "swoosh" has a customer demand that drives sales and gross profits. By contrast, retailers who handle less popular brands have to sell their products for less money in order to create sales, and in turn make less money for every item sold. This is a reality that is often disregarded when owners are evaluating opportunities.

Whether your business sells a high-demand product or brand or one on the opposite end of the spectrum, the basic rule of thumb for operating a business is that you sell for gross profit and manage for net profit. This means there are basically two areas you have to concentrate on in order to make an acceptable profit. The first is finding ways to maximize your gross profit through volume sales, achieve a significant gross profit on every item you sell, or a combination of the two. The second is managing expenses. Once you calculate your anticipated gross profit, you have to manage your expenses in order to make sure you have more gross profit than expenses.

The fact that these product inequities exist also presents three operating issues that impact on profits and the need for operational skills. The first is how A-list product owners operate their businesses and the effect it has on the entire market. Since markets are finite, the more market share these owners have, the less there is left for the smaller market niches. This is true basically because of price. By choosing to operate with fewer sales but higher gross profits on what they sell, A-list owners leave more buyers for the inexpensive brands. However, if one of these A-list owners decided to lower its prices and operate on very little gross profit but more volume, the other A-list owners would have to lower their prices as well, thereby attracting and selling to more buyers, and in turn limiting the number of buyers for the inexpensive brands.

Second, owners who represent products on the A list have to operate their businesses better than their head-to-head competitors in order to get the lion's share of the brand's business. For example, two NAPA parts stores compete for business with those customers who prefer NAPA brands as well as with the rest of the market. But the NAPA store that meets more of the customers' expectations—that is, the one that operates better—will be more successful.

Third, owners who don't have the advantage of a strong market presence should use a different business model than those who do, because they usually have smaller gross profits when compared to their counterparts. That means they have to make up for those lower profits in different ways. For example, Maytag appliance stores don't make money on repairs (or so their marketing suggests), they make it on selling their appliances. But those selling brands with less of a market presence, who will therefore sell fewer appliances and realize lower gross profits, can only increase their profits by selling more items, providing service, and possibly by selling add-on products. The point is that the products you sell, service, or manufacture have to dictate how you operate your business in terms of your expense structure and your gross profits. If you don't operate your business this way, you won't have one for long because in the war zone it's survival of the fittest, and the fittest is measured by net profit.

How Your Business Competes—The "X" Factor

Competitiveness, the third element of the marketplace war zone, also has a direct connection to the product or service you sell and how your business is operated. For example you can have a great product and develop a great marketing campaign that attracts hundreds of potential customers. But if they discover that your business is disorganized, or that your staff is discourteous or lacking in product knowledge, it's not going to do you much good. However, when you have a great product and creative, targeted, and aggressive marketing and advertising, and your business is operating well, you will have developed the X factor. And it's developing that X factor that will enable you to increase your market share and take business away from your competitors, whether you have an A-list product or not. So while it's true that owners who represent top brands can dominate their markets, even those who have lesser brands can work their way up the market share ladder and be strong market competitors.

Unfortunately, the X factor, like the other elements of the marketplace war zone, can't increase your business's market share over an extended period of time—at least it can't do it alone. In the end, being competitive is not just about having an aggressive market reputation and creative marketing and advertising. It requires additional weapons to be fully competitive, including price, customer service, selection, convenience, and location, just to name a few. And, because of the way the war zone works, that is, because the competition continually heats up, these weapons have to be continually redefined. It's not easy, but if you want your company to move ahead, it has to be done. As I said at the beginning, that's just the way it is. The marketplace is a war zone, and the battle never ends.

Level 1: Ownership and Opportunity

As is always the case, regardless of which Fact of Business Life is being discussed, Level 1 is essentially about looking into the future and asking yourself two questions—"Do I want to be an owner?" and "If I do, what opportunity do I want to pursue?" This is essentially how Level 1 works—if you decide that ownership is for you, then you begin to look for opportunities. As you do so, though, you'll soon begin to realize you are not alone. That is, there are others who are exploring opportunities, including already established companies that are using Level 1 research techniques to expand their businesses. In other words, you have competitors even before you've started. Welcome to the war zone!

One of the benefits of looking at opportunity through each Fact of Business Life is that it enables you to see it in several different ways. This is important because opportunity comes in many forms, and studying it from different perspectives allows you to see opportunities others may have missed as well as recognize potential threats or problems. The war zone perspective on opportunity begins by focusing on the market's dominant brands, or A-list products, their market share, and the impact they can have on the market you are interested in. If, for example, you're considering opening a home improvement store, you have to bear in mind that Lowe's and Home Depot already have 60 percent of the market, so that if you want to compete, it will have to be for part of the 40 percent that remains. Of course, if you were the only competitor outside of the A list, you'd be in great shape, at least until other competitors enter. But if your business were one of 20 competitors, the size of your market would be extremely limited.

In addition, when A-list companies command such a large part of the market, they can make the environment even more difficult for competitors. If, for example, Lowe's or Home Depot decided they wanted to squeeze out some of their competitors, either one of them could do it by lowering its prices. And if one of them lowered its prices, the other would certainly do the same, which would have an enormous effect on the entire market because by expanding their sales and market share, they would be lowering the market share available for their smaller competitors. And even if one of those smaller competitors decided to lower its prices, all it would serve to do would be to put a squeeze on the company's gross profit, which would have a negative effect on its bottom line. A true lose–lose situation.

These are important points to consider in any opportunity evaluation because they take into account both market share and gross profit, the two variables that ultimately define opportunity.

The preceding example also indicates the importance of price in the market. Pricing is important in any opportunity analysis because it defines gross profit or lack of it. However, some industries are more price sensitive than others, and if this price sensitivity (also referred to as price elasticity) is an issue in the market you're looking at, you should consider it to be a red flag. This is because if A-list brands like Lowe's and Home Depot want to expand their market and have a pricing war, they will still be standing when it's over, but not all their competitors will be. The market is a war zone, and it has many victims. The opportunity decision, then, should be focused on determining if there is enough opportunity outside the dominant brands in the market and, if so, whether it can generate enough gross profit to make it worth your while well into the future.

The Benefits of Understanding the Marketplace War Zone at Level 1

- Understanding the marketplace war zone gives you an additional means of evaluating the opportunities you are considering, whether you are just starting a business or expanding an already existing one.
- Understanding the marketplace war zone provides you with a competitive edge by enabling you to prepare for it even before you enter it.
- Understanding the marketplace war zone forces you to consider the strengths and weakness of your potential competitors in terms of product, operations, and competitiveness.
- Understanding the marketplace war zone helps you determine which brands dominate in the markets you are considering as well as identify the effect pricing has on the total market.
- Understanding the marketplace war zone enables you to determine if the market is overcrowded, or could become overcrowded, by the dominant and nondominant brands.
- Understanding the marketplace war zone allows you to identify and use the weapons you will compete with to measure— and decide on—your opportunities.

The Products or Services You Sell at Level 1

The primary focus for products or services at this level is on the size of the selling opportunity and the gross profit attached to those sales. Again, a good way of looking at opportunity is by looking at the dominant brand or brands in the areas you're considering. If, for example, you find out how well those dominant brands sell, and determine the size of their national and regional market share, you can compare those figures to their share in the market area you are studying. Doing so will give you a good idea of how the market you're considering compares to the industry or national sales averages, and the result may well show some inequities you could take advantage of. If, for example, you are thinking of opening a high-end furniture store, and you find a city in Florida that compares favorably with other Florida cities in that it doesn't have any stores selling A-list furniture, there may be an opportunity there. Similarly, if you are looking at a market where there is an A-list retailer, like a McDonald's, whose sales are weak compared to national and regional sales, you might consider approaching the owner to suggest purchasing his or her business.

Once you have determined that there appears to be ample sales opportunity in the business you are considering, and approximately what those sales might be, the next step is to calculate the gross profit attached to them. Sales information is relatively easy to find through public records or industry reports, but determining gross profit can be more challenging. If you are familiar with the industry, though, you can usually find many people who can direct you to places where this information is available. Gross profit can be calculated in two ways—the gross profit made on each sale or the gross profit made on all sales. The first can be determined by subtracting your cost for the product from what the products sells for in the market. If a package of razor blades cost you $4 and you can sell it for $7, your gross profit is $3 per sale. To find the gross profit from all sales, you simply multiply the number of packages you expect to sell by the expected gross profit per sale. So if you anticipate selling 10,000 packages, your gross profit would be $30,000. Your new sales and gross profit estimates should line up with your other gross profit calculations from the other Facts of Business Life, and if they don't, you need to find out why.

Since the war zone is such a competitive arena, there is one other issue you should look at after you have calculated sales and gross profit. This is the matter of whether it is likely that other competitors might enter the market. This issue presents two questions you have to answer—"If there are few barriers to entry, how will this affect my operations and forecasts?" and "Once my business is up and running, is there anything I can do to discourage others from trying to enter the market?" Unfortunately, at this point there is no way to answer either of these questions. Only time will tell. They are both, however, questions you will have to think about and address if you choose the opportunity.

How Your Business Operates at Level 1

The basic purpose of a business's operations is to make a profit. The goal at Level 1, then, is to define the opportunity in terms of how much money (profit) can be made each year over an extended period of time. Since this is a preparation level, you don't have to concern yourself with how well you will operate the business, but rather with how much potential there is to make money. Up to now I've been talking about sales and gross profits because they are product or service issues. But on the issue of how your business operates, the focus is on net profit and how it relates to the opportunity. Net profit can be calculated by subtracting the cost of products and services from the revenue generated from sales, which, as noted above, leaves you with your gross profit number. Once you have the gross profit, you subtract all your costs for operating the business, and the difference—whether positive or negative—will be your net profit.

For example, if you owned a clothing store and your sales over the course of a month added up to $200,000, and your cost, or what you paid for the clothes you sold, was $125,000, your gross profit would be $75,000. If you then subtracted your total monthly expenses of $20,000, your net profit before taxes would be $50,000 for the month. Net profit gets extra attention in the marketplace war zone because it can be a tactical as well as a strategic weapon both offensively and defensively. For example, on the offensive side, the stronger you are financially, the more money you can spend on marketing and advertising, generating additional sales as well as gross and net profit. Defensively, profit can be used to fend off any attack on your turf from a competitor.

A War Zone Story

I was once very familiar with a market area in which there were four dominant companies. These four businesses were owned by four different individuals, each of whom had been in business for nearly 20 years. They all had their own turf, and they were all content with their sales, gross profit, and net profit. Then one of the four sold his business. The new owner, wanting a make a name for himself and increase his market share, decided to lower his selling prices.

For the first few months the new owner had impressive sales increases. And then, four or five months after he had taken over, one of the other three owners dropped in to welcome his new competitor to the city and the market. After some general pleasantries, he brought out his financial statements and showed the new owner his impressive financial position. Then he told the new owner that unless he increased his pricing he would begin selling his products at a loss and bankrupt the new owner. The market returned to normal very quickly.

It's not a pretty story, but it's a war zone reality, and a good example of how financial strength can be a strong defensive weapon.

Insofar as your goal is to make as much money as you can, the obvious question is, how do you do it? You start by having as few limitations as possible. For example, trying to sell a product or service for which there is little demand limits your profit potential. So does being in a market where there is a lot of competition. In other words, if you want to make a lot of money, you have to first make sure the market is big and growing bigger so your talents as an owner can be maximized. This is a key concept because, regardless of how talented an owner you are, unless the market is sufficiently large and presents sufficient demand for whatever you're selling, your ability to exercise your talent, and your profit, will be limited.

You also have to take extenuating circumstances into consideration when you're making the opportunity decision. For example, smaller markets require less funds to enter, and when you're beginning your ownership career, money is usually a qualifier to opportunity. At the same time, some markets are extremely competitive and require considerable ownership skills to make money, so unless you want to see your dream die right at the start, even if you have the money, it's best for you to avoid situations like this. However, you may find yourself presented with an opportunity that doesn't match a lot of your criteria in terms of market size or brands but is appealing for other reasons. For example, an owner may offer you a strong ownership position in his or her profitable company if you'll agree to operate the business. This becomes a win–win situation for you because not only does the financial risk decision evaporate, but so do other barriers that you would normally have to consider.

How Your Business Competes—The X Factor—at Level 1

As important as product, sales, and gross and net profit are, they are all tied in one form or another to the owner's competitiveness—the X factor. There are very few things that can influence a business like the competitiveness of an owner, and it's one of the few factors over which owners have complete control. Even if, for example, an owner represents an A-list product and operates a good business, if he or she is a weak competitor, the business will never make the money it should. Conversely, an owner with a strong competitive drive can get a foothold in the market even with a weaker product line, as long as he or she is a good operator, the overall market is fairly passive, and especially if the owner's overhead or expenses are significantly lower than his or her competitors. That's how important the X factor is.

Other than products, the three most common weapons owners use to compete are customer service, price, and location/convenience. In fact, the competitive climate usually forces owners to have all three of these elements in play to some degree at all times. It's the price of admission to the marketplace war zone. And not surprisingly, it's the businesses that implement these weapons with more skill than others that are generally the most successful. But knowing what should be done and doing it are altogether different things, and it's the gap between what your competitors know—or should know—and what they do that creates opportunities for you.

There are numerous ways to use these weapons, either individually or in combination. In a situation in which your competitors think of customer service as an expense and try to minimize it, for example, if you have processes in place that optimize the customers' experience, such as a means of dealing with customer complaints quickly or using the latest technology to serve them, you will in all likelihood realize more sales, better profits, and more control over your customers. Price can also be a very effective weapon, particularly if you have lower overhead than your competitors, because you can lower the price, sell more, make more profits, and use those profits to be more aggressive in your marketing strategy. Finally, the Internet and social media have redefined convenience, and when markets change, it invariably means new opportunities for anyone quick enough to take advantage of them. For example, eBay used the new technology to create the world's largest buying, selling, and auction business, and in the process instantly expanded the market far beyond any particular location or marketplace. Similarly, Barnes & Noble could have sat back and let the new online book sellers take away their business, but instead they fought back using their well-known brand as a launching pad for protecting their market share by developing their own electronic reader, giving customers a choice of instantly downloading books or buying them in their stores. Of course, at Level 1, it's far too early to start making use of any of these weapons. However, if you have done the kind of marketing research I've suggested, you will have learned your competitors' strengths and where they are most vulnerable to attack.

Ultimately, though, being competitive doesn't just mean knowing about an opportunity and acting on it—it means acting in such a way as to get the most out of it. That is the primary purpose of being competitive. Level 1 is where current and potential owners define what getting the most out of an opportunity means in terms of the investment of their time and money, how long it will take to get there, the net profit and market share it will produce, and the benefits that can be derived from the opportunity. Being able to make the most of every opportunity is what separates the average entrepreneur from the great one. So the opportunity question ultimately comes down to you, the owner, and the X factor.

Level 2: Creating Your Company's DNA

One of the realities of the marketplace war zone is that not everyone conducts business in the same way. All of your competitors want to succeed, and most of them will play you smart and straight up, and won't cross the line between right and wrong. There are others, though, who will do whatever it takes to succeed—say things about your business that aren't true, use false advertising to attract customers, and lie to those customers when it's in their best interests to do so. In other words, the war zone is not fair, and someone is always looking for an advantage, whether it be legitimate or not. And you have to prepare yourself for it.

To do so you have to ask yourself how you will react to this kind of pressure, that is, how you will compete. Will you be the kind of owner who wants to "win at all costs," or will you try to dominate your competitors without crossing the line? Only you can answer this question. It is a serious question, though, and every successful owner at one time or another has to answer it. In fact, because markets and competitors invariably change over time, most owners have to answer it more than once. Unfortunately, sometimes owners wait too long to take a firm stand and are forced to make a choice in the heat of battle when emotions are high, and this is never the best time to make a critical decision.

So the sooner you make that choice, the better off you will be. And the best time to make it is now, at Level 2, when you're creating your company's DNA. That is, you need to decide on the ethics you will apply when competing externally, the weapons you will use, and the kind of battle strategy you will implement. You will also have to develop systems and processes that will back up those external weapons to make sure that what you want to happen actually does happen, every time, and be prepared to discipline those who choose to bypass these procedures. Doing so will give you a competitive edge because you will have thought these processes through and prepared yourself and your business even before the battle begins at Level 3.

Unfortunately, too many owners underestimate the intensity of the war zone and what is at stake. They analyze the market at Level 1 but neglect to think about how they will fight or how their competitors will. To compound the problem, the majority of owners, particularly first-time owners, frequently fail to set up the internal processes that are needed to back up their external marketing efforts. Just throwing wild punches at a market without a plan or preparation is not a strategy—it's a recipe for failure. The way it should work is that your marketing and advertising attracts interested buyers, and your internal processes—and the people who operate them—make the sale. Making these kinds of preparations will not guarantee you will beat out all your competitors, but it will provide you with a leg up compared to those who don't make such preparations.

The Benefits of Understanding the Marketplace War Zone at Level 2

- Understanding the marketplace war zone helps you develop strategies to maximize the opportunity.
- Understanding the marketplace war zone enables you and your key employees to create a step-by-step plan for implementing your strategy prior to entering or reentering the battle.
- Understanding the marketplace war zone gives you time to communicate to your employees the intensity of your competitive drive, your definition of appropriate behavior, and the discipline they can expect if they cross the line.
- Understanding the marketplace war zone enables you to establish the procedures through which you want your company to operate and compete.
- Understanding the marketplace war zone allows you to synchronize the business's overall marketing and business plans

with its marketing war zone strategy and make sure all the company's operations are coordinated.

- Understanding the marketplace war zone keeps owners and employees from making often unfortunate impulse decisions because the boundaries will have already been set.
- Understanding the marketplace war zone enables you to analyze what you are currently doing in the war zone and determine what you could do better.

The Products or Services You Sell at Level 2

If you want to compete successfully in the war zone, there are two issues at this level that must be resolved regarding the product or service you're going to be selling. The first is defining your product or service and creating a means of communicating that definition to your employees. The second is, having analyzed your product or service's potential at Level 1, devising a strategy to maximize both sales and gross profit.

The primary reason for defining your product or service is to make sure your employees understand exactly what it is. That may sound like nonsense—after all, a product is a product—but it's not. Here's an example. Your company makes pies that you serve in your own shops, which according to numerous food critics are the best pies in the country. If, though, a customer comes in to one of your shops and is served by someone who looks like he or she hasn't bathed in weeks, and smells like it, is the customer really going to care how good the pie tastes? Is she going to enjoy it? Is she even going to eat it? The point is that your product or service isn't just what it is, it's also how it's delivered or served to the customer. And how you want that to happen has to be communicated and constantly reinforced throughout the company. Of course, you don't *have* to do it. If you don't, though, it's likely that your business will get crushed in the marketplace war zone when your reputation and lack of repeat customers catches up to you. Again, this can be avoided by making sure your employees understand exactly what you expect of them and what is unacceptable.

By the time you get to Level 2 you will have already determined your product or service's market potential. At this level, what you have to do is create an operational DNA strategy that will enable you to maximize that potential. That means you will have to devise a marketing strategy that will capture market share and increase both sales and gross profit. One way of doing this, if you are selling a product, is to have loss leaders to help drive traffic, and train your employees to up-sell customers to more expensive products that have more benefits as well as more gross profit attached to them. If you are providing a service, you might offer some special pricing on items that are connected to this service. For example, if you are servicing air conditioners, you can train your technicians in selling and offering specials on safety inspections, dehumidifiers attached to the air conditioner, or upgrades on a customer's entire air conditioning system.

Whatever strategy you decide to pursue in the war zone, it's important to remember that it cannot be operated in isolation. That is, it has to be balanced and coordinated with the other Facts of Business Life. You will, for example, have to draw on the facts concerning planning and knowing business if you are planning to market more aggressively because you will have to budget not only for increased marketing and advertising costs but for other associated expenses, such as increased personnel or an increase in your credit line with your lender. You will also have to adjust your overall financial forecast for more sales, additional gross profit, and increased inventory, so you can see what the expected results look like on paper. However, doing so may show that you can't take advantage of the opportunity because your current financial resources will be stretched too thin. Similarly, drawing on the facts concerning leadership and planning, you may discover the pricing strategy you're thinking of using won't generate enough gross profit to adequately cover your operating costs. In addition, referring back to the facts concerning marketing and knowing business, you may find your strategy to be so rewarding that you want to double down and expand your market presence, and change your business model and business plan in order to maximize your opportunity while it's hot and your competitors haven't figured out what you're doing.

How Your Company Operates at Level 2

In the marketplace war zone there are generally four types of business operations. The first has a poorly performing owner-operator who is selling or servicing a limited-demand product or products. This company's likelihood of success is nonexistent. The second has a good owner-operator who is selling or servicing a limited-demand product or products. This kind of company can survive, but it will be a constant battle. The third type has a poorly performing owner-operator selling or servicing a high-demand product or products. This company's likelihood of success is average. That is, it will probably succeed but never attain its full potential. The fourth and final type has a good owner-operator who sells or services a high-demand product or products. It is only this kind of operation that's likely to not only be successful but, potentially, dominate its market.

This reality, however, raises the question of exactly what a well-run business is. That is, what traits does an efficiently operated company have that others do not? This is important because unless you know exactly what you're trying to create, you won't know how to create it. Ultimately, this is something you have to decide for yourself. To my mind, however, a well-run business is one in which the owner:

- Understands the importance of customers and communicates it to his or her employees.
- Values the importance of gross profit and manages the business accordingly.
- Is willing and able to explore alternative ways to add sales and gross profit.
- Establishes processes and trains employees to operate them.
- Works to make sure that every department supports the overall goal of creating and keeping customers.
- Understands the Facts of Business Life and applies them appropriately to the company's operation based on which of the five levels the company is on.

These are obviously not all the things the owner of a well-run business has to do, but you can use it as a starting point for creating your own list. Of course, creating the list is just the beginning. Once it's done, the next step, as is always the case at Level 2, is to develop the processes that will enable you to make sure your business does in fact operate this way. How your business operates is obviously a DNA function. So unless you have thought through how you want your company to run, and developed processes that are manageable and focus on results, your business will never operate the way you want it to. It's that simple—and that complex. And whether you like it or not, it's a reality of the war zone.

How Your Business Competes—The X Factor—at Level 2

Some people refer to the X factor as the "great intangible," and to a certain extent doing so isn't entirely unreasonable. The competitive spirit that makes some companies successful can appear to be something of a mystery. At the same time, if you want to compete successfully in the marketplace war zone, it cannot remain a mystery. That is, you have to make sure you know what it is and build it into your company's DNA. It's only by establishing this kind of firm foundation that you will be able to enter the war zone at full speed when you get to Level 3. But doing so requires you to take three steps.

The first step is to educate your staff about the level of competition in the market; what it will take to attract, sell, and keep customers; the necessity of being better than your competitors if you want to become successful and remain that way; and the part they must play if it's going to become a reality. Doing this makes it clear to them that you are serious about what you're doing, while at the same time showing them that the business won't succeed without their front-line knowledge of both the overall market and your competitors' actions.

The second step is to explain to your staff exactly why you have chosen the weapons you have to compete externally and how you're going to use them. This is because if the weapons are going to be effective, they must be backed up by your employees' actions. If you're trying to develop a professional image, for example, it is essential that your employees make sure your premises are clean and that they dress, act, and exhibit their product knowledge appropriately. This will enable them to understand that the business will have to be a coordinated machine in which they play an essential part.

The third and final step is to make sure your employees understand which skills you expect them to have and the tempo at which you expect them to work when dealing with both customers and each other. The reason these two items are so important is that if every one of your competitors is well run, and has equivalent products and prices, it's your employees' skills that will make the difference. The best way to bring this about is to explain the role processes play in the company's operations and the reason they are so important. At the same time, you should tell them how their performance will be measured, the benefits of performing well, and the disadvantages of performing poorly.

Being competitive clearly doesn't necessarily mean being the most aggressive. What it does mean is being the most competent, that is, displaying certain basic skills such as product knowledge, pride in professionally caring for customers' needs, and enthusiasm when dealing with customers. In other words, competitiveness begins with your marketing and advertising and ends with your staff demonstrating how well they are trained by doing what you expect of them. This is the daily blocking and tackling of business, and how well this is executed will be determined by your company's competitive DNA—the X factor.

Level 3: From Survival to Success

Being able to enter the war zone at Level 3 with a detailed plan of attack developed at Levels 1 and 2 gives your business an immediate advantage over a lot of your competitors. This is because you have prepared and planned, know the latest market facts (including some your competitors may not know), and have set your business up to attack a market opportunity backed up by well-thought-out internal processes. In other words, preparing in advance of entering the war zone not only enabled you to come out swinging and make sure your swings have an impact, it also made the chances of your succeeding much better. The importance of this concept cannot be exaggerated, nor should it ever be taken for granted. This is because the journey from the survival end to the success end of the spectrum can be a marathon, and it's a marathon most businesses do not complete. And in almost every instance, failure can be attributed either directly or indirectly to a lack of appropriate planning and preparation for the realities of the war zone.

Some companies fail as a direct result of something that happens or doesn't happen in the market. For example, a new business enters the market with a plan to undercut its competitors' pricing because they believe the market is price sensitive and will react favorably to this strategy. A few months into the strategy, sales are a bit better than expected, but the business is losing money, and cash reserves are being depleted because of the continual losses. The problem, of course, is that lowering prices lowers gross profits, which affects the company's ability to make money on the bottom line. The flaw in this business model is that the owner either misunderstood or underestimated the expenses the company would have on a regular basis and/or didn't understand the overall effect lowering prices has on gross profits or how lower gross profits affect net profits. Obviously, better planning beforehand would have, at least in part, alleviated these problems. Sometimes, in situations like this, it's possible to go back to Level 1 and start over, but the chances of being successful at it are not good unless the company has large cash reserves and the time for this new business model to develop and catch on in the market.

But companies also sometimes fail because they beat themselves. The war zone not only creates competitive pressure externally, as shown in the preceding example, it also creates pressure internally. And the problems that internal pressure causes generally come from a lack of preparation, planning, and process development, the result of which is chaos. And due to this chaos, the owner and his or her key employees are forced to concentrate on fixing the internal issues, which is never easy, and are seldom able to identify the core problem. The core problem, in turn, continues to resurface in a variety of guises throughout the business. Under these circumstances, because the owner is consumed with resolving internal problems, he or she has little time to focus on the external market, which means the company is less able to battle in the war zone.

Think of what would happen if the coach of a football team neglected to prepare his team for a game or plan for how it would attack its opponents. Without any predesigned offensive plays the coach would have to constantly be explaining what went wrong on the last play and wouldn't have much time to figure out what to do on the next. And if this weren't sufficiently chaotic, the coach would also be yelling at the players and the other coaches, the players would be yelling at the coaching staff, and in the end no one would have any idea of what to do. Business is just the same. Just as the onslaught of the opposing team in football exposes a team's weaknesses, the pressure brought on by war zone competition does the same to a business. And the more weak areas there are, the more time the owner and key employees have to spend shoring them up instead of preparing for what happens next. In other words, it isn't necessarily market competition that beats you—sometimes companies fail simply because of internal issues and pressures brought on by the war zone and by the lack of planning and preparation.

The goal at Level 3 is to become consistently successful. In order to do that, as we've discussed in other chapters, you have to develop a series of goals and objectives that will enable you to reach the point at which you consider the company to be a success. In the beginning, that is, at the survival end of the spectrum, your sales will be largely made up of "gimmes" due to your location, the fact that your business is new, and because people you know will buy from you. Some of your sales will also come from competitors whose operations are poorly run and who can't hold on to their customers. However, it's important to understand that as your business moves toward the success end of the spectrum, the realities of the war zone will in all likelihood slow your growth rate. As you work your way along the spectrum and grow your business, you will begin to challenge the better-operated businesses that have loyal and satisfied customers who will need good reasons to switch from where they are now to you. In other words, the more success and market share you attain, the more difficult it becomes to attain it. But just as planning is the key to successfully launching your business in the war zone, it is also the key to growing it.

The Benefits of Understanding the Marketplace War Zone at Level 3

- Understanding the marketplace war zone fosters a sense of urgency rather than a laissez faire attitude in both you and your employees.
- Understanding the marketplace war zone focuses your employees on what is expected of them, why, and what will happen if those expectations are not met.
- Understanding the marketplace war zone establishes individual pride in accomplishing specific tasks as well as group pride in the company's overall achievements.
- Understanding the marketplace war zone helps you show your employees what they must do individually as well as what has to happen around them to keep the businesses moving forward.
- Understanding the marketplace war zone enables you to not only make appropriate plans but also to make adjustments quickly if the market is found to be different than you anticipated.
- Understanding the marketplace war zone makes it possible for you to anticipate changes and make proactive strategic moves ahead of your competitors.

The war zone is essentially about success or failure. And it's not a friendly place, because you and your competitors both want the same thing—each other's customers and gross profit. What that means is that your customer base is never secure, so you have to be constantly on the attack. But the battle against your competitors is not the only one you have to fight. You also have to constantly push your employees to improve because the market and customers' demands competence, and the better your employees are, the better your bottom line will be. Neither battle is easy to win, but if you want to succeed, you need to win both.

The Products or Services You Sell at Level 3

The first rule of the marketplace war zone is: you can't beat yourself. There are enough ways for your business to fail without committing suicide. That means you have to make sure you have as much control as possible over everything within your control, and that starts with the product or services you sell. Either can be a powerful weapon and can be used both defensively and offensively, that is, inside your company and outside in the war zone.

The defensive use of your products or services is essentially dependent on your planning, preparing, designing processes, and making sure those processes are executed by employees who are skilled, well trained, and ready to handle the action at Level 3. In other words, by setting up your internal processes to back up your products or services, you are providing protection not just for them but for your entire business. Succeeding in the war zone is difficult enough without beating yourself, and since this is one of the few areas in which you can have control, it simply makes sense to exercise it. The offensive use of your products or services similarly depends on a number of factors. These include the skill of your employees in making sales, how competitive your company's climate is, your pricing strategy, the demand for your product or service in the market, the aggressiveness of your business, and how well your product is delivered to your customers and how it meets their needs. Your offensive weapons are on display every day, but in order to be effective, they require consistency in the way your business operates.

But at the end of the day, it's your products or services that customers come for and, hopefully, come back for. No matter how well your employees treat them or how efficient your internal systems are, if you don't have something customers want to buy, you aren't going to have much of a business, much less a successful one. A great example of this is Firestone tires. For years Firestone retailers had a reputation for quality, aggressive pricing, and selection.

But in the late 1990s, Ford Explorers had rollover issues and it was determined that Firestone tires were a factor in the rollovers. As a result, Firestone's business dropped off the cliff. Overnight, every Firestone dealer learned the importance of product and what the loss of customers and their confidence could mean to a business. Although this might seem like an extreme example, it's unfortunately not all that unusual. It does, in any case, point out the fact that in the war zone, if you don't have product power, you don't have anything.

How Your Company Operates at Level 3

If you look at virtually any successful company, you will see that a great sales operation invariably goes hand in hand with a good business operation. That means that in order for a company to move from the survival to the success end of the spectrum, the internal business operation has to do its part in supporting what is happening on the front lines of the war zone. That is, internal processes have to be effective and, perhaps even more important, relevant to war zone participants and your customers. Moreover, your talent, and the talent of your key employees, is reflected in the processes you design and how aggressively and enthusiastically your employees operate them. Processes bring efficiencies and coordination to any business and eliminate the problem of the "left hand not knowing what the right hand is doing," as well as the embarrassment and frustration that inevitably follow. Perhaps most important, how well your war zone processes operate is a major factor in determining whether you will achieve your net profit goal.

But having a well-run business is about more than just that, and the Firestone story provides a good example. The first casualties of the Ford Explorer problem were the Firestone owners who had sloppy business operations, and those who just relied on selling tires. Not surprisingly, the better operators were the ones who, prior to the emergence of the problem, not only sold tires but pushed their businesses to find other ways to make sales and gross profits, that is, those who diversified. In other words, the retailers who survived the storm were those who weren't dependent on just one item but also sold accessories, provided car maintenance, or offered other products or services. The point is that if a business is well run, it can withstand unforeseen events as long as its owner has learned to be innovative with its products and continually find ways to expand its business and profits.

How Your Business Competes—The X Factor—at Level 3

To succeed at Level 3 an owner obviously has to demonstrate his or her competitiveness to the market. That's a given. But an often neglected and important aspect of success is getting your employees to be equally competitive. The customer who walks in the door, calls on the phone, or sends an e-mail should be your employee's main focus. All owners want this to happen, but in practice it rarely does. And the reason it happens so infrequently is that your employees' performances are more important to you than they are to them. But there is a way to change that. It's called internal competitiveness, and it's another element of the X factor.

Virtually all professional athletes exhibit internal competitiveness. In fact, professional teams have it down to a science—the science of statistics. Statistics are fundamental to sports because they enable players to measure themselves and then work to become better, that is, more competitive. And it can work as well in business as it does in sports. By focusing on results versus expectations, both employees and their managers can see where the employees are strong and where they can improve. And since most employees want to improve, if you show them how to do it, they will repay you by becoming more competitive.

Another particularly good way to get your employees to be more competitive is to be more competitive yourself. Competiveness is like measles—they are both contagious. What this means is if you show your employees that you like a market showdown, and show them what and how they can improve, most of them will become enthusiastic and step up their game. At the same time, it's important for you to remember that, for an owner, being competitive doesn't come cheap or without risk. If you want more sales and profits, you have to be willing to take chances. For example, in order to increase sales, you usually have to increase your marketing and advertising budget, add more personnel, add to your inventory, or spend accumulated profits on equipment and other capital expenditures. In other words, becoming more competitive costs money, which increases your risk as well as your possible rewards. To my way of thinking, though, if you have an accepted product, a well-run business operation, and especially competitive employees, you should be "pushing the pedal to the metal." And there are a number of ways you can do that.

Among the less risky efforts you can make is to offer specials on certain products, expand your inventory and create a well-designed sale, or target a specific area in your market where sales have been weak in the past and you know you can improve on them. You can also become more aggressive in pricing and/or advertising on a product you're well known for in order to capture more market share, which will in turn draw more customers and give your staff the opportunity to sell them related products or services. However, if you are willing to take a chance—and you should be—there are more aggressive, and potentially more rewarding, efforts you can make.

One of these is expanding your business or adding new products or services. Expanding can mean adding another location or enlarging your current facilities, but either way you will give yourself the opportunity to increase sales, which in turn can get your employees excited about possible promotions, and raise their confidence level not only in the business's future but also about their place within the company. In fact, you can even get your competitors' employees—particularly the good ones—thinking about your company as an employment option. You can also add new products or services, like the Firestone dealers who sold accessories to go with the tires and offered additional services to their customers. The bottom line is that while expanding your business does mean added risk, it also tells both the market and your employees that you're a force in the market and that you're dialing up the competition.

Another, more aggressive way of increasing sales is to buy a competitor. In fact, this might be the most aggressive competitive move you can make. It is a strategic way to quickly add market share, customers, and, hopefully, some great employees. And if purchasing a competitor provides you with economies of scale, you can become more efficient overall and make both companies exponentially more profitable. It also means, though, that some competitors will step up their game to meet your challenge in whatever ways they feel comfortable, whether it be with price, selection, quality, service, or other means. Some of those competitors will be able to keep up, but some will fall behind. Even those who fall behind, though, can provide you with an advantage. Not only can you target their customers, their weakened states could make them additional opportunities for ownership.

Most people think of being competitive as having great prices, large inventory, quality products, or other similar characteristics. These all help, of course, but being competitive in business also means being internally competitive and getting better every day. Over time, your business's overall competitiveness sets it apart from most of your competitors and gives you the power and financial strength to take the war zone battle to others, on your terms, and make the kind of net profit you can be proud of.

Level 4: Maintaining Success

You will have attained Level 4 when your business has consistently achieved your net profit goals over a period of time. And when it does, you might think you can lie back and rest on your laurels. Unfortunately, you can't. The fact is that you still have a challenge to meet. That challenge is no longer trying to *become* successful but, rather, trying to *remain* successful. And this is a formidable challenge, because the trappings of success will more than likely have changed both you and your company. That is, the drive for success both you and your employees once had will begin to fade, so much so, in fact, that you could find yourself back at Level 3 fighting not for success but for survival. Unfortunately, there's nothing particularly unusual about this—it's a natural tendency. The constant fear of failing you once had will have been replaced by the satisfaction success brings. But as a result, the aggressive, competitive, fast-moving company you had when you were approaching the success end of the spectrum at Level 3 is not the same company you have now. In the war zone, though, your business is always under attack because competitors want your customers, just as you want theirs. And that means that you have to keep fighting, albeit with some different weapons.

Maintaining success essentially requires you to do two things. The first is to take what the war zone gives you, and the second is to not dwell on what the war zone takes away. That is, you have to be quick to adapt to new market opportunities and just as quick to respond to any problems that may arise. And doing so may require you to make internal adjustments, which in effect can mean changing the composition of your business. For example, being able to adapt quickly to new market opportunities means you should be constantly looking for ways to bring in additional revenue. This means that if you are a heavy-duty truck dealer, you could expand your service department from one working shift to two, which would not only attract some after-hours emergency work but would also help your current service customers by giving them the option to have their trucks fixed in the off-hours instead of having to bring them in during the day and lose a day's work. The new service shift would also require an additional shift in the parts department, which would mean additional parts sales, as well as other changes. This kind of change—that is, a change in the composition of the business—is typical of market expansion at Level 4. The point, of course, is that very little remains the same in business, and if you want to maintain your success, you have to stay on the top of the market so you can take advantage of what the market gives you and defend yourself against competitors who try to take what you have earned.

It's also essential that you understand that things can move incredibly fast in the war zone and that, accordingly, you will have to develop new battle plans. Doing so will require you not only to continue researching and studying both the industry and the market as thoroughly as you did at Levels 1 and 2, but also to make sure you don't rely on misplaced assumptions based on what happened in the past. By the time you get to Level 4, you may not be as lean and hungry as you once were, but there are others out there who are just as lean and hungry as you used to be. And since you have a successful business, they will take runs at you, just as you took runs at successful businesses when you were starting out. If you want to maintain your success, then, you must point your big weapons at them so you can either kick their butts out of the market or inflict enough pain on them to make sure they leave you and your business alone.

The Benefits of Understanding the Marketplace War Zone at Level 4

- Understanding the marketplace war zone enables you to recognize the pitfalls of success and counteract them.
- Understanding the marketplace war zone enables you to review your business in light of mistakes that have been made and develop plans to avoid such mistakes in the future.
- Understanding the marketplace war zone allows you to define new success points based on your experience and knowledge of the market and to take your company there.
- Understanding the marketplace war zone makes it possible for you to overcome the apathy of the success comfort zone by developing new strategies and adding new, high-energy managers to your team.
- Understanding the marketplace war zone enables you to redefine opportunities that were unachievable or unthinkable at the survival end of the spectrum and take advantage of them with your new strength.
- Understanding the marketplace war zone helps you protect your company from beating itself out of its past gains.
- Understanding the marketplace war zone gives you the opportunity to begin considering what will happen when your new success objectives have been accomplished and what your next market move will be, and begin planning for it.

The Products or Services You Sell at Level 4

By the time you achieve this level, your product or service—as well as your business—will have been fairly well established. You also will have a good understanding of what customers want in terms of their tolerance for pricing, likes and dislikes, and expectations. Now, taking advantage of this understanding, you have to either enhance those products or services that are already widely accepted or develop new ways to create revenue and gross profit using those products or services as a weapon.

One way to enhance an already existing product or service is to look for natural add-on items that are likely to interest your customers. Amazon and iTunes do this particularly well by recommending books or songs other people who purchased what you're looking at have bought and, of course, making it easy to purchase the additional items. In fact, iTunes takes this a step further by also listing the most popular songs by the artist whose song you are considering buying. Similarly, Pandora Internet Radio asks you to rate a song by giving it thumbs up or down, and when you have, opens a window that lets you connect directly to iTunes so you can buy it. This provides sales and gross profits for both companies, a win–win all around.

Another means of bringing in more revenues and gross profit is to find and/or create ways to increase your customer-to-contact ratio, that is, to convert more contacts into sales. In base-ball terms, this would mean increasing your batting average by working on your swing or preparing yourself better for each pitch. In business it means increased training for your sales presentations, being more focused on the benefits of your product or service and on buying from you rather than a competitor, offering daily specials, or giving employees bonuses for improvement. In fact, just letting your employees know that you are monitoring their performances is likely to result in increased sales per customer contact.

These tactics represent only a few of the many ways you can bring in more revenue. It's important to remember, though, that increased performance in the war zone depends not only on your external efforts but also on the internal efforts you make to support them. For example, your marketing and advertising budget affects the number and quality of customers you attract, so the more money you spend, the greater your sales traffic is. But in order to capitalize on this added traffic, you may need more inventory, additional personnel and training, new or revised operational controls and processes, and/or enlarged or additional facilities. And all of these, of course, have to be planned for, which takes time, coordination, and patience. While you are likely to know this because of your past war zone success, what may come as a shock is how expensive it is to accomplish and how growing your business increases the risk due to the additional investment you're making.

How Your Company Operates at Level 4

At Level 3, "the office"—that is, what I refer to as business operations—tends to take a backseat to products or services, sales, and gross profit. At Level 4, though, it's essential that you pay more attention to the office because the better your internal operations are, the more competitive your business can be. Put another way, if your costs are lower than your competitors', your net profit will be higher on a sale-for-sale basis. And having more profit than your competitors can be a powerful weapon when and if you choose to use it in the war zone.

There are many ways that business operations can take the lead in helping your company increase efficiency, bring down overall costs, and increase net profits. It can, for example, analyze existing contracts and competitively shop them when they become due, find ways to create economies of scale within the business, and negotiate for bulk purchase pricing, as well as others. Any and all efforts like these can help provide you with increased profits and, in turn, a competitive edge that your competitors may not be able to duplicate. Finding a competitive edge like this isn't necessarily difficult, but you do have to look for it, and most owners at Level 4 do it as diligently as they can, because they know how powerful an effect it can have on profits.

However, while finding ways to increase efficiency and bring down overall costs can provide you with an additional weapon, it's important that you do it without jeopardizing your customer's experience or interfering with your other war zone activities. Let's say, for example, that your operations manager comes and tells you that by releasing two of your customer retention employees and hiring an outside service to handle the activity, the company could save over $50,000 a year in payroll and benefits. On the surface, this sounds like a compelling argument. The flip side, however, is that you would be giving up oversight and losing control of one of your most important business functions. Successful owners know that making decisions based only on expense can actually cost more in business than the saving you thought you were going to realize. The point is that at Level 4, it is particularly important that business operations function as an integral part of the company and its efforts to reach its goals.

How Your Business Competes—The X Factor—at Level Four

When Hollywood bad boy Charlie Sheen described himself as having "tiger blood," he was essentially defining competitiveness. But Sheen's tiger blood isn't what's required at Level 4. What's required is the competitiveness of people like basketball's Michael Jordan, football's Bart Starr, NASCAR's Jimmy Johnson, track and field's Wilma Rudolf, and hockey's Sidney Crosby. All of these people were or are great athletes and great competitors. What makes them great is their work ethic, their desire to be the best, and their ability to win by bringing their teams along with them. Even more important, instead of resting on their laurels after they became successful, they overcame the trappings of success and rededicated themselves to become even more competitive. It's this same spirit of competiveness that drives Level 4 owners to do what needs to be done to maintain their continued success or make their companies one of the great privately owned businesses.

There are, however, two major headwinds that make this competitive push difficult. The first, and biggest, of these is you. Just getting a business to the point at which it is consistently successful tires most owners out, and the thought of trying to take it to another level is sometimes just overwhelming. However, it's the willingness to take this additional step that's an important ingredient in maintaining success at Level Four. Some owners don't want to take this step because they're content with just being consistent in their profits, and care little about being the best or the most dominant in their markets. Some owners, however, want to dominate and become the benchmarks others aspire to. If you are in this latter group, however, the best way to get what you want isn't necessarily to work harder but, as the old saying goes, work smarter.

Working smarter starts with identifying the very top owners in your industry and learning what they do that makes them so successful. The next step is to move outside your industry to find out what best practices other industry owners use to be the best. Doing so essentially enables you to find common best practices you can put into effect in your own business. In addition, in the process of communicating with great owners, new ideas can be born, explored, and, if applicable, injected into your company. The net effect of all this effort, interestingly enough, is that it gets you motivated and reenergized and fires up your competitive juices. In the end, though, after finding other owners' best practices, getting advice, learning new ways to do old tasks, and reenergizing yourself, it still comes back to one thing—the X factor, that is, having the determination and the guts to do something that few others do.

The second obstacle you're likely to encounter is, not surprisingly, some of your competitors and their strength and determination to dominate the market. That's because they don't want to lose their grip on the market any more than you do, so when you launch an attack, they are going to react; that is, they're going to fight back in order to maintain their own positions. Even so, you have an advantage at this point that you did not have when your company was still trying to become successful. Your relatively weak financial condition when you first started out, and your lack of seasoning in the war zone, made you vulnerable in a way that's no longer true. That is, now that you've had years of consistent profits, you're in a much better position to attack your competitors using smart marketing techniques you have developed during your time in the war zone.

Earlier, in the discussion of Level 3, I made the point that the war zone requires owners to be both defensive—meaning the internal side of the business is operating on all cylinders and supporting your marketing efforts—and offensive—by attacking the market. This is important at Level 4 as well because as the internal side of your business improves and best practices are added, those improvements becomes unique to you and in turn become one of your offensive marketing weapons. In other words, however you choose to attack the market, you have a weapon few, if any, competitors have. At Level 4, this weapon is more often than not found in the efficiencies and innovations your business has developed. And in practical terms, that means your business will have significantly higher sales revenues than your competitors.

This strength in the market gives you a tremendous amount of flexibility in how you choose to attack your competitors. You could, for example, tackle the entire market using a shotgun approach and attract customers from many if not all of your competitors. Alternatively, you could be more tactical and target just a couple of your competitors with the overall objective of hammering away at their strengths and eventually weakening them. Attacking your competitors as I've described it may seem cold, but this is the way the war zone is—if you want to grow your business, you have to take it from someone else. As I've said before, the market is finite, so the law of the jungle prevails—be strong or die.

Of course, as at every other level, you do not go into battle without a plan. Also as at every other level, that plan must incorporate the products or services you sell, the way your company operates, and, especially, how your company competes. In developing this plan, it is essential that you follow these guidelines:

- Make sure you're well prepared, that is, that you've done the research, know the market's strengths and weaknesses, and know how to use them in your attack.
- Develop unreasonable sales, gross profit, and net profit goals, and then back them up with a very high level of offensive support.
- Create strong financial incentives for your employees to help motivate them to work with you to obtain the results you want.
- Support your employees' and customers' expectations with asset expenditures geared toward internal efficiencies and

customer satisfaction. In other words, put your money where your expectations are.

- Pound at the market's strengths and opportunities, as well as your competitors' strengths and weaknesses so you can focus your time, money and efforts where they will bring you the greatest returns.
- Give your employees all the support, training, and leadership they need, and react to any failure to achieve objectives as a challenge to improve.
- Have patience and strength and be ready for a wild ride.

Level 5: Moving on When It's Time to Go

There is a saying that all good things must come to an end, and it's as true of ownership as it is of everything else. And the war zone plays a significant role in that. Being able to compete successfully in today's marketplace requires a lot of effort, and eventually the time, energy, money, and other resources you have to expend on it can get to be too much. Of course, very few owners wake up in the middle of the night and say, "That's it. I'm done." More often, what happens is one day they realize that charging up yet another hill is going to take more energy than they have left, and that's when they make the decision to move on.

As I've said repeatedly, the best time to exit a business is when you don't have to, and if you don't choose when to exit yourself, someone or something else will. One of those "something else's" is the war zone and the toll it takes on owners. In fact, even though every owner who steps aside does so for his or her own reasons, the vast majority of those reasons are connected to the war zone, either directly due to the day-to-day competition owners have to face or indirectly due to the internal issues that arise from the war zone.

Of course, every successful owner has a choice when the time comes to leave—he or she can sell the business, pass it along to a son or daughter, or just close the doors. If you choose to pass the business along or simply close up shop, the war zone will make no further demands on you, except to maintain what you've accomplished until you pass it on to your successor. Ironically, though, if you choose to sell your business you will soon find yourself, at least temporarily, in an entirely new war zone. This war zone is different because it's one you basically have to go through alone, without the help of your business team, so it's entirely up to you to make sure the process moves along. It's also up to you to make the final decision, which can be the most important decision in your ownership career. Interestingly, the situation is very similar to the one you faced when you first went into business yourself.

You do not, however, enter this new war zone as soon as you've made a decision to sell. First, you do what you have already been doing for years—you think through what you have to do, then you make preparations and plans. This means you decide how best to showcase your company and make it ready for sale, develop criteria for picking your best candidates, create a list of those with the ability to pay, choose whether you want an asset or a share sale, and put together the information your potential buyers will need to evaluate the business, among other things. The point is that, just as you have throughout your ownership career, you don't go into the war zone, even this different one, until you are as thoroughly prepared as you can be so you can maximize your payout potential.

That's because the ultimate goal in this new war zone is to sell your business for the most money possible, and under the conditions that you consider optimal. In order to accomplish this, the three elements of the war zone—products or services, operations, and competition—have to be operating on all cylinders as well as coordinated with each other, which means your business should be running as smoothly as possible. The best way to guarantee this happening is to make sure your products or services are being aggressively marketed, your operations are backing up your offensive efforts in order to attract, sell, and retain as many customers as possible, and your employees are continuing to exhibit competitiveness at every level of the business. In addition, you will want to develop an understanding of how these three elements factor into the exit decision, both separately and in coordination with each other at this level.

The Benefits of Understanding the Marketplace War Zone at Level 5

- Understanding the marketplace war zone enables you to recognize and deal with war zone fatigue.
- Understanding the marketplace war zone allows you to think about what comes next in your personal life and factor it into your exit decision.
- Understanding the marketplace war zone allows you to evaluate all the pros and cons of selling the business, passing it along, or closing it.
- Understanding the marketplace war zone gives you time to prepare your business to be attractive to potential buyers if you choose to sell it, or to a successor if you decide to pass it on.
- Understanding the marketplace war zone enables you to learn about the professional side of selling a business, the tax consequences, and the legal issues involved.
- Understanding the marketplace war zone makes it possible to prepare for the new war zone and develop a selling process that will enable you to get and maintain control over it.

The Products or Services You Sell at Level 5

At Level 5, the product you are selling is your business. And as with any product or service, market preparation has to begin by focusing on price. In fact, deciding how much you want for your business should be your first step. In most cases, the money you receive from the sale will have to last through the remainder of your life, so if the company's value doesn't match your financial needs, you have to determine where to go from there. You options include holding off on selling the business until you can build up the value of the company, negotiating with a new owner for you to stay on for a number of years as a paid employee, or selling the business and finding a job elsewhere, among others.

It is essential, of course, that you have a clear idea of how much money you want to receive for your business before you start negotiating in the new war zone. As I've already mentioned, the price of a business is usually determined on the basis of three factors: the value of the company's assets, the value of the company's real estate, and goodwill, that is, the company's yearly net profit multiplied by a certain number of years. Once you have determined what you consider to be a reasonable figure, you should find someone you know and trust in the industry, or an attorney or accountant who deals in buy/sell contracts, to get a second opinion on the value of your business. This is important because an owner's opinion of his or her business's worth is usually more optimistic than the actual market value. Once you have worked out a reasonable valuation, the next step is to see a banker or lender you trust to discuss the sale. The banker or lender should be able to tell you what type of individual or business would be able to afford to buy your company, what he or she would look for in a candidate who wants to borrow money, and what your company's strengths and weaknesses are as far as he or she is concerned. This is a step that sellers often miss, but it's an essential one because it helps clarify who would be an ideal candidate for your business.

The point is that your product and the market price for a business like yours go hand in hand; that is, the better the business is operated and the more money it makes, the more valuable it will be to a buyer. And the better the business, the more demand there will be for it, and the more banks will be willing to lend money to someone who wants to buy it. As you've learned in the war zone at earlier levels, greater demand generally means higher prices because there will be competition for the product—in this case, your business. And it's when you get to this point that you enter the war zone at Level 5.

At the end of the day, then, the real war zone issue is how much you get paid for your business; the rest is just semantics. Unfortunately, deals like these are rarely finalized without some bumps along the way. But if you have a qualified buyer, it's your responsibility to take a leadership role and keep the negotiations moving along. After all, the product is yours to sell. Hopefully, you will be able to strike a deal with the first serious candidate you talk to, but even if you can't, the exercise will be good practice for the next buyer you take into the war zone.

How Your Company Operates at Level 5

As was just noted, one of the keys to a successful sale is making sure all three of the elements of the war zone—products or services, operations, and competition—are operating on all cylinders. What that means for business operations is that the company must continue running as it has all along, even with the distraction caused by the rumors that inevitably fly around the office as well as the overall market. There are two important reasons for this. The first is that it shows the prospective buyer that the business can run successfully without your active participation on a day-to-day basis. This is a major selling point because it means the business will not collapse around him or her as soon as you leave.

The second reason is that no sale is final until the last legal document has been signed and the money is in your bank. And the fact is that things happen during negotiations that can not only put a deal on hold but even stop it altogether. Let's say, for example, that you are negotiating the sale of your company and there is another earthquake in Japan, which keeps you from getting critical parts for your product. In a situation like this, it's possible that your buyer will say that it's your problem and suggest you contact him or her when your business is back to normal. It's also possible that the buyer may decide at the last minute that your business is not for him or her. The point is, if negotiations stop for any reason, the more smoothly your business is operating, the easier it will be for you to slip back into your ownership role and keep the company doing what it's been doing all along—running well and delivering profits.

How Your Business Competes—The X Factor—at Level 5

Competitiveness—the X factor—was an integral part of your company's success in the war zone at all the previous levels of business, and it serves the same purpose at Level 5. But there is a difference. At the earlier levels, both your competitiveness and that of your employees played a role in your success. At Level 5, though, it's primarily your employees' competitiveness and drive for success that's so important, because it's that attitude your buyer wants to purchase. In fact, when your employees demonstrate their willingness to compete in the war zone, it can be every bit as powerful a selling point as showing positive sales, gross profit, or net profit trends.

How do you demonstrate a company's competitiveness? One way is by showing potential buyers how well your employees can attract, sell, and deliver the business's products, as well as maintain contact with customers. Another is to demonstrate your processes and how efficiently your employees operate them. Not only do such demonstrations give your potential buyers confidence in the business, it also helps justify whatever price you're asking for the company. Perhaps the best way to make sure potential buyers see all of this is to walk them through your business and point out what happens in different areas of the company, how you or your managers keep track of expectations, and in turn how each department supports the others in a coordinated way to achieve the expected outcome.

■ ■ ■

The war zone isn't for everybody. And even among those who are willing to enter it, no two will attack it in quite the same way. But the reality is if you don't recognize the war zone for what it is, and what it can do to benefit—or damage—your company, your business model will have a serious flaw that will cause your business to seriously underperform, if not fail altogether. In order to be a success in the war zone, your business has to be focused on three elements—the products and/or services you sell, how your business operates and supports your offensive weapons in the war zone, and the X factor, that is, how competitive you are. Each of these elements is an integral part of war zone success, and together they make the point that success is far more than just aggressiveness in marketing. In fact, it requires many different skills, including leadership, planning, control, and all the other Facts of Business Life, as well as understanding how to navigate your business as it moves from one level to the next.

Fact 7: You Don't Just Have to Know the Business You're In, You Have to Know Business

Being an entrepreneur is about making choices. Even this book is a result of choices made. For example, I have chosen the seven most important and relevant business concepts owners need to understand in order to be successful. They don't cover every aspect of business, but that doesn't mean the business disciplines I didn't choose to discuss aren't important. It simply means that some concepts are more important to business owners and their success than others. In fact, the more you know about business in general, the wider your overall understanding of business becomes, and the more likely you will be to attain the kind of success you're looking for.

This hasn't always been true. In the past, if you were an expert in your field, even if you had only a limited knowledge of business outside that field, it was possible for you to be business success. For example, in the 1950s, 1960s, or even 1970s, if you were a good car salesman, you could be a candidate for owning an automotive franchise. Today, though, car manufacturers judge candidates much differently, using criteria such as overall experience in business, strong capitalization, understanding of the importance of customer satisfaction, personal background, experience in leadership, and skills in accounting and finance, among other business abilities. That is, they look for well-rounded individuals with track records of business success. The reason for this, of course, is the enormous change that's taken place in the market over the past 50 years. The increased demands of customers and employees, as well as the increased challenges of the marketplace and the pressures of a changing war zone, have forced owners to become more knowledgeable, more innovative, and more focused on their customers and employees than they ever had to before. And since this heightened level of competition is not going away, there will be more and more pressure on owners to comprehend a broader range of business issues.

Of course, it isn't possible for any individual owner to know everything there is to know about business. Even if it was, having that much information in your head would probably gridlock your brain! What's most important, though, is not how much you know but what you know, and what you do with that knowledge. For example, it's important to know what's going on in your market, but it is just as important to know what to do with that information and how you can translate it into more sales and gross and net profits. This knowledge will come from many sources, like learning from mistakes as well as successes, mentors, books, speakers, and, of course, your successful peers in other markets. In the end, though, it's your responsibility to make sure what you're learning is correct, as well as relevant.

The Benefits of Knowing Business

- Knowing business enables you to recognize areas in which you are less knowledgeable and seek help in them.
- Knowing business means understanding you can't know it all, but you can hire good employees who do have this knowledge, and then use your combined knowledge to build a great company.
- Knowing business enables you to make better hiring decisions because you will know what questions to ask of candidates and be better able to evaluate their answers.
- Knowing business helps you evaluate your employees' performance and be better at selecting those to groom for more responsibilities.

- Knowing business helps improve the odds of your making a good decision because the more you know and the wider your business perspective, the more information goes into making the decision.
- Knowing business and understanding how all its elements are interrelated helps you build your staff into an effective and efficient team that can move your company quickly from the survival to the success end of the spectrum and on to Level 4.

The Realities of Knowing Business

- Ownership requires expertise in areas most nonowners and underperforming owners don't appreciate.
- Knowing all there is to know about your industry is a good start, but it's not enough.
- Thinking you know it all, or acting like you do, is the first step toward problems in the future.
- The more you learn, the more you realize how much you don't know.
- The more you know about business, the better your chances of survival and success.
- Making mistakes is expensive, but as long as you learn from them, it will have been worth it.
- You always need to know the score, or at least have a very good idea of what it is, and the more business you know, the easier it is to read the scoreboard and react to it.

■ ■ ■

There are essentially four elements that owners should consistently pay attention to in order to round out their understanding of ownership or entrepreneurship. We have dealt, at least to some extent, with all of them before, but it's in this fact that we focus in on them. These four elements are product, people, accounting and finance, and, finally, you, the entrepreneur.

Product

Although product is something I've discussed in virtually all the previous chapters, the fact is that you can never underestimate its importance or forget that it should always be a focal point. One of the main reasons for this is that product and the potential of an opportunity are joined at the hip and together drive net profit. For example, if you had a product that was designed specifically to be used on the NASA space shuttles, your market would be very limited and controlled by the number of shuttle flights. However, if you had a product that could be used in both military and commercial airplanes, your market would be significantly broader, as would your opportunity for success.

Product represents the sum total of all a company does to attract and sell to its customers. That is, your business can do all the right things, but doing all the right things is irrelevant if there is little or no demand for your product. It's also essential that you always consider not just the demand for your product today but what the demand will be well into the future. For example, 10 years ago there were relatively few people who could have imagined the effect electronic books would have on the dynamics of book buying and the sustainability of the brick-and-mortar businesses that depend on books to attract customers. In situations like this, not recognizing the possibility of a decreased demand can mean more than a loss of sales revenue and profits—it can mean the loss of everything you have worked for, including the value of your business.

People

As an owner, employees represent not only one of your biggest concerns and costs, but also one of your biggest opportunities. The problem with people, however, is that they are people, and open to all the faults and attitudes human beings have, faults and attitudes they tend to bring to work with them. As one of my colleagues once told me, there is nothing like going to the storage room looking for an old file and finding two of your employees half naked on the floor. But you've got to love them, because they do make it so interesting—and challenging.

It's been said that it's an owner's responsibility to "motivate, educate, and entertain" his or her employees. And if there is one thing that's true about a company's owner and its employees, this is surely it. It's also been said that "Good owners are created, not born," and I believe that's true as well. But some owners clearly have a God-given ability to be great motivators and educators and to do both entertainingly. If you have this ability, it's a valuable tool, and if you apply it skillfully, you can help employees who are only average performers become excellent employees by teaching them to maximize their abilities through a combination of confidence, knowledge, enthusiasm, and understanding that their daily performance matters to their coworkers, their customers, and the business.

This ability to motivate, educate, and entertain creates something owners without these skills can't duplicate—transforming their business from a company to a team. Getting your employees to perform different tasks at different levels, and coordinate their efforts to focus on the same objectives and goal, is a beautiful thing. Unfortunately, this kind of teamwork is commonly uncommon in business, just as it is in sports. One of the main reasons success eludes some businesses and sports teams while others enjoy continued success is the ability of a coach or owner to motivate, educate, and entertain. And doing so not only differentiates your business from your competitors, it also gives you a major market advantage.

Accounting and Finance

It is nearly impossible to evaluate an opportunity or effectively run and grow your business without doing financial projections and understanding your financial position. Unfortunately, although virtually all owners know this, many do not have strong accounting and finance skills, and accordingly don't have the knowledge they need to match the demands of their businesses. To make matters worse, many owners rationalize their weakness in this area by telling themselves they can hire someone to look after it, and do little to improve themselves except, hopefully, learn when they make mistakes. But no matter how much an owner rationalizes his or her lack of knowledge in this field, there are two underlying factors that can't be rationalized away. The first is that if you can't measure it, you can't manage it. And the second is that in order to know where you're going, you have to know where you are.

There are other reasons that support the importance of understanding accounting and finance, but for an owner who is serious about being successful, these two factors say it all. Although most owners don't start out with a strong background in the "numbers," there are lots of ways to improve your knowledge. One way is to take your banker to lunch, ask what the bank looks for when making loans, and get him or her to explain how they analyze your statements. You can also ask your accountant for an hour of his or her time to teach you the basics. Neither of these will make you a "numbers" pro, but they are good starts, as are the numerous online courses and free information available on the Web. It's important to remember that ownership is a career and should be treated as such.

You

To my mind, too little is discussed about the successful owner. Because our businesses are private, little is known about us, except for what we choose to let our staff and customers see. While a lot is written about what owners have to do, little is said about how we view business, what drives us, what our concerns are, and so on. For example, some of us never lose the fear of failing. Many people believe that once an owner achieves success, that fear evaporates, but the truth is that sometimes it's the fear of failing and losing what we have that drives us to keep going. One thing is certain: what joins us—being owners and entrepreneurs—is also what separates us. What we share is having money and pride on the line, but beyond that most owners have different business styles, talents, goals, concerns, and dreams, all of which show up in how we operate our businesses.

Owning a business is more of an art than a science, because at times the owner has to feel his or her way through a mine field. Look, for example, at the difference between entrepreneurship and sports. Sports have easily recognizable rules, statistics that show how well everyone is doing their job, specific goals, and obvious accountability. Rules offer parameters within which to operate, the goals are clearly visible, and a scoring system offers immediate feedback so everyone knows how well they're doing, both individually and as a team. Entrepreneurs, however, have only the rule of law to work within, and have to create their own rules, goals, and means of measuring performance, whether it's on a daily, weekly, monthly, or even yearly basis. In business, too, every day is game day, with little time for practice—except on the job. In other words, while owners have the "freedom" to choose how they want their businesses to operate, with that freedom comes an enormous challenge, a challenge that, unless you have a good understanding of business, can be very difficult to meet.

Level 1: Ownership and Opportunity

Level 1 is always a mental concept, or preparation, level, where ownership and opportunity are analyzed and evaluated before determining what action should be taken. And in that respect, this fact is no different than any of the others. What is different about this fact is that instead of focusing on a particular aspect of business, it covers a wide range of important ownership issues. As a result, when combined with the other six facts, it allows you to make more informed Level 1 decisions by providing you with a broader perspective that enables you to use previously unknown business criteria to gather additional information and, accordingly, improve your chances of making the right decision.

As I have pointed out throughout this book, it is essential that you always let facts guide your decisions. But what makes ownership and opportunity decisions so difficult to make is that even when all the facts are lined up, not everyone will see it the same way. A perfect example of this is a story a friend of mine once told me. Many years ago, the president of a shoe manufacturer sent two men to study the market in the Amazon Basin of South America. One morning he received a cable from one of them saying, "No one here wears shoes. Selling shoes would be disaster." Later on that afternoon, though, the president received a cable from the other man: "No one here wears shoes. Huge opportunity. Must move fast." In other words, while the facts are clearly important in making any decision, what's also extremely important is the person making the decision. And the truth is that the more you know about business and its many disciplines, the clearer the facts will speak to you. That's why you don't just have to know the business you're in, you have to know business.

Most people understand this concept in general, but it can get confusing. Let's say, for example, that your cousin Vinnie asks you to invest in his new computer repair business, but he doesn't have any experience repairing computers or, for that matter, in any other business. Family responsibilities aside, you'd probably tell him he was nuts or fake a heart attack and tell him your health won't take the stress. However, if Vinnie had 10 years of experience as a computer technician and was generally regarded as one of the best in his field, you'd listen to him when he told you about the great opportunity for competent computer repair people. He could make a persuasive argument based on his knowledge of the industry and the work he knows.

This, however, is where the confusion comes in. Vinnie may be able to discuss the opportunity based on what he knows, but he can't explain in dollars and cents how much cash will be needed because he hasn't been exposed to that part of the business. He also can't tell you how good the opportunity is from a profit standpoint or how the business will grow. And, finally, he can't conceptualize what needs to be done from an organizational standpoint to make the business operate properly. Going into business without this kind of information is a mistake new owners often make, and it's something that must be considered when ownership and opportunity are being analyzed. The fact is that, although Vinnie may not realize it, fixing computers is only one piece of the pie where ownership and opportunity are concerned, and unless he takes the other pieces into consideration, the chances he will fail are high.

In other words, while Vinnie may be an extraordinary computer technician, unless he familiarizes himself with other aspects of business, he's going to have a problem. He would probably be fine as long as he's the only one doing repairs, but if that's the case, the company will never be able to grow and all he will have done is buy himself a job. Once he starts hiring other people to repair computers, answer the phone, handle Internet inquiries, do the books, and even clean the office, he is no longer a computer technician but a businessperson, which is something he knows little about and may not even want to do. There is no escaping the fact that if you don't know business and its various concepts, you are setting yourself and your business up for failure, not because you were wrong about the opportunity, but because without a general understanding of business, you're not ready to be an owner. That's why it's so important to take this into consideration at Level 1.

The Benefits of Knowing Business at Level 1

- Knowing business enables you to evaluate ownership and opportunity decisions from a broader perspective.
- Knowing business helps you understand the importance of making a correct decision as well as the costs of getting it wrong.
- Knowing business enables you to discover your weaknesses and find ways to overcome them, before you go into business or expand an existing business.
- Knowing business helps you realize you don't have to know it all, but you do have to be willing to admit it and find a way to upgrade your business knowledge.
- Knowing business provides you with a better chance of recognizing an opportunity because having a broader perspective could enable you to see an opportunity that you might not have otherwise seen.
- Knowing business makes it more likely that you will be able to create an opportunity because you have more tools to work with in your toolbox.
- Knowing business helps you understand that ownership and opportunity have to work in conjunction with each other, and that in most cases having one without the other means failure.

Product at Level 1

Since product is what your business offers the customer, it speaks directly to the question of opportunity. Opportunity, in fact, is a measurement of the demand for the product. For that reason the two are essentially joined at the hip, so without one the other has little meaning. Since Level 1 is a preparation level, one at which your business is still only a mental concept, the goal is straightforward. You have to determine the continuous demand for the product and find out if the demand is strong enough to produce adequate profits. And the more you know about business in general, and how successful businesses operate, the better your decision is likely to be.

For example, if you are an owner who has only industry-specific knowledge, the chances of your knowing and understanding product innovation will be remote. While it's true that product innovation can mean different things to different people, in this context it means how you differentiate your business and products from your competitors and their products. And product innovation is one of the key concepts you should review at this level because it speaks to expanding the opportunity beyond the present, that is, it addresses not just what your company will be offering its customers when you first open the doors, but also what it will be offering them in the future.

Here's a good way to look at product innovation. It might seem that a shot of Jack Daniels is the same at any bar, a Toyota Camry is the same from one dealer to the next, and watching a movie is the same regardless of which movie theater you go to. The fact is, though, they're not. That's because product isn't just about what a customer buys, it's about how his or her needs are served. A shot of "Jack" tastes a lot better if it's served in a clean glass and delivered by a friendly bartender, as opposed to one who hasn't shaved or combed his hair in days and looks like he's been up all night sampling "Jack." The point is that customers have expectations, and when these expectations are met, it separates the winners from the losers. That's why some businesses selling the same product excel, some do just all right, and others fail. The key to product innovation lies in your creativity, your willingness to compete, and your not letting the thought of constant innovation and changes intimidate you. But unless you understand the importance of knowing business, you may never appreciate the importance of product innovation and the role it plays in opportunity.

People at Level 1

Since at Level 1 the business doesn't exist yet, it might not seem like people or employees are an important factor. The fact is, though, that considering your potential staff and the type of talent you will need is something you need to do because it speaks to your ability to manage them, which in turn speaks to your ownership ability. This is an important point because if you're starting a new business or expanding one, you will have to recruit some experienced people, and both your knowledge and ability will be evaluated by those you recruit. Similarly, if you're buying a business, the current employees will be judging your every move and every statement. The question you have to ask yourself, then, is whether or not you're ready for this challenge and/or scrutiny. If, as an owner, you can't lead, market the business, and "motivate, educate, and entertain" your employees, the strength of the opportunity will be of little importance because you'll never get there.

One of your responsibilities as an owner is to tell your employees how you want them to execute their jobs. But you also have to be able to back it up through determination, persistence, and a willingness to discipline those employees who don't do what you want. In regard to the question of ownership, then, you have to honestly evaluate whether you will be able to do this consistently. *Consistency* is a key word because owners and managers often have a different view of how things should be done than their employees do. That means conflicts are going to occur, and they will need to be settled. And it's the willingness to address those conflicts that separates the good owners from the poor ones. In other words, the tail can't wag the dog, and if you're not willing to mix it up with employees on occasion, you shouldn't become an owner. So your ability—or inability—to deal with people is something you need to take into consideration in making the ownership decision at Level 1.

Accounting and Finance at Level 1

Up until now, I have not singled out accounting and finance as a subject of its own, although I have made numerous references to it, because I wanted to make it clear that it doesn't represent a separate discipline but one that is woven into the fabric of your business. Unfortunately, despite its importance, it's one of the subjects owners and entrepreneurs understand the least. As a result, there are many owners who should have been successful but never were because they didn't understand how important it is.

At Level 1, accounting and finance come into play in the opportunity analysis in two areas, cash and profits. We all know the saying "cash is king," but the reality is that some owners don't really understand why it is so important, particularly at this level. One of the reasons is that cash—or more correctly, the lack of it— can keep you from becoming an owner in the first place. Unless you have it, or have access to it, the likelihood of fulfilling your dream of starting or buying your own business is pretty remote. Moreover, the larger the business you want to buy, the more cash you will need to buy it.

In addition, even if you have enough cash to start or buy a business, you will need still more cash to operate it until the business is bringing in enough money to cover your expenses and provide a profit. In other words, "cash is king" means more than just having cash available. It also means having a solid understanding of how much overall cash will be needed to operate the business on a day-to-day basis, and of the positive and negative effects cash can have. Let's say, for example, that you believe there is sufficient market demand for you to buy an expensive piece of equipment that will create more sales and gross profit. The question, then, is whether you should buy the equipment outright, finance it through your lender, or lease it. This is a "cash is king" decision. If you buy the equipment outright, the cash drain on your business could be severe, but if you combined cash with some financing, while it would increase the breakeven point, it would also enable you to keep more of your hard-earned cash. The point is that you have to take these considerations into account in making such decisions, because not understanding their impact can create serious financial difficulties.

Most business owners actually understand this concept, but making it work in the real world is a different story. In order to do so at Level 1, you need to familiarize yourself with the use of three essential financial tools: the cash flow analysis, the income (or profit-and-loss) statement, and the balance sheet. The cash flow analysis is a tool that tells you how much money has come into the business, how much has been spent, and how much remains. Without the cash flow analysis you would be operating in the dark in terms of what you should and shouldn't do as far as using cash is concerned, and that's a dangerous spot to be in even for a successful owner.

The second tool, the income (or profit-and-loss) statement, shows you sales revenue, cost of sales, gross profit, expenses, and net profit. This tool is essential because it enables you to see how much net profit you've made. In addition, when you are looking at an opportunity, it can show you how lucrative the opportunity may be based on certain facts, such as normal expenses, or educated assumptions, such as sales revenue and gross profit, and tell how much money drops to the bottom line. That is, by "playing with the numbers," you can get a feel for various levels of sales revenue, gross profits generated from those sales, and expense levels, to determine where your breakeven point is. Without this knowledge every scenario becomes a surprise, and that's not the way successful businesses operate.

The balance sheet, the third tool, shows current and long-term assets on the left side of the statement and the business's liabilities and net worth on the right side. The reason it's called a balance sheet is that the asset side of the page has to balance with the liability and net worth side. This tool essentially provides a picture in time that shows you, at the time it's prepared, where your cash is located in terms of current and fixed assets, your working capital, net worth, and retained earnings. Having this information is important because it provides you with basic facts about the business's operation, such as the amount of cash on hand, receivables, business liability (including payables owed), and others. In addition, it's a good tool to understand because most lenders rely heavily on the balance sheet for their lending criteria. In fact, it's a more important document than most owners realize, because it can be the determining factor in a lender's decision to give you money to buy or expand a business.

The bottom line, figuratively and literally, is this: if you don't use these financial tools at Level 1 to analyze an opportunity in terms of how much cash is needed and how much profit is available, you haven't done an adequate job in analyzing your opportunity decision. And in that case, you will be operating more on the "I hope this happens" theory than on the one that suggests "opportunity is there, I just have to make it happen."

You at Level 1

By now, you may have made up your mind about ownership and opportunity, or at least have a pretty good idea of what your decision will be. I do, though, have a further word of advice: this is not the time to be impatient and hurry your decision. If you don't take all the various considerations into account, and rush toward either starting a business or giving up on the idea, you will more than likely have neglected to take into account one of the most important elements in the ownership and opportunity decision process—you. This is because of all the many questions you have asked yourself in trying to make the ownership decision, it really comes down to one overriding question: "have I really been honest with myself?"

This is not the time to let the fear of the unknown get in your way. It is, however, the time to reanalyze and question your abilities, your determination to succeed, and your commitment to compete every day. Entrepreneurship is serious business played by serious people, and if you want to be an owner or expand your business, you need to consider that you will eventually come up against owners like me who don't want you to be successful and are committed to growing their business at your expense. And if you can't honestly say that you feel up to the challenge, ownership is not for you.

There is also, however, one more reality you have to face in regard to the ownership decision. Some decisions in our lives are not based on facts but driven by some unfilled need. This need is what pushes you toward the success you have defined for yourself, mixed in with some pride and a bit of ego. At times it can be overpowering and therefore dangerous. Would-be or current owners wanting to grow or expand their businesses have to recognize this drive for what it is, hold it in check until all the facts are in, and control it when analyzing their circumstances because it can make a questionable opportunity look attractive. And finally, if after you've done all the analysis, you continue to see the risk side, walk away because you might be right.

Level 2: Creating Your Company's DNA

Every successful business has goals and objectives they want to achieve. The trick, of course, is to make these goals and objectives a reality, which is a formidable challenge. One of the things that makes it such a challenge is that in order to get your company to where you want it to be, you have to get your employees to do what you want them to. In other words, although your employees are an integral part of your achieving your goals, it is still up to you to determine how your business operates, and you can't leave it to chance or to your employees' interpretation.

As I discussed earlier, in successful companies, processes operate the business and employees operate the processes. That is, processes tell employees the "what" and "how" of their jobs, as well as help coordinate the activities of the overall business. But there is a rub, which is what makes this fact so important at Level 2. The rub is that the more you know about business, its principles, and concepts, the better the processes you develop will be, and the better your business will operate. But the opposite is equally true, so if you want to run your business as effectively and efficiently as possible, it's important that you have a good overall understanding of all the various facets of business.

As I've also said before, very little in business operates in isolation, which means that virtually anything that happens in one part of your business will have an effect on some or all of the other parts. For example, if you don't watch your accounts receivable you can quickly find yourself short of cash to pay your employees or suppliers. Similarly, if the individual responsible for ordering your stock doesn't order sufficient quantities for the demand, your sales will be affected. In other words, a problem in one department can create additional problems not only in another department but throughout the company. We've all heard the expression "the left hand doesn't know what the right hand is doing." When that's said of a business, it means the owner does not understand that business principles are interrelated and that, in fact, success depends on knowing what both hands are doing.

The Benefits of Knowing Business at Level 2

- Knowing business helps you develop a stronger appreciation of the importance of goals and objectives in the development of processes.
- Knowing business enables you to understand that the most effective processes are those developed by combining industry knowledge, overall business knowledge, and experience.
- Knowing business shows you the benefit of analyzing both mistakes and successes because both add to your understanding of how best to operate a business.
- Knowing business shows you the importance of continually upgrading your business knowledge as well as understanding how it applies to your business.
- Knowing business enables you to understand the importance of having a good basic understanding of accounting and finance as well as of its influence throughout the levels.
- Knowing business provides you with a deeper appreciation of how the three "P's"—process, product, and people—are interrelated, and how this interrelationship develops the fourth "P"—profit.

■ ■ ■

The point of this Fact of Business Life is a simple one—the more you know about business, the better your business will operate. However, a lot of owners do not appreciate its importance, and it's primarily because most of them know their businesses well. I know that on the surface this doesn't seem to make sense, but it's true nevertheless. These owners confuse knowing what they do well with knowing how to run a business and, as a result, are totally unprepared for the decisions and problems they have to face as owners. Owners in situations like this often become frustrated and disillusioned with their decision to become owners, but are nevertheless reluctant to walk away from their investments. It's a tough situation to be in and one with few options. If, however, you understand the significance of the four elements of knowing business—product, people, accounting and finance, and you—your chances of success will increase several-fold.

Product at Level 2

Although it's seldom understood as such, how your employees act and perform their jobs is an extension of the products you sell, manufacture, or service. The reason it's so rarely understood is that many owners don't realize product is tied to two important overall success goals: to create sales and generate your desired gross and net profit, and to make sure your customers are sufficiently satisfied with the product and its delivery to come back and buy from you again.

Product plays a key role in achieving both of these company goals, but in order for it to do so, you must draw on the other Facts of Business Life to maximize its sales and gross profit potential. For example, you have to draw on the defensive side of marketing (that is, your internal processes) to support the offensive side (that is, attracting and selling customers) to make sure the product is delivered the way you want—and the customer expects—it to be. Similarly, it falls on accounting to guarantee that your products' sales will be accounted for accurately. You also have to draw on leadership to make sure your employees are trained to do their jobs properly. And you must rely on several facts, including those concerning marketing, controls, and the war zone, to see to it that slow-selling inventory will be minimized and not tie up cash that the company needs to grow. All of these issues relate to product, and all of them rely on effective and efficient processes.

Perhaps the best way to see the difference that understanding the interrelationship between the Facts of Business Life makes is to show how two different individuals might create processes for their products. The first, someone with years of experience in the same industry but with little training outside his or her specialty, might design a process like this:

1. Order the product.
2. Accept delivery and set up an inventory stocking system.
3. Sell the product.
4. Reorder the product.

It's a simple process, and it would work. However, an owner who has a deeper understanding of the various aspects of business and how they are connected to each other would probably set up a process like this:

1. Determine the dollars available for inventory and products.
2. Order products with a sales plan in mind based on the money that's available and the anticipated gross profit from sales.
3. Receive the products, balance them against what you ordered and were charged for, and fix any discrepancy.
4. Set up an internal system to determine both fast- and slow-turning inventory, as well as to track gross profit from actual sales.
5. Continuously compare actual sales to forecasted sales and gross profit.
6. Sell inventory from a predetermined step-by-step sales process covering everything from greeting a customer to closing the sale.
7. Proactively attack the problem of slower-selling inventory in order to minimize its potential loss rather than waiting until it becomes stale and creates a drain on gross profits and cash.
8. Readjust the inventory value based on actual sales, and readjust the inventory itself to concentrate on what sells and delivers gross profits.

I can go on, but I'm sure the point is clear. If you have any doubt, just ask yourself which business you would like to invest in, or which business you think will perform better and attain success first. It should be obvious that the second process has definite advantages over the first in that it not only takes into account a wide range of the Facts of Business Life but also guarantees that both the right and the left hands know what the other is doing. In fact, a lot of businesses have failed or underperformed, not because their products weren't in demand, but because their products were not coordinated with other important operations, including selling, accounting and finance, control, and others. This example also speaks to the goals of Level 2, that is, to create sales and generate your desired gross and net profit, and to make sure your customers are sufficiently satisfied with the product and its delivery to come back and buy from you again.

People at Level 2

In the introduction of this chapter, I said that employees are both one of your biggest concerns and one of your biggest opportunities. In fact, there are two respects in which they must be a concern. The first has to do with what can happen if you rely on a few key employees for your success. Putting all your eggs, so to speak, in one basket is never a good idea. In this particular case, those eggs can quit, go to a competitor, or tell you to stuff it when you tell them how you want your customers handled. In other words, if you count very heavily on a small group of employees, they can put you in a box that you can't allow yourself to be put in. That is, you can wind up giving them the run of the business at the expense of the processes you've established, your beliefs, your control, your goals, and ultimately your success. This may seem unlikely to you, but the fact is that the problem is much more prevalent than you would think.

The second issue, to my mind, is at least as serious as the first. It concerns how employees react when owners exhibit what appears to be a double standard in regard to how they treat those who don't follow the processes the owner has established. When an owner behaves like this, it makes him or her look weak in the eyes of others, including those he or she is favoring. Moreover, it makes others employees question the owners' commitment to follow through with any serious penalties for not doing what they are expected to do. And if this isn't bad enough, even in the best of circumstances, such behavior can only lead to frustration and constant complaints among the staff.

While it is certainly true, as I mentioned earlier, that owners have to "motivate, educate, and entertain" their employees, when attitudes are corrupted like this, little motivation or education will occur, and the entertainment you provide will be exactly that—entertainment without substance. If you're a one-dimensional owner, that is, if your knowledge is confined to your industry and/or to your specialty within the industry, it will be impossible for you to understand the consequences of your decisions or how they will affect your employees until you get blinded with a sucker punch.

Of course, since at Level 2 your business is still in the planning stages—that is, you are just starting to develop the processes under which your company will operate—it would seem that you needn't concern yourself with issues like these. In fact, though, if at this level you remember that very little in business takes place in isolation, and that whatever decisions you make will have ramifications, you will be able to recognize in your own mind that behaviors like this can create problems, and make sure that you do not allow such problems to surface when the business is actually in operation.

Accounting and Finance at Level 2

The "office," as I think of it, is the place from which, and to which, all your business's information flows. In other words, your "office" is the heart of your business. As an owner, it's your responsibility to determine how to use the office and what demands will be made on it. However, if you don't have a good understanding of business in general, you won't know what's needed to help operate the business and won't be able to make the appropriate demands. And if you don't know what demands must be made, you will not be able to exercise control over your business, and will find yourself facing unpleasant surprises month after month.

For example, owners who don't have strong business experience tend to be unsure of how to control expenses, which is as important as sales and gross profits because of the effect expenses have on net profit. The key to control in this instance is to start thinking of expenses as occurring when you approve them rather than when you pay them. In other words, you should set up a process that covers all the business's purchases and funnels them through the office for your—or one of your trusted employee's— approval before the purchase is made. Of course, this is just one example of the kind of controls that need to be put in place. The point, though, is that unless you have a good overall grasp of business and understand how the various parts of your business interrelate, you will not be able to set up such controls.

You at Level 2

In one way or another, your business and the way it operates is a reflection of you. If your business is disorganized, it will reflect on you. If your employees act in an unprofessional way, it will reflect on you. And if you allow any kind of questionable activities to take place in your business, that will reflect on you as well. But if you, as an owner, don't understand how the various Facts of Business Life work and depend on each other, you will be helpless when it comes to operating and overseeing your business. The problem essentially is that on a certain level, it all comes down to you.

At the same time, a business can't be a one-person show. You can't work all day bringing in sales revenue, then work to all hours of the night purchasing supplies, doing the accounting, and so on. Well, actually, you can, but that's not owning a business—it's being a slave to it. To become successful you have to rely on others to do their jobs, and that's the catch. In order to know what their jobs are, you have to be able to define them, and before you can define them, you have to understand their importance to your business and your success. For example, you may know everything about selling your product or service, but that means you have to rely on others to make sure they order what you want to sell, inventory it, account for it when it's delivered to your business, track it as it moves from your stock to your customers, and so on. But unless you understand how important all those functions are to the successful operation of your business, you will not be able to oversee them effectively.

The bottom line is that in order to create your company's DNA, that is, set up the processes you will need to operate the business successfully, it is essential that you have as broad a background in business as possible. If you don't, your tenure as an owner may be short lived. And even if you manage to survive, it certainly will be extremely frustrating and painful as you try to solve issues that you are unequipped to deal with.

Level 3: From Survival to Success

Whether you're starting, buying, or expanding a business, or reinventing the way your business is run, Level 3 is the point at which you start implementing all the plans you made at Levels 1 and 2. In other words, it's where you switch from theory to reality. But no matter how well you have planned and prepared for the reality of entering the market, there is a catch. And the catch is that the market will stay the way it is only for a short time. The reason, of course, is that things change. And it's these changes that make it so important for you to not only understand all seven of the Facts of Business Life but, even more important, how they relate to and support each other. The better you understand this, and the more you operate your business accordingly, the stronger your company will become, and the quicker it will move from the survival to the success end of the spectrum.

In fact, unless you do understand this, you will inevitably run into problems. Let's say, for example, that your business has a great product, but you don't really appreciate the importance of Fact 1, If You Don't Lead, No One Will Follow. And because of that, you haven't emphasized the importance of product to your employees, so they have little sense of purpose or understanding of the product, and it doesn't get very much internal attention. The result, of course, is that the business's product takes a secondary position to other, less important activities, such as a manager having a conversation with an employee while customers are waiting and phones are ringing. Similarly, if you have a poor sense of Fact 5, If You Don't Market Your Business, You Won't Have One, and as a result don't market the company aggressively, few people will be attracted to it. But even if your marketing is great and you're attracting thousands of potential customers, if you don't understand Fact 6, The Marketplace Is a War Zone, and make sure your employees understand it, too, you will never be truly successful. In fact, the real secret of success, and the one that every successful owner knows, is understanding the importance of these facts both individually and as an interrelated and interdependent group.

It's also important to remember, though, that any group is only as strong as its weakest link, and when pressure is applied to that weakest link, it will give out. This concept applies to ownership as well as it does to everything else. What this means for an owner is that problems are most likely to occur in the facts where they are their weakest because they are restricted by their knowledge and are unable to see the problems developing. The results of this can vary from being a continuous and annoying problem to creating a catastrophe. However, when owners have a good understanding of all the facts and of how they are connected, the strength of the facts becomes greater than the sum of their parts.

Benefits of Knowing Business at Level 3

- Knowing business enables you to understand how all seven of the Facts of Business Life are interdependent and interconnected and how you can use their combined strength to build your business.
- Knowing business helps you recognize problems as they arise and take steps to stop them before they become more serious.
- Knowing business makes you better prepared for the road ahead, better able to analyze what happened when something does goes wrong, and better able to permanently fix it.
- Knowing business helps you focus on moving your business forward rather than dwelling on what went wrong in the past.

- Knowing business helps you understand that when you realize your success goal, more opportunities will appear due to
  the maturity of the business and your increased knowledge
  and experience in using all seven Facts of Business Life.

Product at Level 3

As your business goes "live" at Level 3, you will inevitably come face
to face with two inescapable—and related—truths about product.
The first of these is that at times it feels like you have very little
control over your product and its sales. And, unfortunately, sometimes it's true. For example, you can't control how your competitors
market their products, or how aggressively they attack the market
and promote themselves against you. In addition, since competition
usually dictates the selling price of products, your gross profit margins are also essentially controlled by competitive pressures.

The second inescapable truth is that products are rarely successful unless the owner understands and applies all the Facts of
Business Life to them. In other words, products cannot stand on
their own, and even good products die without internal help. For
example, how your business advertises and markets your products
and how effectively it's done will have an effect on sales. Similarly, if
you have few controls in place for supporting your product, you will
probably experience shortages of your faster-selling products and
inventory overages on your slower selling ones, both of which cost
the business money.

So while it's true that as far as product is concerned your control of the competitive marketplace is limited, what isn't limited is
how you can control your product internally. And, in fact, if you do
it right, this internal control—that is, applying the Facts of Business
Life to your products—can be used as a very effective competitive
weapon. For example, if you have a Wal-Mart-type competitor that
has lower product costs and can therefore charge lower prices, you
can use what you control—expenses, internal processes, product
knowledge, and training—to fight back. Unfortunately, if you don't
realize that product, its sales, and its gross profit depend on other
business principles, you'll find out the hard way—while you're competing in the war zone, and hopefully before it's too late.

People at Level 3

There is no more important time in a business to constantly "motivate, educate, and entertain" your employees than when you are starting a business, taking over an existing one, or changing the way your business is operated. The reasons for this should be obvious: it's the difference between teaching employees how to do their jobs and what you expect of them, and just telling them what you want and leaving them to figure the rest out for themselves. At Level 3, then, in regard to people, there are two things it is essential you do as an owner.

The first of these is creating an atmosphere of success. You do this by finding ways to remove, or at least limit, the kinds of things that employees feel get in the way of their doing their jobs well. Let's say, for example, you have a saleswoman who feels her sales are low because of the business's lack of marketing and advertising—in other words, providing herself with an excuse for her lack of productivity. By simply pointing out that other salespeople are doing well and that your business spends as much on marketing and advertising as your comparably sized competitors, you can eliminate the excuse and get to whatever the real problem is. Similarly, you might have a service technician who complains about the type of work he's being given compared to other technicians. If, however, you point out that the other technicians have more training than he does, as well as greater knowledge of the proper use of certain tools, you can make it clear that it's his own lack of initiative that's holding him back and disqualifying him from getting better-paying work. By doing this you can eliminate any—or at least most—excuses employees may have for not performing up to your expectations and focus them on making sure they do.

The second thing you have to do is be courageous. If there are people in your company who are not doing what you expect of them, it's actually fairly easy to ignore them. Being an owner, though, is not about being easy, it's about constantly improving your business. Even so, it does take courage to stand up for yourself, especially when, as is normally the case, there are more of them—that is, your employee—than there are you. Of course, most of us like to avoid confrontations when we can, but if you do so in this kind of situation, you will be neglecting to provide the leadership your company needs. And without leadership, it's unlikely that your business will improve, which in turn means it will probably underperform, if not fail altogether.

There are also times, though, when owners don't act courageously not because they want to avoid confrontations but because they don't understand the importance of leadership and how not

More of Them than You

It was in the fifth or sixth year of our ownership of a business in Texas that we began getting disturbing news from the informal employee grapevine about some possible thefts in a department that employed about 10 people. Two of our managers took it upon themselves to investigate and set up a minor sting operation. The results of the sting showed that the employees and their manager were from time to time bringing unauthorized vehicles into our service department, using company equipment and products to repair them, getting paid in cash, and then pocketing the money for themselves. It was clear I had to take some action.

This department was not only important to customers and other departments on a daily basis, it also impacted significantly on our gross profit. At first, hoping to find an easy way out, I tried to figure out some way to minimize fallout. But I realized taking such a tack would conflict with the DNA we'd created for the company, and as my past experience had shown me, not following my own rules would lead to a loss of respect and have a negative effect on how my managers would act or react if they were faced with a similar situation. Plus, I would miss an opportunity to send a strong message throughout the company.

I made a decision and called a meeting for the department's employee's one Friday evening right after closing time. I took the department's manager into my office, told him he was fired, and turned him over to the police, who were also present. At the same time, three other managers told the department's employees their jobs were terminated and why.

Doing that was not easy, but it enabled me to let everyone in the company know where I stood on certain issues. The message was clear. And in the end, we barely missed a beat. We got the department up and running very quickly because we were swamped with applications from our competitors' employees. And it was a good lesson for all of us—one I might not have been able to provide if I'd had less experience and less overall knowledge of business.

applying all the Facts of Business Life can have a negative effect on their entire business. For example, if you allow your employees to perform their jobs the way they want to rather than the way you want them to, you're going to have the "tail wagging the dog," and you can't allow that to happen. However, if you don't understand all the various areas of business, you may not even realize it's happening, and you can't fix what you don't recognize is a problem. Generally speaking, the more experience—and the more knowledge of business—you have, the more courageous you become, because you have a clearer understanding of the ramifications of neglecting to act when you should.

Accounting and Finance at Level 3

Since at Level 3 the business is "live," there is a lot of activity going on, particularly around your company's accounting department in trying to get its processes up and running. A mistake many owners make at this level is neglecting to take advantage of the financial tools I mentioned earlier in this chapter—the cash flow analysis, the income (or profit-and-loss) statement, and the balance sheet—to keep track of their financial condition. In fact, this mistake is one of the leading causes of early business failure. If for no other reason, it just makes sense to use these tools because they can alert you to possible problems before they blow up in your face. They can also help you make decisions because they provide the kind of information you need to make those decisions.

Specifically, the balance sheet helps you understand where your cash is located—that is, inventory, receivables, and fixed assets—as well as the effect your decisions will have on your cash position. In other words, the balance sheet gives you important information about your internal operation. The income (or profit-and-loss) statement shows you where you are in terms of sales dollars, gross profits, expenses, and overall profit or loss at a particular point in time. The benefit of having this information is that it enables you to see whether you've made money and, if so, how much. It also helps you determine what you can do to improve your company's revenues. The bottom line, then, is really the bottom line. That is, eventually everything flows through your business's financial statements, and if you know how to use them, it will significantly increase your chances of success.

You at Level 3

When your business is operating at Level 3, there are two situations in which you particularly do not want to find yourself, as least not for long. The first is operating at a pace at which your knowledge and talents can't keep up with your business's growth. Being in a situation like this may not seem all that bad at first, but it opens up the possibility of the wheels eventually falling off the bus, most likely due to poor decisions made as a result of inexperience and lack of knowledge. The second is not knowing how to "jump start" your business, that is, fix a problem when you have one. This problem, too, is a result of an owner's having only a limited knowledge and/or understanding of business. Unless you take action quickly to remedy this lack of experience and knowledge, the fate of your business will be fairly predictable, especially when you consider that the marketplace if full of owners who have more business knowledge than you do.

The point here is that, ultimately, it's your business, and how well it performs falls on your shoulders. No one is going to force you to do anything about improving your overall business skills. But unless you take steps to do so, it's unlikely that you will be able to move your company along the spectrum from survival to success. At Level 3, things can hit you fast, like an important employee quitting, a large customer refusing to pay its bill, or a sexual harassment suit being filed by an employee. And how you react to this kind of pressure sends a message throughout your company. If you react calmly, it boosts the confidence of all those around you. But if you "blow your top," particularly if you do it on a regular basis, your staff is going to start wondering what they've gotten themselves into. Ultimately, how you react is a result of how much experience and knowledge you have about business because when you have this knowledge, you know you have more options than getting upset, and you are more likely to stay calm, analyze whatever problems may arise, and gain control over them.

If you have any doubt about why it's beneficial to have this knowledge, you might think about it in terms of how your employees might describe you. How they do so not only says a lot about your business to their friends, relatives, coworkers, suppliers, and others, it also has an enormous effect on how they react to you and your ownership style. For example, I've always wanted my staff to see me as a fun-loving guy but one who is deadly serious about his business and the processes that run it. I also want them to see me as honest, fair, a motivator and educator, aggressive in the war zone, and unrelenting in demanding accurate information and delivering on expectations. Whether or not I achieved this is something only my employees can say. What I can tell you, though, is the more you know about business in general, the more your employees will recognize and appreciate it, and the more they will be not only willing but anxious to help you achieve your goals.

Level 4: Maintaining Success

It may actually be impossible to maintain success without understanding all seven Facts of Business Life and how they depend on each other. Without leadership, for example, a company won't have direction, and without direction, controls and management mean very little. Without planning, there will be no destination, and without a destination, any road will take you there. Similarly, instead of having a war zone mentality, your employees may develop its opposite, an "I couldn't care less" attitude, toward customers. And customers, in turn, will in all likelihood start staying away in droves. If you do understand business and its important concepts, however, while Level 4 will be a challenge, it will be no more of a challenge than what you have overcome in Level 3. As a matter of fact, the more you understand about business, the quicker you will discover the easiest path to maintaining success, and the sooner you will get there.

The first step in setting up your business to maintain success is to reevaluate both your internal and external environments. By the time you get to Level 4, since your business knowledge and experience will have expanded, your views on business and how it operates will have expanded as well. As a result of this increased knowledge and experience, you will see some of the decisions you made previously may not have been as good as they could have been. These decisions may have been made in leadership, control, asset protection, planning, marketing, the war zone, or any of the remaining areas of business, that is, in any and/or all the Facts of Business Life. For example, some of the processes you first created may actually be hurting the business in that they were not created with the customer and the company's goals sufficiently in mind. Alternately, an opportunity that you judged to be questionable in the past may now look both good and doable when viewed through the prism of your expanded knowledge and ownership experience. In other words, in reviewing your situation you are more than likely to find errors to correct, better ways to do things, and new opportunities to explore.

As I mentioned earlier, if on arriving at your success destination you decide to stay there and rest on your laurels, you will not be able to maintain success. Not only won't your competitors allow you to maintain your position, your customers' wants, needs, and expectations will change over time, which in turn will impact on your marketing, products, and war zone strategy, among other things. In other words, there is no standing still in the market. Whether you like it or not, it's the way it is, and it's out of your control. But there are things you can control, and if you want to maintain success, you must know what they are and how you can use them to your advantage.

There are basically two things you can do in order to maintain success, and all of them require you to exercise all of your knowledge of business. The first is to develop a market share strategy focused on small but continuous market share gains. This might include visiting an industry peer in another market to look for sales you may be missing in your own or testing the price sensitivity of a product by finding a way to lower your cost, then lowering your price accordingly to see if sales increases match the lowered pricing. You might also attack a particular segment of the market or look for a way to overpower one of your weaker competitors. This is a conservative approach to maintaining success in that it's focused on moving the business forward in a way that minimizes risk to the overall business. The downside to this approach is that it can feel like you're swimming against the current because your progress is slow when compared to the energy you are devoting to it. And, in fact, it's not your imagination. This is an example of what economists call the "law of diminishing returns," that is, as your market share increases, it takes more and more effort to move your business noticeably forward.

The second strategy you can use is to purchase a competitor or competitors, or expand your business to a significantly new level so you can permanently shift market share in your favor. Unlike the first strategy, this one can enable you to increase your market share immediately. However, using it also exposes your business to added risk because it generally requires you to take on more debt, which can become a company-wide problem if the expansion doesn't work. But if the expansion plan does work, the rewards are considerably greater, including increased market dominance, increased profits, and additional cash flow. If you are considering such a move, however, you must essentially go back to Level 2, Opportunity and Ownership, and do the same kind of evaluation you did when you were just starting your business. And if after that evaluation you find that the opportunity meets your goals and makes sense financially, you have to begin working your way through the levels again, one at a time, because if you expand your business or buy a competitor, you will not only have to redefine what success means but also determine how you will get there.

The Benefits of Knowing Business at Level 4

- Knowing business helps you understand and evaluate how best to maintain success and/or expand your business.
- Knowing business enables you to focus your new knowledge and turn it into added profits and market share.
- Knowing business helps you understand the numerous barriers to maintaining success, such as the law of diminishing returns.
- Knowing business helps you realize that market growth—or slippage—depends on the accumulated knowledge gained, and that the better you pass that knowledge on to your employees, the more likely you are to maintain success.

- Knowing business helps you recognize that some of the employees you have counted on may begin to disappoint you at this level, while others surprise you by stepping up their performances.

Product at Level 4

Whichever strategy you choose to maintain your company's success, product will inevitably lead the way. As I have pointed out before, the more natural demand a product has, the better the chances you have of succeeding. And it's no different in maintaining success. That is, the greater the demand, the easier it will be to maintain success because a great product and the gross profit it generates cover a host of sins.

As far as product is concerned, however, there is an important difference between Levels 3 and 4. At Level 3, your business and its products were offensive in nature, trying to punch a hole in the market big enough to allow your business to succeed. At Level 4, though, your product is both a weapon and an asset that needs protection, especially in the war zone, where you have to protect the market share you have already won. And this isn't something over which you have a choice—it's your reality. Every one of your competitors wants what you have, and you have no choice but to defend your position in the market. Actually, the stronger and more aggressive your attack on the market is at Level 4, the easier it will be to defend your product lineup. That's because if your competitors are busy reacting to what you're doing in the market, they can't be thinking about how they are going to attack your customers and market share.

To be honest, though, defending—and increasing—your market share is not easy to do, and it can't be done without understanding the effect your increased sales will have on your overall business. In fact, making an aggressive effort to maintain success is more of a balancing act than anything else. That is, by Level 4 you will have realized that business decisions have consequences, and little happens in isolation, all of which has to be taken into consideration. For example, being aggressive will mean your war zone strategy will have to be rethought because you're going for more sales. That means more money will have to be spent on marketing and inventory. It also means you will have to ramp up expectations of your staff, possibly even add people and then train them, to meet the increased demand for your product. That, in turn, means you will have to have more or at least improved controls, and that accounting and finance will have to make sure the proper information is flowing in and out so you and your managers can monitor important variables like gross profit margins on your product lineup, mix of business, cash flow, and others.

People at Level 4

At this level, there are some serious owner–employee issues you have to be concerned with. Until success has been achieved, it is essentially you who are leading the charge and making sure your employees are operating the processes the way you want them to and with the results you expect. But even before you get to Level 4, you can no longer risk the business being entirely dependent on you, and for three very good reasons. First, you can burn out and, despite your best intentions, start leading the business on a downward slide. Second, if you were to suffer a serious injury or worse, the business would lose its only leader. And third, if you choose to micromanage your company, you are likely to retard its growth because if everything has to go through you, everyone else has to wait for your decision before moving ahead. The answer to this problem is to develop and educate key staff members so their collective knowledge and talents can be focused on maintaining success. Basically, this means you have to remove yourself from any day-to-day operations, which is something some owners are reluctant to do. Nevertheless, if you want to maintain the success you've worked so hard to achieve, it is necessary.

The first step, of course, is to select appropriate employees to take over your responsibilities. This is usually not particularly difficult because by now you will have developed a very good sense of your key employees' abilities, as well as their ambitions. The difficult part, in fact, is molding these key employees to work as a team and get them to understand what you have learned—that a successful business depends on a number of business principles operating in unison. Perhaps the best way of doing this is to widen their perspective of the business by concentrating on teaching them about how the various parts of the business operate and interact with each other rather than focusing on their own departments. While it is possible for egos and/or attitudes to get in the way of this process, it is essential that you, as the owner, be prepared to take swift and decisive action if they do. Eventually, your employees will figure out that they need each other's wisdom to grow their departments, solve problems, and help move the business forward, and the result will be continued success for everyone involved.

Accounting and Finance

As I've already noted, the vast majority of owners would not list accounting and finance as one of their business strengths. However, after a couple of "rude" and expensive surprises and lessons learned, they begin to realize the value of financial analyses and the proactive power they give company. They realize, for example, that such analyses can protect them from making bad decisions based on wrong information and assumptions, or alert them to problems that need attention before they become crises. Accounting and finance can also help an owner fine-tune the business by proactively controlling expenses, working on inventory turns, identifying which products are hurting the business's overall gross profit margins, and generally providing the owner with "what-could-be" scenarios if he or she did this or that. At the same time, though, even having this kind of important information will be of little value to an owner who has limited overall business knowledge, simply because he or she won't know what to do with it.

All successful owners, depending on their experience and business knowledge, have certain "key" ratios, asset or liability balances they look for, or industry standards they measure themselves against. It's these warning signs and measurements, used skillfully, that can make the difference between a good business and a continuously great one. Benchmarking, for example, is a great way for owners to measure their business performance as it is usually a summation of their industry's best practices. In fact, for owners who benchmark and drive their businesses toward these key measurements, owning a great business may only be a matter of time and talent. What is perhaps most important is knowing what needs to be measured and what the measurements mean. And, again, unless you have a good understanding of business in general, you will not be able to do that.

In addition, sharing your knowledge of business with key employees and exposing them to accounting and finance is a great way to teach them how their departments work in conjunction with all the other departments, and how the success of one department helps the overall business achieve its goals. For example, by sharing how your managers' departments are measured by the company's balance sheet and profit-and-loss statement, you not only increase their knowledge, you show them how you are judging and grading them as well. Teaching your key staff members how everything in business is related changes their paradigms about the business, and generates efficiencies within departments that move the business closer to the benchmarks, positively affects the bottom line, and helps maintain success.

You at Level 4

One of the things that happens at Level 4 when you start letting your employees take on more responsibility for the company is that you begin to see yourself and your life as separate from the business. For the first time, in fact, you realize that your personal goals and the company's goals can be separated, and that's when you begin thinking about how you will exit the business. This is not to suggest, of course, that it isn't something you won't have thought about before. Rather, it's at this point that it starts to take on a reality it never had in the past, and it's now that your paradigm begins to change. That is, you begin to wonder how much your business would be worth if you sold it, or what you might need to do to make it easier for a successor to take it over. You are also likely to feel a greater urgency to increase both sales and profits, as well as look for other ways to add value to your business to make it more attractive to possible buyers or successors. Eventually, this change of paradigm leads you to define a new destination for the business, that is, new objectives and goals, as well as a new idea of what maintaining success means.

You may decide, when you first start thinking along these lines, that you're not ready to exit the business yet. Even so, it won't stop you from wondering what could be, or from focusing more carefully on how your business operates and how it generates its profits. In other words, you will begin to realize what happens from one year to the next has a new and different meaning than it did before. However, if your understanding of business is limited at this point, your ability to exit the business successfully will also be limited. You will not, for example, be able to identify who your best buyer is, point out the upside potential of the business to a buyer, or increase profits in order to maximize your payout. You also may not be able to choose the most appropriate successor or give that successor the best possible chance of success. In other words, as in virtually everything you do in business, the more you know about business in general, the better off you will be.

Level 5: Moving On When It's Time to Go

On one level, the decision to exit your business may seem fairly simple—you have to decide if the reasons to stay outweigh the reasons to go. Unfortunately—and perhaps not surprisingly—this is not as simple as it seems. In fact, as I've already discussed, there are a great number of issues you have to take into account when you're thinking about moving on. Some of those issues are of a more personal nature, but from a business point of view there is perhaps nothing more important than the question of valuing your business. And, perhaps also not surprisingly, the greater your understanding of business, the easier that valuation will be.

In determining the value of your company there are essentially two questions you must ask. The first is "how much is the business worth now?" As I've already discussed, there are three elements that have to be taken into consideration in valuing a business—assets, real estate, and goodwill. Adding these three figures together will give you, as close as possible, the amount of money your business is worth at the moment, which is the figure you will take into account in devising an asking price when you offer the company for sale. The second question you must ask is "how much will it be worth at some specific point in the future?" Determining this figure is considerably more difficult. The reason for this is that there are many more things that have to be taken into consideration. And this is where your general knowledge of business—or lack of it—comes into play. In order to calculate the future value of your company, you must consider the strength of the market today and in the future, how much your employees and processes are likely to improve over time, and how this will affect profits; and demonstrate through the profit-and-loss statement exactly how these positive changes will affect future profits. Beyond this, however, you should also take into consideration such items as the strength of your competition going forward, that is, their performance in the war zone; the life of your products (marketing); possible changes in the industry (leadership); maximizing the business's assets (asset protection); and others. The point is that determining a business's future value is not as easy as it might appear to be, and to do it well it's important that you have a broad understanding of the various aspects of business.

Being able to accurately value your company is not the only advantage of knowing business at Level 5, and some of the additional advantages are discussed later. What is ironic about all this, however, is that the more you know about business, the more complicated the exit decision becomes, but also the more likely you are to make the right choice. Conversely, the less you know about business, the easier the decision-making process will be, and the more it will be based on erroneous assumptions, unsubstantiated claims, and emotion, which is obviously not the way to attract serious buyers.

The Benefits of Knowing Business at Level 5

- Knowing business enables you to more accurately value your business today and in the future.

- Knowing business helps you use valuation as a "compass" by which you can determine the best direction to move your company in order to realize its maximum exit value.
- Knowing business shows you the importance of facing the inevitable, and gives you the time you need to set the business up for maximum payout, to create the best possible situation for your successor, or to close it down.
- Knowing business enables you to develop an appreciation of the many business concepts the exit decision entails.
- Knowing business helps you understand your exit decision is about business and not just about what you want and need.

Product at Level 5

If you don't know all the Facts of Business Life at this level, you will be severely limited in your understanding of the value of your product, that is, your business. And if you are, you will be handicapped in determining, creating, and explaining its optimal value to any potential buyer, whether you decide on an asset or a share sale. In fact, it could mean that your buyer will have a better understanding of the value of your business than you do, and that is not a position you want to be in. But it's a position a buyer would love to be in because he or she would then be given the opportunity to possibly "steal" your business. In business, knowledge is king, and not least of all when you are exiting it.

When you are selling your business as a product, the more you understand about business, your product, and your buyer, the easier it is to explain and justify the price. For example, if you can tell a prospective buyer about future opportunities and how your employees are trained to take advantage of these opportunities, and tie it into expected future profits, you can make a compelling argument that adds value to your business. Similarly, if you can explain to a competitor who is considering buying your business how the economies of scale will lower the overall costs of both businesses, and the profit windfall this could create, you are much more likely to get the optimal price for your company.

Having a good understanding of business is important if you choose to pass your company to a family member as well. Not only will it help you determine the best candidate to take over, if you pass along not only the company but also your understanding of business, you will be doing all you can to ensure his or her success. Bear in mind, too, that when there is a successor, the "fair value" of the business can become a family issue, especially if the successor becomes the owner. Others in the family will have to be convinced that their payouts are adequate compensation for their loss of the benefits and income from the business. In addition, the more you know about business—including issues like taxation, asset protection, and prospects for the future—the smoother the transition will be for you, your family, and the business.

Finally, if you choose to close your business down, you must remember that your business assets have value and should accordingly be sold for as much as possible. For example, your business's customers can have value to some of your competitors, so knowing who these competitors are and who would pay the most for this asset is obviously important. Similarly, if your business has been around for a while, your company's brand name may have value. In addition, knowing accounting and the difference between book value and market or replacement value can mean more money in your pocket. The point is that just because you're closing down your business doesn't mean the business assets don't have value, and the more you know about business the easier it is to determine which of those assets have value, what that value is, and who would pay the most.

People at Level 5

One of the basic facts of business is that successful businesses are invariably built on the relationship between a company and its customers. Most successful owners realize this, and when they can show prospective buyers their employees have good relationships with their customers it increases the good will or blue sky value of their companies. If, for example, when selling your business you can give the buyer confidence that it will continue to run as it has in the past, even without you, the higher your payout is likely to be. However, if you don't show a buyer that you understand the importance of people and processes in operating the business, it will likely be viewed as a flaw and probably result in a lower price being offered. Similarly, if your employees are poorly trained and exhibit unprofessional attitudes, a prospective buyer is likely to pick it up quickly, and to take it into consideration in making an offer, to your detriment. The point, of course, is that the more you know about business, and the more you make sure your people act the way they should to foster success, the more likely you are to realize the greatest amount possible from the sale of the company.

Your employees also play a critical role when succession is involved. No successor wants to lose good employees, their knowledge of how the business operates, or the relationships they have with customers. The best way you can avoid this is to do all you can to make sure the employees do not feel threatened by the change and to make your successor understand the importance of upholding the companies DNA. It is also essential that you give your successor the room to develop his or her own relationship with the key employees as well as with the rest of the staff, and not cast too large a shadow.

Finally, if you choose to close down your company, even though your employees will no longer have any business value to you, they will have value to the companies you used to compete against. Helping them find new places to work, and explaining their value to one of your former competitors will not help your business, but it's the right thing to do, and it's a gesture your employees will always appreciate, however things work out in the future.

Accounting and Finance at Level 5

Accounting and finance has a unique place at virtually all five levels of a company's life. From the creation of pro forma financial statements showing the cash needed and potential profits at Level 1, to providing support for your business's growth at Level 3, to helping you maintain success by alerting you to threats and opportunities at Level 4, to moving onto center stage as you begin developing and implementing your exit plan at Level 5, it is the one department that can tie all the business functions together. In addition, accounting and finance can describe and demonstrate how processes operate the business, how they work, and how they are controlled. What all of this means is that it is in a unique position to not only tell the story of the business's success but also to back it up with facts. And facts are what's needed whenever an owner exits because they help justify the value of the business to the buyer, to the owner's family if succession is chosen, and to whoever may buy the company's assets if it closes down.

When you are selling a business, for example, potential buyers will rely on those facts to make both their valuation and buying decisions. Buyers will also spend countless hours reviewing your financial statements, checking the balance in accounts such as inventory, and checking your business's use of generally accepted accounting principles (GAAP). This is critical for educated buyers because it tells them a great deal about the business, builds trust in what you are selling, and gives them an overall sense of how the business works and how it will work when you leave. This in turn gives them confidence, which will be reflected in how much money they will be willing to pay for the business. However, if your books are sloppy and don't accurately reflect the business, important questions will go unanswered because there are few facts to fall back on, except for whatever claims you may make, which will mean little without backup. And this, too, will be reflected in the money paid for the business. In other words, if you don't understand the power that financials have when selling your business, you will pay a huge price for it.

Accurate financial information is also important in a succession because it helps you justify the business's value to your family as well as back up any claims or questions. It also plays a role in calming emotions among family members, and is critical when an estate has assets to divide or sell, as well as when the government is to receive a percentage of your windfall. In addition, in a situation in which some members of the family know little about business and its complexities, if the information is accurate they can have an accountant review the business's accounting practices and satisfy themselves that they are being treated fairly. Not surprisingly, there have been many instances in which the lack of such information has resulted in families becoming divided.

Finally, as mentioned earlier, you may prefer to simply close your business down. In situations like this, the more you know about business in general, the better you will be able to improve the timing of your exit, prepare for it, and weigh your options and recognize what assets others may be interested in buying.

You at Level 5

Making the decision to leave the company you've spent years building into a successful enterprise is in many cases a very difficult one. And to make matters worse, there are several traps you can fall into while you are in the process of deciding when and how you should leave. The first of these has to do with age. As with virtually everything else in life, the prospect of leaving your business looks different at 30 or 40 than it does at 50 or 60. Not surprisingly, the idea of exiting usually seems considerably more viable at higher ages. Someone at 60, for example, who wants to exit before he or she turns 65, is likely to be a lot more receptive to offers, or more aggressive in finding someone to buy the business, than someone who is only 40. And, in fact, a majority of owners do use age to determine when they will retire. I believe, however, that doing so is a mistake.

To my mind, age should have very little to do with your exit decision. We are all programmed to think of retirement in terms of age because the vast majority of people work for someone else, whether it be the government, large publicly traded companies, or small businesses. But as an owner, and therefore self-employed, you do not belong in this category. Unfortunately, some owners fall into this age trap. But you don't have to. You should make an effort to be more aware of your business value, your health, your interest in continuing to operate the company, and what you want for your family. Only when you have taken these into account will you be able to make a truly considered decision. And if you do, you will be able to make the decision that's right for you.

Another trap that some owners fall into is an emotional one. The bottom line, so to speak, is that the more emotional you are about the exit decision, as is true of virtually all decisions, the more likely you will be to make a mistake. The decision to leave, as well as such decisions as how much to accept for your company or what kind of conditions are included in the contract, should be made with as little emotion as you can manage. Doing so is not always easy, but it's nevertheless important that you make these decisions the same way you made all the other important decisions in your career—carefully, intelligently, and dispassionately. In fact, having a good, strong understanding of business will actually help you do this because when all the reasons to retire are compared to all the reasons to leave, what appeared to be a difficult decision can become remarkably clear.

A third trap you should do your best to avoid in making the exit decision has to do with, for lack of a better expression, exhaustion. The reality is that most owners can only take a business so far, not from a lack of talent or knowledge but from a lack of energy, that is, not being able to maintain the continuous mental discipline needed to run a business or keep up with the constant change that is a given in the war zone. In other words, owners get tired, and some things that used to be easy become challenges, just as they do for professional athletes. No one likes to see a great athlete stay too long and embarrass him or herself, and it's the same in business. At some point every owner reaches the top of his or her game, and they have to recognize when this is beginning to happen and start making decisions based on what's good for them and for their businesses. Not surprisingly, the more you know about business, the more likely you will be to recognize when that time has come, and the more effectively you will be able to deal with it, regardless of how you choose to make your exit.

■ ■ ■

Knowledge, as the saying goes, is power. And that's as true in business as it is in every other endeavor. As I have essentially argued throughout this book, you don't just have to know the business you're in, you have to know business. In other words, while the first six Facts of Business Life are all essential tools for you to use in starting, building, maintaining, and eventually leaving your business, the seventh fact is ultimately the one that ties them all together.

The market is a very rough place, and there's no room at the top for people who aren't willing to do what has to be done to be successful. Ultimately, though, what is comes down to is owner vs. owner, and it's the owners who have the most business skills and knowledge who will always remain standing while their competitors wonder how they are able to do what they do so well.

Conclusion

Success—it's why owners do what they do. And one of the really cool things about success is that you have the freedom to define what success means for you and your business. Unfortunately, that freedom is also a trap. The trap lies in that if you don't define success for yourself in financial terms and map out how you will achieve that success, the odds of your business failing or having limited success are significantly higher. That's just the way it is. But it's your choice.

Success, in my mind, is made up of two macro realities. First, having defined what success means to you, you need to have the courage and drive to commit yourself to achieving it. Second, in order to improve and grow your business, you have to be willing to try new and different ideas and take additional risks. It's true that when you do this, mistakes—and even failure—will sometimes result. But failure can be a bittersweet pill because by learning from your mistakes and understanding why they occurred, you can turn them into opportunities you may have never realized existed if you hadn't tried to stretch and improve your business.

For example, after nearly 100 years, Babe Ruth is still a baseball icon, especially for the home runs he hit. The truth is, though, that while he hit an extraordinary number of home runs, he had nearly twice as many strikeouts. Even so, he would never have hit the home runs he did if he hadn't stretched his talent and learned from his strike outs. Michael Jordan understood this success/failure concept as well as any athlete has. He was cut from his high school basketball team, and was not heavily recruited for college. He's even admitted that, "I've missed more than a thousand shots. I've lost almost three hundred games. Twenty-six times I've been trusted to take the game-winning shot, and missed." But like the Babe, he took his mistakes, or failures, in stride, and used them to make him a better player. And the result, of course, is that he became one of the greatest professional athletes in the history of sports. And it's no different in business. If you want to succeed, you have to continuously challenge yourself and your business to improve. And if you don't, it will leave you and your business to the not-so-tender mercies of your competitors who do.

One of the other particularly interesting things about success is that, to some extent, it is an elusive target. It's not that you can't attain it, but rather, that as your ownership career develops, your definition of success changes. This happens because once you reach your success destination, moving on to another success destination doesn't look as formidable as it once did. It's the competitiveness in you, which continually drives you and your business forward, through Levels 3, 4, and 5. In fact, when most successful owners look back on their careers, they realize that where they finished is not where they thought they would end up. This happens because in your search to improve and challenge your business, you are essentially always changing your definition of success. And this, in fact, is one of the great benefits of being a business owner—having the flexibility to create something better, if you choose, and ending up with greater success than you ever dared to dream about.

There is one last point I would like to make. On the day you welcome your first customer, you will be beginning a marathon in which you will be competing not just against other companies in the marketplace, but against time. A successful ownership career is measured in time, usually decades, and it goes by faster than you can imagine, especially when you look back on it as I have on mine. You remember the successes and how they were achieved, and you remember the painful experiences and realize what you learned from them. You remember the great partners who teamed up with you, and the great employees who helped make your dream a reality. And you realize that all of these individuals changed your life, as you hope you changed theirs, knowing that together you beat the odds and proved wrong those who said it couldn't be done.

Ladies and gentlemen, start your engines. And enjoy the ride.

About the Author

A graduate of Mount Royal College in Calgary, Alberta, and the University of Saskatchewan in Saskatoon, William (Bill) McBean began his career with General Motors of Canada Limited (GM) in 1976. After holding several management positions with GM, in 1981 he accepted a position with the Bank of Nova Scotia (ScotiaBank) as manager of a sizeable commercial lending portfolio. Two years later, however, GM approached him about opening a new automobile dealership in Yorkton, Saskatchewan, and, along with ScotiaBank, offered to lend him the required capital. Accepting the offer, he started the business the following year, and it became profitable from the outset.

Although the Yorkton business became one of the most profitable GM dealerships in the region, in 1992 McBean was presented with an even greater opportunity in Corpus Christi, Texas, where he and his friend Bill Sterett purchased an underperforming automobile dealership. Applying his business expertise, McBean not only turned the company around, but bought out several additional poorly-performing import and domestic automobile franchises. Under his leadership, the company grew from $32 million to $160 million in sales and from 75 to 300 employees over a period of 11 years. During that period, the car manufacturers he represented continually awarded him and his companies honors for business excellence. Because of its success, the automotive group attracted the interest of several major public companies, and in 2003 was purchased by AutoNation, the world's largest automotive retailer.

Both before and since selling the group, McBean has started several new businesses, and he is currently general partner of McBean Management, an investment company. He is also executive director and chairman of the board of both Our-mentor.com, which provides mentoring to business owners (including buying and selling companies), and Net Claims Now, which provides companies in the restoration industry with invoicing, collection, and business lead-generation services. McBean and his wife, Lynnda, reside in both Texas and Florida.

Index

A-list products, 239, 243–244
Accounting and finance, 283–284,
    289–292, 298–299, 305–306,
    318–320
Added value, 107, 186
Advertising, 7
Amazon, 156, 211, 267
Apollo 13 mission, 45–46
Apple Computer, 195
Ashley Furniture, 216
Asset protection, 1, 121–123
  benefits of, 123–124
  creating company, 137–139
  customer-employee-owner
    dynamic, 132–133
  maintaining success and,
    150–152
  maximization of, 123, 131
  ownership and opportunity,
    129–134
  protecting products/services,
    126–127, 139–140, 155–156
  survival to success, 147–149
  tangible/intangible assets,
    125–126, 146–147, 153–155
  when moving on, 159–164
Assets/asset sale, 229–231
Automotive sales, 223–224

Balance sheet, 291
Barnes & Noble, 249
Benchmarking, 312
Bennis, Warren, 47
Brands, 239, 243
Business acumen, 2
Business failures, 1, 14, 63
Business knowledge
  accounting and finance,
    283–284, 298–299, 305–306,
    312–313, 318–320
  benefits of, 280–281, 294–295,
    301–302, 309–310, 315–316
  employees and, 282–283,
    297–298, 303–305, 311–312,
    317–318
  product focus, 281–282, 295–297,
    302, 310–311, 316–317
  realities of, 281
  successful owner, 284–285,
    292–293, 299–300, 306–307,
    313–314, 320–321
Business life
  control and, 4–5
  facts of, 1–3, 53
  leadership, 3–4
  marketing, 7
  marketplace as war zone, 8

Business life (*continued*)
  preparing for the future, 6–7
  protecting company's assets, 5–6
  understanding the industry, 8–9
Business life cycle, 2, 9–11, 13
  creating company, 10, 14
  maintaining success, 10, 14
  moving on, 10, 14
  ownership and opportunity,
    10, 14
  stages of, 10, 14
  successive levels of, 15
  survival to success, 10
Business plan. *See also Planning*
  analysis of, 19
  destination or vision, 171
  development of strategies, 20
  elements of, 170–171
  finding right opportunity, 54
  goals, 171
  implementation, 171
  mission statement, 171
  objectives, 171
  review, 171
  strategies, 171
  summary and communication,
    171
Business purpose, 36
Business success, 13–17
Business valuation, 314–315

Cash and cash flow analysis,
    290–291
Cash flow statements, 147
Caterpillar, 239
Coca-Cola, 194, 239
Collins, Jim, 34

Communication skills, 48, 56
Company assets
  benefits of, 123–124
  protection of, 2, 5–6
  realities of, 124
  tangible/intangible assets,
    125–125
Company culture
  expectations of, 3
  leadership and, 3–4
Competitive advantage, 34, 74, 268
Competitive analysis, 8, 18,
    245–246, 255. *See also*
    Marketplace as war zone
Competitiveness, 33, 236, 241, 264
Consistency, 258
Control, 1–2, 4–5, 87
  benefits of, 88–89
  defined, 87
  of employees, 96–97, 101–102
  of information, 90–91, 95–96,
    99–100
  procedures and, 93–94
  of processes, 91, 96, 100–101
  of product, 92–93, 97–98,
    102–103
  realities of, 89
  of self, 92
Control balance, 94
Core values, 56
Covey, Steven, 16, 89, 204
Creating company's DNA (Level 2),
    10–11, 14, 22–23
  accounting and finance,
    299–300
  achieving objective or goal,
    58–60

analysis, planning, and
implementation, 177–179
asset protection, 134–136
attracting the customer, 208–209
benefits of control, 94–95
benefits of leadership, 58
benefits of marketing, 208
benefits of planning, 176–179
building/maintaining a team,
60–61
business knowledge, 293–300
business owner, 299–300
control and, 93–98
control of employees, 96–97
control of processes, 96
control of product, 97–98
employees, 297–298
external marketing, 207–208
from survival to success, 62–64
gathering information, 176–177
how company operates, 254–255
individual development, 61–62
information control, 95–96
internal marketing, 205–207
keeping the customer, 211–212
leadership, 23–24
management and, 24
marketing and customers, 26–27,
204–212
marketplace as war zone,
250–256
mental image to actuality, 56–57,
59
planning and people, 24–25,
175–179
prioritizing and meeting
financial goals, 59

product/services you sell,
252–254, 295–296
protecting company's assets, 137
protecting employees, 140–142
protecting products/services,
139–140
protecting tangible/intangible
assets, 137–138
selling the customer, 209–211
takeover attempt, 136
Customer base, 5, 31
Customer delivery, 4
Customer-employee-owner
dynamic, 132–133, 149, 157
Customer retention, 216–217, 223
Customers, 16, 140
attracting the customer, 196–197,
201, 208–209, 214–215,
220–222, 226–228
creating a customer, 36
customer-employee-owner
dynamic, 132–133, 149, 157
keeping the customer, 196, 198,
203–204, 211–212, 216–218,
223–224, 231–233
marketing and, 21–22, 26–27,
31–32, 36, 195–196
over delivery for, 185
selling the customer, 197,
202–203, 209–211, 215–216,
222–223, 228–231
targeting of, 31

Data mining, 109
Decision making, on facts not
emotions, 52
Destination, 171

Dillard's Department, 216
Drucker, Peter, 36

The E-Myth (Gerber), 97
E*Trade, 214
Economy, Peter, 47
Employee-owner dynamic, 157–158
Employees, 16, 20–21, 25
  business knowledge and, 303
  control of, 96–97, 101–102,
    108–109, 117–118
  creating company, 61–62
  developing individuals, 70–72,
    76–77
  exiting/succession planning and,
    83–317–318
  fostering positive attitudes, 71
  motivation of, 28
  ownership and opportunity level,
    55–56
  planning and, 29–31, 35, 40–42
  protection of, 127–128, 149–149,
    157–158
Empowerment, 76, 101
Encyclopedia of Business and Finance
    (Kaliski), 87
Ethical environment, 58–59
Exiting a business, 37–40, 77–79,
    112. *See also Moving on (Level 5)*
  information control and, 112–113
  marketing and customer, 42
  points for consideration, 78–80
  professionals involved in, 41
External marketing, 207–208, 251

Family business, 9
Fannie Mae, 33

Finance, 283–284, 289–292,
    298–299, 305–306, 318–320
Financial forecast, 18
Financial statements, 154, 189, 291,
    319
Ford Motor Company, 6, 261

"Gears of War" video game, 214
General Motors, 33, 105, 107,
    109–110, 194
Generally accepted accounting
    principles (GAAP), 319
Gerber, Michael, 97
Goals and objectives, 19, 171
  external requirements for, 66–67
  internal requirements for, 66
  review questions for, 67–68
Good to Great (Collins), 34
Goodwill, 159, 161, 230
Gross profit, 198, 245–246

Harley-Davidson, 107, 239

Improvement goals, 106
Income (profit-and-loss) statement,
    291
Industry knowledge, 8–9
Information
  control of, 90–91, 95–96, 99–100,
    106–107, 112–114
  data gathering, 90, 173–174,
    176–177, 180–181
  data mining past sales, 109
  internal financial information, 189
  market information, 189
  prioritizing and defining, 90
  use of, 90

Internal financial information, 189
Internal marketing, 205–207

John Deere, 107

Kaliski, Burton, 87
Key jobs, 21
Killer instinct, 109, 203
Killing ground, 98, 212
Kouzes, James M., 34
Kranz, Eugene, 45–46
Kroc, Ray, 217

Law of diminishing returns, 309
Leaders, 45
  being responsible, 48
  communication and, 48
  courage, tenacity, and patience
    of, 48
  empowerment and, 76
  flexibility of, 47–48
  humility and presence, 48
Leadership, 1–4, 16, 18, 45
  achieving objective, 50
  benefits of, 48–49, 51–52, 58
  building/maintaining teams, 50
  by example, 45–46, 56
  common goals and, 46
  company cultures and, 3–4
  defining reality, 28
  determining objectives, 28
  in exiting transition, 81
  maintaining success, 73–74
  motivating employees, 28
  ownership and opportunity,
    50–51
  realities of, 49–50

self-analysis, 17
survival to success level, 64–65
in team building, 60
vision for, 23
The Leadership Challenge (Kouzes
  and Posner), 34
Lombardi, Vince, 50
Long-term plans, 169, 174
Lovell, James A., 45–46
Low-hanging fruit, 201, 213

McDonald's, 217
Maintaining success (Level 4),
    10–11, 14, 32–34, 72–73
  accounting and finance, 312–313
  achieving objectives/goals, 74
  analysis, planning, and
    implementation, 184–187
  asset protection and, 150–152
  attracting the customer, 214–215,
    220–222
  benefits of control, 105–106
  benefits of knowing business,
    309–310
  benefits of marketing, 219–220
  benefits of protecting assets,
    152–155
  building/maintaining team,
    75–76
  business knowledge and, 307–314
  control of employees, 108–109
  control of information, 106–107
  control of processes, 107–108
  control of product, 109–111
  how company competes, 269–272
  how company operates, 268–269
  information gathering, 183–184

Maintaining success (Level 4)
(*continued*)
keeping the customer, 216–218,
223–224
leadership and, 34, 73–74
management and, 34–35
marketing and customers, 36–37,
218–224
marketplace as war zone,
264–272
planning and people, 35–36, 183
products or services that you sell,
266–268, 310–311
protecting people, 157–158
protecting products or services,
155–156
selling the customer, 215–216,
222–223
successful owner, 313–314
tangible and intangible assets,
153–155
Management, 16, 29, 87
competitive analysis, 18
exiting a business, 37–40
financial performance and
customers, 34–35
leadership and, 18
processes/procedures, 24
Managing for Dummies (Nelson and
Economy), 47
Market information, 189
Market share, 243
Market turf, 148
Marketing, 1, 7, 193–195
assessment of opportunities, 199
at ownership and opportunity
level, 198–204

benefits of, 195–196
costs and, 31–32
creating company's DNA and,
204–212
customers and, 16, 21–22,
26–27, 36
elements of, 196–198
from survival to success,
212–218
internal marketing, 205–207
macro concepts of, 193
maintaining success and,
218–224
monitoring the results, 215
moving on level, 224–232
niche marketing, 221
realities of, 196
Marketing research, 226
Marketplace reputation, 61
Marketplace as war zone, 8,
235–237
benefits of understanding, 237
creating company's DNA,
250–256
financial strength as defense,
247
from survival to success, 256–264
how business competes, 241–242,
248–250, 255–256, 262–264,
269–272, 276–277
how business operates, 240–241,
246–248, 254–255, 261–262,
268–269, 276
maintaining success, 254–272
moving on and, 272–277
ownership and opportunity level,
242–250

products or services for sale, 238–240, 245–245, 252–254, 260–261, 266–268, 274–275
realities of, 237–238
understanding of, 259–260
Mental concept, 16
Microsoft, 156
Mission statement, 171
Moving on (Level 5), 10–11, 14, 37–38, 77–80
accounting and finance, 318–320
achieving objectives/goal, 81–82
analysis, planning, and implementation, 190–192
asset protection, 159–161
attracting the customer, 226–228
benefits of control, 111–112
benefits of planning, 187–192
business knowledge and, 314–321
control of employees, 117–118
control of information, 112–114
control of processes, 114–117
control of product, 118–119
employees and, 317–318
gathering information, 188–190
how business competes, 276–277
how company operates, 276
keeping the customer, 231–232
leadership and, 38–39, 81
management and, 39–40
marketing and customers, 42, 224–232
marketing research, 226
marketplace as war zone, 272–277
planning and people, 40–42

products/services you sell, 274–275, 316–317
protecting employees, 164–166
protecting products/services, 163–164
protecting tangible/intangible assets, 161–163
questions for consideration, 79–80, 114–115
selling the customer, 226–231
successful owner, 320–321
succession process, 115–116
teams and, 82–83

Nelson, Bob, 47
Net profit, 246
New market entrants, 248
Niche markets, 221, 241
Nike, 195, 239–40, 296

Objectives, 171
On Becoming a Leader (Bennis), 47
Opportunities, 13, 17
evaluation of, 52, 243–244
finding right opportunity, 52–54, 248
Opportunity evaluation, 52, 243–244
Ownership control, 4, 89
Ownership and opportunity (Level 1), 10–11, 14
achieving objectives or goal, 52–54
analysis, planning, and implementation, 174–175
asset protection, 129–134
attracting the customer, 201

Ownership and opportunity
(Level 1) (*continued*)
benefits of knowing business, 287
building/maintaining a team, 55
control and, 89–93
control of information, 90–91
control of people, 92
control of processes, 91–92
control of product, 92–92
customers, 21–22
developing the individual, 55–56
finding right opportunity, 53–54
gathering information, 173–174
how business operates, 246–248
keeping the customer, 203–204
knowing the business, 285–293
leadership and, 17–18, 50–56
management and, 18
marketing and, 198–204
marketplace as war zone,
242–244
people and, 20–21
planning and, 19–20, 172–175
products or services you sell,
245–246, 287
protecting employees, 132–134
protecting products or services,
132
risk vs. reward, 17
selling the customer, 202–203
tangible/intangible assets,
130–131
without leadership, 52

People. *See Employees*
Pfizer, 197

Physical concept, 16
Planning, 16, 19–20, 24–25,
167–169
analysis, planning, and
implementation, 174–175
art and science of, 168
benefits of, 169, 172–173
determining where business is
headed, 169
employees and, 40–42
goals and objectives, 19
information gathering,
173–174
long-term plans, 169
moving on and, 187–192
people and, 29–31, 35
realities of, 170
as science and art, 6–7
short-term plans, 169
Planning levels, 15
Policies and procedures, 1
Posner, Barry Z., 34
Potential buyers, criteria for, 227
Preparing for the future, 6–7
Price strategy, 249
Pricing, 244
Process control, 91, 96, 100–101,
107–108, 114–117, 178
Product control, 92–93, 97–98,
102–103, 109–111, 118–119
Product/services, protection
of, 126–127, 132, 139–140,
147–149
Profits, as sufficient, 53–54

Quality definition, 22

Real estate assets, 161, 230–231

Return on investment (ROI), 18

Risk, 17, 134

Sales information, 245

Self-analysis, 17, 52

  for ownership fit, 52–53

Selling process, 230

Services, 239

Seven Habits of Highly Successful People (Covey), 16, 204

Share sale, 229

Short-term plans, 169, 175

Social media, 249

Strategic planning, 1, 20, 171

Strengths and weaknesses, 52

Successful owner, 284–285, 292–293, 299–300, 306–307, 320–321

Succession plan, 80, 84, 115, 189–190

Survival to success (Level 3), 10–11, 14, 62–64

  accounting and finance, 305–306

  achieving objective or goal, 65

  analysis, planning, and implementation, 181–182

  benefits of control, 98–103

  benefits of planning, 180–182

  benefits of protecting your assets, 145–146

  building/maintaining a team, 68–70

  business knowledge and, 300–307

  business owner, 306–307

control of information, 99–100

control of people, 101–102

control of processes, 100–101

control of product, 102–103

employees, 303–305

how business competes, 262–264

how company operates, 261–262

leadership and, 27–29, 64–65

management and, 29

marketing and the customer, 31–32, 212–218

marketplace as war zone, 256–264

planning and, 29–31, 179–182

product/services you sell, 260–261, 302

protecting people, 149–150

protection of assets, 142–145

protection of product/services, 147–149

tangible/intangible assets, 148–147

Takeover, 136

Tangible/intangible assets, 125–126, 130–131, 137–139, 146–147, 153–155

  ownership and opportunity, 130–131

Teams, 4, 36, 57

  binding elements/chemistry of, 60–61

  building/maintaining of, 50, 55, 60, 75–76

Teams (*continued*)
creating atmosphere for, 69–70
developing individuals in
the company, 50
exit plan and, 82–83
Threats, 13
Tickle process, 118
Training, 21

Vision, 23, 56, 171

Walton, Sam, 186
Warrior mentality, 2
Working smarter, 270

X factor, 255–256, 262–263, 269,
276–277

Stay in touch!

Subscribe to our free Finance and Accounting eNewsletters at
www.wiley.com/enewsletters

Visit our blog: **www.capitalexchangeblog.com**

 Follow us on Twitter
@wiley_finance

 "Like" us on Facebook
www.facebook.com/wileyglobalfinance

 Find us on LinkedIn
Wiley Global Finance Group

WILEY Global Finance
WHERE DATA FINDS DIRECTION